D1030116

The Patriarchs of Israel

THE PATRIARCHS
 OF ISRAEL

John Marshall Holt

VANDERBILT UNIVERSITY PRESS

Nashville 1964

Copyright © 1964 by John M. Holt

LIBRARY OF CONGRESS CATALOGUE CARD NUMBER: 64–13543
COMPOSED, PRINTED, AND BOUND BY KINGSPORT PRESS, INC.
KINGSPORT, TENNESSEE, U.S.A.

S30787

222.11
H758

❧ FOREWORD

IN THIS BOOK I deliberately address myself to the interested reader of the Bible who lacks detailed acquaintance with the methods and findings of Biblical archaeology. Such a reader will probably want to pass over much of the bibliographical data in the notes, which the technical reader will peruse closely, but even the general reader will find the material in the notes indicative not only of the sources of this study but also of the places he may go for further reading. They are mentioned to give a view more representative than exhaustive of the literature available. Any reader will need to have his Bible close at hand as he reads this, and a good Bible atlas will serve him well, also.

Professors J. Philip Hyatt and Lou H. Silberman of Vanderbilt University have shown me patience and encouragement since the beginning of this study, and my affectionate gratitude to them continues for their many helpful suggestions along the way. I also here express my thanks to the Dean and Board of Trustees of the Episcopal Theological Seminary of the Southwest, who allowed a leave of absence for the preparation of this work.

JOHN MARSHALL HOLT

Jerusalem
October 1963

❧ CONTENTS

THE PATRIARCHS OF ISRAEL

✑ I

THE PATRIARCHS OF GENESIS

The Story of the Patriarchs

ALTHOUGH the word *patriarch* is the frequently found epithet for any revered ancestor in antiquity of many peoples, when one comes to speak of Israel, the people of the Bible, customary usage narrows down the reference of the term. Out of all the heroes remembered and venerated in Israelite tradition, the patriarchs *par excellence* are the leading characters of the twelfth through the fiftieth chapters of Genesis: Abraham, Isaac, Jacob, and Joseph. It was to them that historical Israel traced her origin, once the tradition reached the full form in which we now have it in the Bible. They hold the pre-eminent position among all of Israel's saints and are looked upon as at least spiritual ancestors by all those who claim any descent from or association with the Israel of old. In their lives, as recorded in the Genesis tradition, the later generations found the first steps toward the formation of that distinct people known since late in the second millennium B.C. as Israel. The patriarchs were those in whom the action of God produced a unique family, whose descendants were to occupy a peculiar position and live with a unique sense of destiny in the history of the world. They serve those who claim to follow in their succession as heroes, pioneers, and exemplars.

As the story about them stands in Genesis, it is familiar to most from the earliest days of their religious training. Abraham was the first of them. Without fixing any definite date for him, the tradition tells how in remote antiquity this man, known first as Abram, left his homeland in Mesopotamia and migrated westward to a new home and a purpose different from any he had previously known. He was a grown man, married but childless, at the time that his sense of vocation came irresistibly to him: the true God dispatched him and his family to a fresh beginning in a land not yet known to him. With obedient faithfulness to the divine impulse, Abram proceeded to Palestine and journeyed here and there in that land, making contact with several places of later importance for their political or religious associations. Before he settled anywhere with any permanency, he and his wife had a most dramatic adventure during a trip to Egypt: Abram came very close to losing his life, and Sarai, his wife, was in grave danger of becoming an adulteress. Fortunately, the patriarch's quick wit and the providential intervention of God prevented either of those calamities from coming to pass.

Once again settled in Palestine, Abram demonstrated his peacefulness, generosity, and magnanimity in dealings with his own relatives, and he likewise proved himself a man of unmistakable valor in withstanding those who threatened the lives and safety of those dear to him. Even the king-priest of Salem recognized these qualities in Abram and pronounced a solemn blessing over him. Having found a regular residence at last in Hebron, where the great King David was later to rule for a time, Abram was indeed a resident of a new land to which his God had brought him, but he had not yet become a father. The divine promise was that he was to sire a family whose descendants would bless the world by their presence and fill it with their multitude, but Abram's only heir was still only a trusted friend and servant, not a son. In view of the solemnity of the divine promise, Abram sought to provide himself with an heir by taking one of his wife's maids as his concubine.

4

Perhaps this might be the way that Abram could fulfil the destiny his God had assigned him.

The concubine did bear Abram a son, but Abram's wife could not long tolerate either his presence in the household or that of his mother. Feminine vanity and basic human jealousy soon soured the otherwise peaceful life the family had known, and Abram was finally compelled to let both the child and his mother go. It was not through the son of a bondwoman that Abram's progeny would come into the world, although the divine assurance came to Abram that the child of the concubine would do very well.

Strange visitors, not clearly identifiable as either divine or human, finally brought the startling news that Abraham would have his heir, the son of his wife, Sarah. (The new form of their names remains in consistent use from this period in their lives onward.) It was difficult to believe such a prediction, in view of the advanced age of both of the supposed parents, but there could be no serious doubt for long of the reliability of the visitors' assertions about the future. They rescued Abraham's relatives from Sodom just before the awful catastrophe that destroyed the cities of the plain, a catastrophe of which they had given explicit warning ahead of time. In the natural course of time, Sarah did give birth to a son, and the delighted parents named him Isaac in commemoration of the laughter, both of joy and of incredulity, that accompanied his birth.

Abraham lived many years at peace with his neighbors, Canaanites, Philistines, Hittites, and the other occupants of the land, as he proudly watched his son grow to manhood. Having successfully passed the ordeal of faith his God forced him to undergo—it almost cost the life of Isaac —Abraham lived as a man well respected by all who knew him and as one blessed with close contact with his God. The story is full of the patriarch's prayerful waiting upon God and his frequent acts of worship. His grief over Sarah's death was soon relieved with happiness over the marriage of Isaac to Rebekah, whom the trusted servant had been able to find in Abraham's own homeland and bring to Palestine to continue the family line. At last Abraham could die full of years and blessing.

Issac and Rebekah continued the family line, all right, but their son Jacob soon moved into prominence, and much of the rest of the patriarchal story is his story. Most charitably estimated, Jacob was a man of ambition who usually managed to make the most of every opportunity for his own advantage. He displaced his brother, Esau, as the favored son of Isaac, and he went on his way to marry and make his own fortune. Returning to the Mesopotamian land of his family's ultimate origin, he married well and profited from his ability to outwit his father-in-law. He continued the worship of the God who had made himself known to his father and grandfather, and the same divine favor earlier generations had known still prospered Jacob on his travels and in his career. More than once this God vouchsafed to Jacob evidence of his presence with him and support of his progress. Relations were not always harmonious within the family, for Jacob, who later became known as Israel, was willing to take on all opponents or exploit all relationships when he set his will to it. His departure with his wives, children, and possessions for residence in the land of his birth was greeted with relief by his relatives by marriage, who at length concluded it best to try no vengeance against Jacob but simply to let him go, and themselves stay, in peace.

Jacob's children bore the names of the tribes known in historical times as the principal components of the nation of Israel, whom we are to acknowledge as the offspring of those children of Jacob. Father Israel-Jacob had not often been on good terms with his relatives, and his children occasionally displayed some of their father's unlovely traits

6

as they grew up. Such a collision of wills and aspirations among the brothers was responsible for the adventures of Joseph, for whom old Israel had shown strong partiality. Sold into slavery in Egypt by his resentful brothers, Joseph had many a close brush with disaster. His chastity was threatened by the attempt of his master's wife to seduce him, and he could have died in prison after her false accusation caused him to be jailed. The favor of the fathers' God was upon this Joseph, however, and the divine gifts of incorruptible virtue and superior wisdom helped him out of prison and into high position at the court of the king of Egypt. Joseph married a daughter of one of Egypt's best families and enjoyed privileges of rank and dignity second only to the king himself.

Joseph had saved the country from starvation at a time of national emergency and thereby built up a strong central government with himself as benevolent and wise administrator under his pharaoh. When his own family could no longer support themselves in Palestine, Joseph was able to override the Egyptian hostility toward foreigners and make a home in the Nile Delta for his aged father and his brothers and all the family. He readily forgave his brothers for what they had done to him earlier, since he could see the hand of God in the whole course of events. So the family were reunited and lived out their days in Egypt, happily and prosperously together.

Behind the Story

The story of the patriarchs stands within the sacred literature of Christians and Jews and for centuries has been read with the reverent attention their standard piety requires in the approach to Scripture. Until late in the eighteenth century of the present era, for the bulk of Bible readers this meant a reverence that acknowledges the truth

7

and accuracy of what the Bible says because the Bible says it. Learned Jews and Christians alike over the centuries pointed out incongruities and implausibilities in the patriarchal narrative, as well as other parts of Scripture, but the prevailing attitude was that what the Bible said, happened so, just so. It was to be taken as true in all its parts, in all its details, and there was no other legitimate way of accounting the Bible as true.

As the intellectual life of Western civilization has come along in the last two centuries, people have learned to use categories of thought in this matter of truth that were largely unknown to the ancients or anyone else before the age of reason and science. Whether the scientific method of arriving at truth is necessarily better or worse than earlier methods is not really the question. It is the way we have learned to think, and exegesis, the science of Biblical interpretation, has kept pace with the rest of our intellectual pursuits. Scientific, critical, rational study of the Bible spread from German universities to Britain and the rest of Europe, then to the rest of the world. It has now become the fundamental orientation of all modern Bible study.

Biblical criticism has taught us to look at the Bible and its individual books in a more analytical way than was possible earlier. Reverent attention to Scripture has become no less devout, only more analytical and indeed capable of a richer appreciation. Critical analysis of the Bible has prevented us from looking to Scripture for geological, anthropological, or biological data, for instance, and, in many instances, for the hard core of historical fact. It has denied, not truth itself, but these kinds of truth to Scripture when not otherwise verifiable. Traditional notions of the authorship of Biblical books, some of them never dependably attestable, have been revised or replaced with understandings admittedly more complex but more closely reasoned from the actual evidence at hand, which is often only the internal content and structure of the books themselves.

The story of the patriarchs has shared in this new evaluation. Genesis, along with the four following books that form the Pentateuch, has come to be recognized, not as the simple, outright composition of Moses straight through, but as the result of a 500-year-long process of compilation of earlier sources, some of which probably existed even earlier in oral folk tradition that gradually became fixed in written form. Thanks to the literary-critical and form-critical scholarship of the nineteenth century, readers of the Bible can now recognize in Genesis, the rest of the Pentateuch, and on into the following Book of Joshua four main sources of tradition that have been combined and interwoven with each other to form the story of the emergence of Israel in the form in which we now have that story. It is as if a publisher brought out four successive editions of a book, each one expanded and improved to put the point across more fully and tellingly than the preceding one. Beginning with the Yahwist, *J* Source in the tenth century B.C., the tradition was expanded by the addition of the Elohist, *E* Source something over a century later, then by the Deuteronomic, *D* Source in the seventh or sixth century, and finally by the Priestly, *P* Source no later than 400 B.C. The devout reader, who keeps his reverent attention alive, perceives in this process the work of the guiding hand of God, of course, operating through several different men over an extended period of time to produce the final splendid proclamation we can now read straight through from Genesis to Joshua.

Critical study of Genesis and its following books has taught us to discover in those books a theologically motivated interpretation of the fact that Israel did appear as one of the nations of the world around 1000 B.C. This is what one should expect from a book that is, and always has been, primarily a source for theological teaching. In putting together the old traditions about the origin of Israel, the writers of the sources we can now recognize sought to explain to their readers and hearers what it meant that they had achieved the status they had. Writing from this fundamentally theological point of view, they had the aim of producing in the people a response of faith and loyalty to the God of whom the tradition spoke, the God who had brought them into being for a purpose not like that of the other nations they knew.

Once we have learned to turn an analytical eye on the composite product of the sources, we can acknowledge that they made their point well, superlatively so. We can further see that the sources made use of material that, with our categories of thinking, we call *myth* and *legend* as well as what we think of as *history*. Biblical criticism has had to fight every inch of the way against the resistance of those willing to recognize only historical fact as truth, as if myth and legend did not proclaim other kinds of truth especially appropriate to those forms of writing and speaking. But a theological lesson can be taught through any of these types of literature; in fact, some theological affirmations can be made only through the use of mythological language and form, as is the case with the basic acts of faith stated by the Biblical writers in the first eleven chapters of Genesis.

In sum, critical study of the Bible has not made us indifferent to the residue of historical fact, often startlingly discoverable in the Bible, but has shown us how to appreciate the other ways, like myth and legend, that the Biblical authors went about teaching us the religious and theological lesson they had to impart.

Archaeological Discovery

One who reads the Bible nowadays can profit not only from critical scholarship in Biblical literature but also from the contributions to knowledge of another science, archaeology. The student of the Bible will naturally be very interested in what archaeology can tell him of Bible times, lands, and peoples, and there is a wealth of material at hand, so much that one must learn to exercise a certain degree of restraint over his imagination to avoid injudicious conclusions from what Biblical archaeology has brought to light.

Archaeologists have been diligently at work in all parts of the Near East that figure in the Biblical story, though not always because of their Biblical association: in some cases the remains of the ancient civilizations were simply "there," demanding to be studied, and the implications for Bible study have appeared after the archaeological work was done. In their pursuit of the study of past civilizations that have left only physical remains, archaeologists have worked throughout the Fertile Crescent and beyond: Egypt, Palestine, Syria, Asia Minor (Anatolia), the Tigris-Euphrates valley once ruled by Assyria and Babylonia and known to us as Iraq—the principal scene of the Biblical narrative. Some sites display evidence of prehistoric cultures alone, and others of later times, but, when one brings all the data together, there can be formed a sweeping panorama of the ancient Near East in its successive stages of historical development and experience. To accompany a study of the patriarchs of Israel there is material available from throughout the Fertile Crescent, dating from a thousand years (some more) before the appearance of Israel, that bears more or less directly on the story we have of Israelite beginnings.

The archaeological remains at many places are stratified in layers, each the remnant of life at one period of history that replaced an earlier and was in turn used as the foundation for rebuilding at the same location later. Stratigraphic excavation exposes each successive level for record and study, and, once the record is complete, the site can be

11

turned up again deeper to expose a lower, earlier period of settlement. Sometimes the archaeologist will dig a trench straight down only one line across the site so as to provide a cross-section sampling of the various levels of remains. What is found is the material remnant of life as it was lived: foundations or other structural parts of buildings of all types from temples to stables, household utensils, weapons of war, personal jewelry, religious objects, works of art, skeletons of buried dead persons—all have something to say about the life of those who left them behind. There are written remains, also, and these epigraphic materials permit us to read literature both sacred and secular, business transactions, personal and official correspondence, public inscriptions, and almost anything else people write down, on stone, clay tablets, or pieces of pottery. When we study Near Eastern epigraphic remains that bear on the patriarchal period, we benefit from the labors of those who have deciphered and translated the hieroglyphs of Egyptian writers; the syllabic characters of Akkadian cuneiform, the international language from Mesopotamia; and other writing something more like the alphabetic type with which we are familiar, to name but a few.

The places all have intriguingly exotic names, some the same as those by which the ancients knew them; others are known by names given in modern times. For the patriarchal period the most important sources of archaeological information are:

Tell el-Amarna, the Egyptian resting place, for centuries, of letters from officials in Syria and Palestine;

Alalakh and *Ugarit,* eastern Mediterranean cities at the crossroads of continental and maritime cultures, both of which sites have yielded structural and literary knowledge;

Mari and *Nuzi,* northern Mesopotamian treasure-troves that have preserved for us an astoundingly complete, often intimate, record of their people's lives and times. In addition to these, of course, are places whose names are probably easily familiar to every Bible reader. However remote in time they are behind us, though, and however foreign some of the names sound at first acquaintance, the archaeologist has so thoroughly done his job that before long one notices that he has available about as thorough a knowledge of the everyday life of the people who lived at those long-ago, faraway places as he does of those who live just across one or two international borders today.

The data from Biblical archaeology become pertinent for us most pressingly when we have first taken to heart the main lesson of Biblical criticism. When we leave off trying to prove or discredit the absolute, factual accuracy of the story of the patriarchs and concede the legendary quality of much of Genesis xii–l, then we can ask the question that Biblical archaeology can most helpfully answer for us: how close to life are these stories? In what details, in which areas of life, and with what degree of exactness do the patriarchal legends reflect the manner of life and times of the people of whom they speak? Are they complete fiction entirely contrived, or are they stories with a discernible historical background?

The Nature of the Problem

This study is not intended for those who are willing to be content with reading the patriarchal chapters of Genesis, or the Bible as a whole, simply for immediate inspirational uplift or for the pleasure of savoring again the familiar stories known by most of us since childhood. In these pages we turn the attention to the events, times, places, and persons of the beginning of the Biblical period of history. Our concern is not with the first eleven chapters of Genesis, the so-called "primeval myths," for they serve to set the general scene for human life as such; they state the

13

broad affirmations of the Biblical authors about certain important aspects of life as it is in fact lived. The patriarchal chapters, the twelfth through the fiftieth of Genesis, focus the perspective of the Biblical writers and their readers on the single, unique line of Israel as it emerges recognizably into human history. This segment of Biblical history we seek to examine as closely as existing records and trustworthy interpretation of them will allow.

Fairness and honesty require that the author of such an examination declare the presuppositions with which he undertakes it, and they follow. First, my acceptance of the Biblical faith in the God who acts in history impels me to re-create as accurately and as fully as may be relevant and possible the beginning days of the peculiar history of Israel. That is to say, an indispensable part of the approach to the understanding of the revelation given through events is the amplest possible awareness of what the situation actually was, what the people were like, just what it was that took place. This is only part of the approach, to be sure, but an irreplaceable one for all who wish to rise above mere literalism in reading the Bible. Further, I am especially concerned with this particular, earliest stage of Hebrew history for no romantic desire to exalt the earliest as the best and purest but rather because it appears to me that in the earliest, often simpler, and more essential form of Israelite experience can be more adequately understood much of the content and structure of what, chronologically and organically speaking, emerged later. Thus we seek to discern how the patriarchal experience was in truth a valid encounter, in miniature and by anticipation, with what was to come in full stature at a later time.[1] Having come to see the patriarchs plain, so far as we can, we hope to discern in them a kind of Old Testament *praepa-*

1. *Cf.* Gerhard von Rad, *Theologie des Alten Testaments*, Vol. I, p. 17.

14

ratio evangelica, as the authors of Genesis themselves seem to have viewed them.

The records of the past, as contemporaneous with the events themselves as possible, are always the ultimate source for the study of what has gone before. For many centuries the only such record of the patriarchal age available was the Old Testament itself, although it was not until the advent of the critical school of Biblical study that the Old Testament could be adequately exploited as a source for the study of history, properly defined. Pre-critical, unscientific methods of study, as we now call them, coupled with a reverence for the sacred text, which to our forebears compelled unquestioning, literal acceptance, prevented any sort of comparison with other data outside the Old Testament such as is now taken for granted by modern students of the Bible. Indeed, the very absence of external data till something over a century ago helps to explain why the Old Testament as it stood had to be taken as the only source available for knowledge of the life and times of the patriarchs, Abraham, Isaac, Jacob, and Joseph.

The nineteenth century saw the full appearance of that "higher" criticism which sought to evaluate the received material of the Old Testament under the rubrics of authorship, date and place of composition, theological bias, and other questions that contribute to the adequate interpretation of any document received from the past.[2] For those of us who live after this movement it is apparent on the face of it that anyone who wishes to acquire a respectable understanding of the past must take such a "critical" approach toward his sources, but when the pioneers of literary criticism proceeded to study the Old Testament this way, a

2. A survey of critical study of the Hexateuch is given by C. A. Simpson, "The Growth of the Hexateuch," *Interpreter's Bible,* Vol. I (1952), pp. 185–200.

storm of protest broke around their heads. It has not entirely subsided yet, but within most circles there is now a genuine and grateful acknowledgement of the fundamental soundness and necessity of the critics' methods and, in the main, of their principal results.

Although much of the abuse heaped upon the critics for their work on Genesis had to do with the first eleven chapters of the book, which the critics have taught subsequent generations to read as myths collected and retold as teaching devices of religious and ethical proclamation, the massive scholarship of the critical generation also broke mightily through toward intelligent study of the patriarchal stories, which occupy the rest of the Book of Genesis. The finest flowering of literary critical study of the patriarchal legends is, of course, that of Hermann Gunkel, whose commentary on Genesis was first published in 1901 and went through successive editions until his death. Much of the problem that now confronts us can be shown by an examination of Gunkel's estimate of the Genesis legends, for his work stands as the best purely literary study of the patriarchal stories: the findings of modern archaeology most relevant to the patriarchs were by and large not available at the time that he wrote.

Gunkel recognized legend as a certain kind of poetry prized by all religions.[3] It is oral in its composition and first transmission, and it is the work of those who cannot write history or are not interested in doing so. Legend concerns itself rather with family matters, those of more personal and simple scope, less "grand" significance. Its aim is principally to please, to elevate, to inspire and move. In keeping with the classifying type of study for which Gunkel is famous, he noticed such types of legend as the aetiological, the etymological, the ceremonial, and

3. There follows a digest of the pertinent material in the introductory section of Hermann Gunkel, *Genesis,* pp. vii–c.

16

even the geological. He allowed that the legends of Genesis probably did contain some historical elements, such as the migrations of tribes; this accorded with Gunkel's interpretation of the figures of the patriarchs themselves as personified tribes, later on taken literally as persons. Beyond that, however, the value of the patriarchal legends as sources, in the scientific sense, for historical study of the patriarchal age was, for the critical generation, negligible. It is remarkable that the stories of Joseph and of the deceitful dealings between Jacob and Laban, which are so helpfully illuminated by modern archaeological discovery, were for Gunkel quite unclassifiable in his scheme of legend and unexplainable as either legend or history.

The sources of the patriarchal legends were, for Gunkel, to be sought in the Canaanite culture into which the Hebrews moved late in the second millennium B.C., and he could not permit any relation between the component parts of any particular legend or cycle. Each legend must be viewed as an individual unit, episodic in nature, and the earliest form of each would be the shortest. In the absence of any such body of external evidence as is now available, and on purely literary critical premises, Gunkel finally concluded that "the religion of Abraham is in reality the religion of the narrators of the legends, ascribed by them to Abraham."[4] With only a slight risk of oversimplifying Gunkel's position we can with fairness still take this last as summary of the best insights of the critical study he carried on.

The work of Wellhausen, Gunkel, and the other masters of literary criticism was informed by the prevailing "developmental" thought of their time and happens to have come before modern archaeology emerged as a proper science. Our present recognition of the fallacy of that reigning philosophy must not, however, drive us to con-

4. Gunkel, p. lxxix.

tempt or disdain for their having not thought ahead of their age or having reached conclusions that must now be modified in view of subsequent discovery. Much of what they had to say remains definitive for study of the Bible, but there are other resources to which we may now turn. Other remains from antiquity, some literary and some non-literary, have come to light and have vastly increased our understanding of the patriarchal age and its peoples. Some modification of the earlier conclusions of literary critical study is called for, even if the new knowledge has raised, as it should, questions of which no one had previously thought.

Interest in the past, even if only curiosity, has surrounded the ancient sites of the Near East at least since the time of the writers of the earliest documents of the Hexateuch. Instances of "archaeological" interest spring out from every page: place names, individual personalities, and people who were to the J and E writers "ancient" are recorded in these first strata of Old Testament tradition. Nor was this a purely Hebrew matter, for we have other examples in antiquity of prescientific archaeological interest. Asshur-bani-pal in the seventh century B.C. constructed and filled a great cuneiform library in which he hoped to preserve the interesting records and literary production of the past.[5] His wish was fulfilled, inasmuch as modern excavation of the site has enabled people of whom Asshur-bani-pal never heard or dreamed to use his collection precisely for the purpose for which he intended it. Herodotus' work fairly bristles with interesting anecdotes, facts, traditions, and tall tales about the places and peoples of the Fertile Crescent. Through the centuries since then travelers have noticed, remarked upon, and sometimes carried away from their original location remains of antiquity that caught their eye as they journeyed through the

5. Jack Finegan, *Light from the Ancient Past*, pp. 181–182.

18

Near East. Motives varying through all degrees from antiquarian fascination to desire for financial gain have stimu-
lated the search for and study of the material remains of
cultures dead and gone in the so-called "cradle of civilization."

The emergence of the two disciplines of literary critical
study and of scientific excavation and interpretation of discoveries is one of the results of the nineteenth century, but
the former reached its pinnacle of achievement before
the latter: while literary commentaries on the Old Testament were being published by the one group of scholars,
the other was only beginning to read with real success the
languages most important for the study of ancient Near
Eastern life. Beyond the confines of the study and the lec-
ture room, though, out in the field itself, it was not until
the turn of this century that scientific method could finally
be applied to the excavation of known or suspected ancient
sites. The judgment of such a competent scholar as Albright can be taken as doing proper justice: Albright
writes[6] of the survey of Palestinian findings, for instance,
since the eighteenth century as vague, resulting from ex-
plorations that were at best haphazard. As something of a
watershed, on this side of which scientific archaeology as
we know it comes to be recognizable, Albright designates
the literally ground-breaking work of Sir Flinders Petrie,
who worked first in Egypt and then in 1890 directed the
first stratigraphical soundings in Palestine at Tell el-Hesi.
Only shortly before, in 1888, the German work at Zenjirli
in Syria marked the beginning there of systematic excavation by layers,[7] with the discoveries at each level carefully
plotted, identified, sketched or photographed, and otherwise recorded before that level had to be destroyed in dig-

6. Elihu Grant (ed.) *et al., The Haverford Symposium on Archaeology
and the Bible* (hereafter cited as *Haverford Symposium*), p. 3.
7. *Ibid.,* p. 4.

ging deeper for the earlier layers. Here is the essence of what we now consider scientific archaeology. Following generations of archaeologists have not felt the need to modify the basic method, although they have been able to refine its application tremendously.

Archaeology reached full stature approximately one generation later than the apex of literary criticism, and that is responsible for the double aspect of the problem we now face in reading the patriarchal legends. On the one hand we have estimates of the historical usefulness of Biblical material on the basis of purely literary study, as with Gunkel. From these, a whole new school of Biblical interpretation resulted, and, since its interpretations were based on the only available method of study, they must now be modified in the light of what the supplementary method has produced. On the other hand, as archaeological discoveries came to light and were interpreted as to their value for historical study, and particularly as the new discoveries came to be seen as often supporting or at least not outright contradicting the Biblical narrative, overenthusiastic application has been made of archaeology. Exaggerated claims were made for archaeology by some of its practitioners, probably in their zeal to convince the world of the significance of their work: Petrie went somewhat beyond his depth and reached conclusions that made students of linguistic science shudder,[8] and Sir Leonard Woolley some years later optimistically announced[9] positive identification at Ur of the remains of the age of Abraham and of the religion of Abraham himself. Successive consideration by many minds has modified the certainty with

8. *E.g.*, his linguistic fantasy by which he identified Tell el-Farah with the Biblical Beth-pelet. *Cf.* the discussion in C. C. McCown, *The Ladder of Progress in Palestine*, p. 123; also, Millar Burrows, *What Mean These Stones?*, p. 93.

9. Leonard Woolley, *Abraham: Recent Discoveries and Hebrew Origins, passim.*

which Petrie and Woolley made their pronouncements, and all would have been well had it not been for the still militant opponents of literary criticism, who have eagerly seized on archaeological data as further proof of the invalidity of critical study of the Old Testament.

There are still thoroughly competent and magnificently trained specialists in the archaeology of the Near East who construct elaborate houses of cards on the shaky foundation of slight, laboriously tenuous parallels between Biblical and archaeological data. It is perhaps better that the error continue to be on the side of boldness, lest the discipline grow complacent and intransigent. More serious is the attempt made by those who cannot brook even the shadow of literary criticism to discredit it as a whole by a tendentious use of archaeological data. One of the most recent instances of this abuse of archaeology is Free's *Archaeology and Bible History,* on whose first page the author writes that "two of the main functions of Bible archaeology are the illumination and the confirmation of the Bible."[10] "Illumination" is well sought, but the set purpose of "confirmation" is one that asks too much and the wrong type of help from archaeology. One who wishes to show up the poverty of literary critical methods as final answers to Biblical questions can do so quite satisfactorily within the field of literary criticism itself and should not bend to his service a study that has proven its right to a respectably independent position. In a more gentle way Cyrus H. Gordon's *Introduction to Old Testament Times* provides comfort for those who wish to do without literary criticism, but his work as a whole is on a much higher level.

The problem is more than merely trying to strike an average between too-eager use of archaeology, which would tie up every potsherd with a specific chapter and verse, and sullen resistance to literary criticism, which would

10. Joseph P. Free, *Archaeology and Bible History,* p. 1.

consciously try to subvert critical study but, probably without intending to do so, would also tend to damage the proper exercise of archaeological science. The challenge that confronts us is that of making a study as nonargumentative as possible of the parallels between Biblical and non-Biblical material, holding in mind all the while that the separate disciplines of Biblical interpretation and archaeological excavation do often coincide but that the former is not entitled to look upon the latter as its constant handmaiden, since that involves a violation of the integrity of archaeology. An articulate exponent of this view is Kathleen Kenyon, who has declared that "archaeology is the method of finding out about the past of the human race in its material aspects, and the study of the products of the past."[11] It is further "a matter of discovering ancient materials and studying them in order to throw as much light on their makers and users as possible."[12] This is the procedure that alone is qualified to be designated scientific archaeology. The Biblical interpreter must restrain his eagerness to find explanations for the material of his study, lest he force both himself and the compliant archaeologist into precipitate and irrelevant conclusions. Biblical interpretation must allow the archaeologist to pursue his study as the methods and procedures of the science lead him and make a simple, fundamental act of faith that out of the process will come illumination for the Biblical passages the exegete wishes to explain. We hold the great affirmations of the Bible to be the results of the divine activity in the lives of certain people in history, and archaeology is important for the understanding of what the life and thought of these people were on the basis of what their material remains show; it enables us "to put the Bible into its contemporaneous setting so that we can more clearly

11. Kathleen M. Kenyon, *Beginning in Archaeology*, p. 9.
12. *Ibid.*, p. 14.

22

discern its permanent timeless element . . ."[13] Historical source is no matter of indifference, for the Old Testament like the New argues from history.[14] But this cannot be forced, and to require of archaeology that it take as one of its prime purposes the "confirmation" of the Bible is to deprive it of that freedom without which it will be less fully able to do the work that will truly aid the Biblical interpreter. Wilson has wisely laid down the *caveat* that must remain normative in the relations between Bible and archaeology: "there is a certain mild irony in the fact that the discoveries in Egypt which have most immediate importance for biblical scholars were made adventitiously, and not through the search for biblical evidence."[15]

The Patriarchal Age

Since this work is a study of parallels between Biblical passages and archaeological data, it is necessary to specify the nature and content of the respective bodies of material between which relationship will be shown to exist or to be possible. The findings of scientific archaeology since 1900 form the one group, and within that category it will be seen that the epigraphic remains constitute the greater part of the sources for comparison. While the architectural and geological aspects of the discoveries are helpful at points, we are still dealing with written accounts in the Bible; consequently, written remains occupy the greater part of our attention. This should not, however, be understood as limited to strictly "literary" writing, since there is pertinent material in legal contracts, business records, treaties, inscriptions on monuments, and other sources that cannot be considered literary in the usual sense of the word.

13. J. N. Schofield, *Archaeology and the After-Life*, p. 11.
14. *Cf.* John Bright, *Early Israel in Recent History Writing*, p. 12.
15. J. A. Wilson in *Haverford Symposium*, p. 220.

The patriarchal legends of Genesis bear the literary marks of having passed through the hands of Yahwist, Elohist, and Priestly authors and editors. In agreement with all modern study of Genesis, the writer allows that not one word of any of the patriarchal legends was written down in literary form at any time contemporaneous with the people described in them. Late literary composition, however, is not in itself invalidating, in view of the tenacity of oral tradition; so I will feel free to discuss any segment or detail of the patriarchal legends without immediate concern as to its literary source and transmission, except insofar as it may be worthwhile to show that critical analysis of the historical verisimilitude of such and such a passage is strikingly similar (or dissimilar!) to that reached by comparison with archaeological data.

In all that Biblical archaeology has brought to light in the past fifty years, not once is there to be found a direct identification of any one of the patriarchs known to us from the Genesis accounts, and we should hardly expect it, much as we might like to have it. It is indeed "impossible to relate the Biblical narratives with even approximate precision to the events of contemporary history," as John Bright has asserted.[16] We must, however, not become overoptimistic because of Glueck's probably extreme assurance that no Biblical reference has ever been controverted by archaeological findings.[17] Furthermore, at no point in the course of the patriarchal legends do the traditions of Genesis provide us with any reliable kind of absolute date for their events. As Gunkel has made so clear, this is the kind of tradition preserved by those who are not concerned with the composition of history as we think of it. In the absence of a direct cross-reference, then, we must seek to locate a period in the retrievable history of the Near East when

16. In his *A History of Israel*, p. 61.
17. Nelson Glueck, *Rivers in the Desert*, p. 31.

events such as are described in the patriarchal chapters of Genesis can plausibly have happened. This is a search for the "balance of probability" with which Bright advises us to be content because of archaeology's inability to provide eyewitness proof.[18]

The lower limit of the patriarchal age is the entry of the Hebrews into Egypt; the oppression they eventually received at the hands of the Egyptians provided the historical situation of the Exodus under the leadership of Moses—a new age. Since the received tradition has it that Joseph died in prosperity and in advanced old age before the Egyptian authorities took their later, hostile attitude toward the Hebrews, we need to begin by looking backward from a point no more than a century prior to the Exodus, in order to find how far back the upper limit of the patriarchal age needs to be placed. If we allow a date late in the thirteenth century B.C. for the Exodus, then the terminal date for the patriarchal age is not long after 1400, in the so-called "Amarna Age."

As we search on farther back, we need to locate a period in which as many as possible of the details recorded in the patriarchal legends can find a place, for it will hardly suffice to choose arbitrarily any given number of years and rule out a longer period. The following items seem to be the irreducible minimum of requirements for identifying the patriarchal period:

1. *Hebrews and Habiru.* If we are to allow any connection between the Biblical Hebrews and the Habiru frequently mentioned in cuneiform records and the Apiru of Egypt, we must have satisfactory demonstration of the linguistic kinship of the names, at the very least, even if no direct etymology can be established. In turn, however, this must be supported by reasonable demonstration that Hebrews, Habiru, and Apiru were approximately the same

18. *Cf.* his *Early Israel in Recent History Writing*, p. 89.

25

kind of people in similar states of life at coinciding periods of time—whatever the relation may be between their conceivably similar names.

2. *World conditions.* Although the patriarchs are principally represented in Genesis as peaceful men, their world was not a stable one. The only secure social order in which the patriarchal generations ever lived was that which they found in Egypt at the end of the period we are trying to fix. Times of unrest and upheaval must be considered as the background of our legends.

3. *Biblical chronology and geography.* If we are to reach any decision whatever, we must be willing to allow, even before it is formally proved, general plausibility to the broad idea of geography and scheme of time presented in the Genesis legends. This must be, if for no other reason, because they have yet to be disproved. It is unnecessary to overlook the schematized and simplified nature of the traditions in Genesis in order to place this much faith in them.

The following chapter on patriarchal origins will deal with the problem of the Habiru. For the present it is sufficient to observe that Egyptian, Mesopotamian, Ugaritic, and Anatolian records mention peoples known variously as Habiru, Apirim, and Apiru; the occurrences of these peoples are dated all the way from the end of the twentieth century in Mesopotamia down to the middle of the twelfth century in Egypt. The linguistic problem is yet to reach its final solution, if there is one, but there is widespread satisfaction that these names are close enough to that of the Hebrews of Genesis to be akin, especially since these people often look like the Biblical people: they turn up at many points in the Fertile Crescent as semi-nomads who reluctantly settled down, were of a sociologically and economically depressed position in society, were looked on as foreigners wherever they lived, and in time of war made fierce fighters. Although the appearances of the Habiru after the Amarna Age are of little help in fixing the upper limit of the patriarchal period, they are found long enough before Amarna to require us to extend the possible patriarchal time limits considerably beyond the three generations before Joseph that the schematized Genesis story gives us. A consecutive chronological list of the references to Habiru and Apiru, which will be given in the next chapter, displays the gratifying pattern of moving progressively westward from Mesopotamia to Egypt with the passing centuries between 1900 and 1400.

Even more indicative of a patriarchal period extending over several centuries than the evidence of Habiru-Apiru people is the troubled nature of life throughout the entire first half of the second millennium. This was not yet the age of the great Mesopotamian empires that came later with their relatively stable order. From 2200 on, successive waves of Hurrian infiltration moved southward across northern Mesopotamia into Syria, Palestine, and on into Egypt. The Gutian invasions came in the same approximate period. The Elamite invasions swept in from the East soon after 2000, followed shortly by the Amorites from the West. Outside the relatively stable reign of Hammurabi himself in Babylon at the end of the eighteenth century and the beginning of the seventeenth, it is difficult to find any place or any time of lasting peace and prosperity throughout the Fertile Crescent in the years after 2000. In the eighteenth century, soon after the Elamites and the Amorites, came the Hyksos movements across the western section of the Fertile Crescent and on into Egypt, and the Amarna Age was no peaceful one in the Egyptian holdings in Asia. In all, it was five hundred years of unrest and insecurity, and, since we can hardly designate any shorter time as "an unsettled world order," we shall do well to allow this entire period of five centuries to serve as the background into some parts of which the lives and times of the patriarchs can be fitted.

As the account stands in Genesis, the patriarchs are represented as having been successive generations. If we take that literally, we should have to settle upon one single period of slightly more than a century; if we take seriously our dating of the end of the patriarchal period, then we should have to take only the very last century in the possible five. There is substantial argument advanced to support precisely that view of the patriarchal age,[19] but such a view requires attributing more and greater precision of chronological detail to the patriarchal narratives than one might expect of an idealized, traditional history. It also involves an arbitrary limitation of the possible period from which we might seek to illuminate the Genesis narrative.

The generally plausible geographical and chronological reference of the patriarchal traditions spoken of previously is essentially this: the Hebrews looked to Mesopotamia as the land of their origin (Genesis xii.5). At least before they moved westward into Palestine and Egypt, Mesopotamia had been as much of a home as they knew until they finally settled down at the end of the patriarchal age. They were not a people with strong national or ethnic ties, nor did they stay in one place long enough to acquire them. At some point in the long, troubled centuries before 1500 they moved westward, but not all of them, for those who did move into Palestine still had relatives in Mesopotamia with whom they continued to have contact from time to time (xxiv.4, xxviii.2). Although these Hebrews worshipped some sort of tribal or ancestral deity, the state of their religious development was seldom distinctive enough

19 *E.g.*, Gordon, *Introduction to Old Testament Times*, p. 102f.; Yehezkel Kaufmann would locate most of the patriarchal age after 1350, as in his *The Religion of Israel: From Its Beginnings to the Babylonian Exile*, p. 219.

to mark them clearly as a people apart. They shared the social, legal, and business practices of whatever people controlled the territory in which they happened at any time to be living. In short, there was little by which one could recognize Hebrews in the patriarchal period except their social status—and even that varied.

As long as we have to do with such a people as this, who were more a social class or an economic phenomenon than a people in the strict sense, who travelled far and wide in their world by small units largely independent of each other, who may well have been a large, amorphous group of whom the patriarchal Hebrews are a summary stylization, we should not narrow our field overmuch. We can still look on Abraham as the ancestor of the Biblical Hebrews even if his migration out of Haran took place early in the twentieth century and that of his "grandson" Jacob into Egypt in the time of the Hyksos or later. The broad pattern of descent and kinship is still there, just as the general geographical and chronological pattern is essentially true to the period as a whole, if we hold with a patriarchal period as spacious as five hundred years.

The Patriarchal Stories as Legend

If one is entirely rationalistic in his view of history, neither legend nor myth is of much value for him in penetrating the life of the past. Indeed, if one holds that only what can be personally experienced or attended by eye-witnesses is true, there is no worthwhile truth for him in most or all of the contents of Genesis. Neither of these positions governs this study of the patriarchal legends, for the writer holds that, just as there are theological lessons to be deduced from history, and moral and religious truth to be learned from myth, so there is available in legend the raw material, if nothing else, of which history can be written.

To be sure, it lacks the precision and exactitude of historical documents, but it fills the gap where they do not exist.

Records of the past, as they have come down to us, are usually categorized as mythical, legendary, or historical, but such a classification must be made with an honest admission that the boundaries between them are vaguely defined: they fade into each other at their extremities. In speaking of the patriarchal narratives as legend we need to recognize, however, the following peculiarities of each.

In the matter of the *where* and the *when,* as well as the *who,* of the past, history deals with what is demonstrated and factually known; *e.g.,* Charlemagne was crowned emperor of the Holy Roman Empire in A.D. 800. Here it is a matter of a man who actually lived and to whom certain things happened, as records close to the events testify. Myth, however, seldom concerns people at all; or, when it does, they are subsidiary characters in the story to supernatural or divine beings, and the setting is not represented as anywhere within time and space but rather beyond them or on the edge of them; the first eleven chapters of Genesis are classic examples of this. Here we find myth as an affirmation of certain points of view held by the author to be generally true of life as a whole, answers to the great questions of the meaning of things. In Finegan's view, myth is a human statement in human language of what is ultimately beyond man.[20] We can legitimately claim that myth treats not so much what once happened as what is perennially held to happen or to be true. Legend presents an account of something which is attributed to an actual person or to one who could have lived, and a possible place and time are ascribed to the event; for instance, the legend of the veracity of George Washington, or the historical fiction of an imaginary woman named Scarlett O'Hara, whose life

20. Jack Finegan, *In the Beginning: A Journey through Genesis,* p. 11.

and times are very much like those of people who actually did live through the Civil War period in the United States.

All three types of record of the past deal with things that happened, or are represented as having happened, but they differ in the agency and causation they specify for the events. History carefully looks for the line of cause and effect drawn between persons and groups in life in this world and thus, for instance, points to the smouldering resentment of the shattered German people after World War I as one of the reasons for their readiness to accept the promises of national rebirth to days of glory in the Hitler program when it came along. Even when history is written from a theologically motivated attitude, as with the Hebrew Deuteronomist, there is still a strong emphasis on the human, this-worldly aspect of events. Myth looks, again, to the level of the supernatural for the inciting force or agent of its events: heavenly beings may act willy-nilly, like Babylonian gods, or with avowed moral purpose, like the Hebrew Yahweh in sending the flood, but the initiative and effective force lie beyond the temporal and the natural. Legend is well aware of the divine activity but usually sees it mediated through natural, human powers and deeds; e.g., God assures Abraham that he may with impunity break the law and cast out of his house the slave woman who has borne him a son.

The very content of the events recorded in myth, legend, and history helps to distinguish them. Myth works with cosmic events that transcend the limits of ordinary happening. The creator God may be represented as a majestic figure, whose simple willing of a thing causes it to come into being, or as a competent workman who bustles about the universe making things; in either case this is exclusively the domain of myth. It is quite the opposite with history, which pays attention to the large movements and proceedings of significant groups of men and their leaders, and

31

thus tells us how the arrogant self-glorification and oppressive conduct of government by the House of David brought about the disruption of the political unit of Israel they had received from Saul.

Although legend may take account of the general social and political background of its characters and their story, its focus of attention is nevertheless on the small scene, the internal life of the family and its thoughts, desires, sins, and achievements. So it is that the legend of Joseph tells how a cocky and conceited brat, the bane of his brothers' existence, grows up to be a competent administrator of the Egyptian government and, more significantly, the savior of the family livelihood. Legend, particularly the legendary tradition in Genesis, has such as this for its content by virtue of its production in a time, when, for the teller, the family or other small group was the limit of human society. It is involved with the family because it is speaking of prenational times and events of a people.

Difference in language and presentation of the material to be communicated sets myth, legend, and history apart from each other. History will methodically, even laboriously, cite and evaluate sources and, when dealing with fact, indicate it as fact; when speaking on incompletely documented or not quite proven subjects, it will, ideally, label the conclusions as speculative or conjectural. Myth, on the other hand, has about it the manner of recital or even ritual re-enactment, as with the solemn recitation of *Enuma elish,* the Mesopotamian creation story, during the New Year's festivities in Mesopotamia; there is about it no sign of proving or demonstrating anything, but rather, one of stating the faith of the reciter and the hearers in a declarative or even liturgical mood. While either of these, myth or history, can be morally edifying and enjoyable, these are side results for them. It is among the principal purposes of legend, though, to inspire, teach, and entertain, and so the narrative technique of the story-teller predominates in legend, with the free use of all the tricks of the trade: suspense, dramatic irony, surprise, heightening of detail, and the rest.

It thus becomes apparent that myth is so far removed from history as to be of virtually no use whatever in any historical study of the people who knew and told the myth. Useful as the myth is for understanding the inner life and spiritual insight of a people, we can safely rule it out as a source for reconstructing the everyday actuality and experience of its people. Myth makes no attempt to deal with the plausible or conceivable; rather, it often makes a strong appeal to the principle of *credo quia absurdum*: "this is my faith, for I cannot prove it."

On the basis of literary analysis of the legend, however, and if need be, on that basis alone, we can see that the student of the past must take the legend much more seriously. Because of its historical background legend lies on the boundary of fact, of documentary source. Once we have clearly marked the distinction between myth and legend, it becomes necessary to keep legend distinct from history but recognize at the same time its relevance for history. It is not the same as that history which is an "authentic record of actual events based on documents contemporary, or nearly contemporary, with the facts narrated."[21] It is, however, the stage of recording the past that immediately precedes or accompanies that kind of history and consequently must be seen as taking the place of historical record in its own age; perhaps it even shapes the pattern for what follows, preparing the way for it.

To an extent beyond Gunkel, Skinner fathomed the relevance of legend for history and its reliability for a general picture of the historical setting of the legendary events. It

21. John Skinner, *Critical and Exegetical Commentary on Genesis* (hereafter cited as *ICC*), p. iii.

was Skinner who went quite beyond his critical precursors and contemporaries by acknowledging that legends "belong to a pre-literary and uncritical stage of society, when the popular imagination works freely on dim reminiscences of the past, producing an amalgam in which tradition and phantasy are inseparably mingled." It is legend that "reveals the soul of a people, . . . its moral aspirations, . . . conception of itself . . . , and, to some indeterminate extent, the impact on its inner life of the momentous historic experiences in which it first woke up to the consciousness of a national existence and destiny."[22]

Because the "reminiscences" are dim, they cannot be pressed to indicate more than a general and largely undetailed picture of the situation they recall. Within those limits, however, they are fair game for the reconstruction of a time and of areas of life for which historical documents are unavailable. Likewise, since legend does indicate the reaction of the people to the external events, the effect and "impact" which the events had on them, it has not been adequately studied until one goes through the hazardous but necessary process of trying to reason from the effect, the impact, to the event or situation that produced it.

Having reached that conviction, one could proceed through the devious paths of literary analysis and speculation, just as Wellhausen, Gunkel, Skinner, and all their generation did; it must have been their conviction, or they would not have felt free, as they did, to identify the patriarchs as personified tribes and their journeys as movements of the tribes whom they represented. (There, now, is an instance of drawing historical data out of legendary narrative.) But, as Skinner himself made clear, legend yields historical matter in another manner; namely, through the comparison of its content, in general and in detail, with the collateral evidence of archaeology. The

22. *Ibid.*, p. iv.

age of discovery was under way at the time the masterpieces of criticism were being produced, and its effects were beginning to be felt. Skinner could in 1910 optimistically state that "it is no longer possible to doubt the *essential* historicity of the patriarchal tradition,"[23] that there was a *"general* compatibility"[24] of the patriarchal narratives with the general conditions of ancient Near Eastern life, and that the patriarchal legends contained a *"substantial* nucleus"[25] of historical fact. The context of these statements is one so filled with caution and reserve that the qualifying adjectives must be emphasized to preserve the tone of the whole passage. The historicity of the patriarchal legends was just beginning to shine through with new force, enough to make it necessary to rule out the possibility of denying *all* connection with history in the legends, even if there was insufficient evidence to allow any equally sure assertion of how close the tie was with history. It has remained for the following rank of students of the Bible to mark the details, though not always with the meticulous caution of Skinner.

23 *Ibid.,* p. xvi. Emphasis mine.
24. *Ibid.,* p. xvii. Emphasis mine.
25. *Ibid.,* p. xxiii. Emphasis mine.

~ II

PATRIARCHAL ORIGINS

G ENESIS gives us no clearly consistent picture of the original home and base of operations of the Hebrews, any more than there is a coherent explanation of the motivation for their various expeditions here and there about the Fertile Crescent. If the authors of the Hexateuchal documents had been trying to manufacture an entirely imaginary people with a completely nonfactual past—if, for instance, there had been no preservation of the early traditions of Israel through oral transmission, or if for some reason the authors of the sacred history had felt ashamed of or embarrassed by their people's history and therefore had set about trying to write an "improved" history of their people—we may feel sure that they would have presented us with a much more logical, internally consistent narrative than they have. The lack of smoothness in the harmonization of detail and the variety of impressions left with the reader about the origins of the patriarchal tribes point not only to the composite literary nature of the sources but likewise to the presence amidst those sources of those dim reminiscences of the past which are the historical "meat" of legend. To state this in terms of the Biblical tradition alone, as it stands, is little more than a fond wish; to state it, however, in terms of a comparison of what we know of the Biblical Hebrews from Genesis with what we know of the Habiru and Apiru, is to approach more nearly that point at which we can use legend to reconstruct the history of an age for which historical documents are not extant.

The Biblical Hebrews

For all its kaleidoscopic detail the Biblical picture of the Hebrews is a fairly simple one. They originated in Mesopotamia; at least, the dawn of the Biblical age of history finds them there. Whether their point of departure was southern or northern Mesopotamia is a matter whose settlement depends not only on the solution of textual problems[1] but also on archaeological remains from the two areas. There is probably evidence in Genesis of an attempt on the part of the authors to reconcile varying traditions on this question.[2] The Biblical tradition does not begin to take interest in the Hebrews, however, until they leave Mesopotamia. Our legends of the patriarchs represent them as living in several places in Palestine, principally southern Palestine and most especially at Hebron (Genesis xiii.18, xviii.1, xxiii.19) and at Beersheba (xxi.32–33, xxvi.33, xxviii.10). Occasionally the Biblical story takes them to Egypt, and in each case the trip to Egypt is brought on by conditions in Palestine that send them to the land of the Nile for food for themselves and their animals (xii.10, xlii.1f.). Although the Genesis narratives do not make it appear that the patriarchs thought they should not live anywhere but in Palestine even on a temporary basis, there is an element of almost dogged determination to avoid taking up permanent residence elsewhere. Thus it is that Abraham forbids his servant to take Isaac to Mesopotamia to find a wife (xxiv.5–6), probably lest he stay there and forfeit the

---

1. Ur in southern Mesopotamia is named in Genesis xi.31 (P); Haran in northern Mesopotamia in xii.4–5 (J).
2. *Cf.* the commentaries on xi.31.

promised inheritance; later Jacob is determined that, even if he should die while living in Egypt, he must not be buried there (XLVII.29–30). So the Biblical Hebrews leave their Mesopotamian home with no great reluctance, even if they do not break all ties with their relatives there, and move into Palestine as their principal center, though their roots are not permanently put down there till after the patriarchs are dead and gone. Most appropriately, the Hebrew of Genesis XII.6 describes Abram's movement with the verb *ʿbr* ("to cross over, to migrate"), a suggested root of "Hebrew."

The Hebrews' tradition of their ethnic origin and connections put them in the line of Shem, one of the sons of Noah (x.21). The earlier and simpler genealogy of J (x.25) divides the offspring of Eber into two groups: Peleg, the northern "Aramaeans,"[3] and Joktan, the southern branch of Semites in Arabia.[4] The later genealogy provided by P (at the key points x.22, xi.10ff.) more or less harmonizes with the earlier tradition but provides a wider picture of the Hebrews' conception of their kinship and a more systematic presentation of it all, as we expect from P. The line of Abraham is traced back to Arpachshad, the eldest son of Shem. The other Semitic peoples are derived from Arpachshad's brothers. Naming them from east to west,[5] P distributes the family thus: Elam represents the Elamites, whose center was in the area of Shushan; Asshur stands for the Assyrians; Arpachshad is named next in line and should ideally stand for southern Mesopotamia but is not so designated (critical attempts to find "Ur of the Chaldeans" in Arpachshad seemed doomed to linguistic failure),[6] Lud can be located as Lydia in Asia Minor

3. *ICC*, p. 220.
4. *Ibid.*, p. 217.
5. Gunkel, p. 154.
6. A full discussion is to be found at this verse in *ICC*.

or, more helpfully, on the upper Tigris; finally, Aram is the ancestor of the Aramaeans.[7]

Thus P's orderly table of nations places Abraham's family in the descent from the eldest son of Noah—and, parenthetically, continues the line in each generation through eldest sons down to Terah and Abram. That there was confusion in the tradition is shown by the muddy text of J and the almost successful attempt of P to bring order into the family line. It cannot but strike the reader of Genesis that, with all his flair for locating all details carefully and usually quite systematically, the author of P was unable to find a geographic niche for the line of Arpachshad. The other lines descended from Shem can be located geographically with fair success; not so the very line from which the Hebrews traced their origin. If Arpachshad did stand for Ur of the Chaldees in southern Mesopotamia—not otherwise provided for in the family of Shem, since Babel is derived, for instance, from the Hamitic line, x.10—then we could associate the ancestry of Abram with southern Mesopotamia. Even if the linguistic problems of this identification were not insuperable, it would still disagree with the majority of references later in Genesis, which point to Haran as the locus of Abram's family. If it is not reading the text too closely, one wonders, for instance, that Abram was grown up and married before leaving Ur (xi.31) and yet, when called out of Haran by Yahweh, is directed to leave "thy country" (xii.1). Classical criticism agreed to account the Ur tradition as P's idea, with the result that he had to construct a story of a double excursion along a roundabout route, to take Abram from Ur to Canaan. For reasons best known to himself P chose to connect Abram with both

7. This distribution of the peoples is fully dealt with in *ICC*, pp. 204–206.

southern and northern Mesopotamia; we can only speculate, but, since P himself does not represent those accompanying Abram as all of the children of Eber (*i.e.*,
Hebrews), perhaps this was P's way of dealing with the
reminiscence that the people out of whom Abram came
were spread over a large area in Mesopotamia and not
organized into any kind of unified structure, despite their
sense of kinship with each other. Inasmuch as what P
gives us does not allow us to locate the line of Arpachshad
in a definite geographical place, perhaps it should be taken
as indicating no definite home at all. If we should find
through archaeological study that a people otherwise very
much like the Biblical Hebrews were scattered far and
wide throughout the Fertile Crescent, the Biblical details are not so uniform as to rule out the identification
and, in fact, may even suggest it.

The Habiru

Ever since the Habiru came to be familiarly known,
principally from the Amarna correspondence at first and
then from subsequent appearances, there have been
attempts to connect this people, or class of people, with
the Hebrews. At the same time the Apiru of Egyptian
records have struck many minds as paralleling the Biblical people in many respects.[8] If the three-way equation of
Habiru-Apiru-Hebrews can be shown to have appreci-
able validity, there is much help to be derived from the

8. A history of the study of the problem is given by Moshe Greenberg,
The Hab/piru, pp. 3–12. Representative views of the matter are those of
Julius Lewy, "Les textes paléo-assyriens et l'Ancien Testament," *RHR*,
CIX (1934), pp. 29–65, and "Habiru and Hebrews," *HUCA*, XIX (1939),
pp. 587–623; E. Dhorme, "La question des Habiri," *RHR*, CXVIII (1938),
pp. 170–187, as amended by his later review of *Manuel d'Archéologie
Biblique*, by A.-G. Barrois, *RHR*, CXXII (1940), pp. 153–158; C. H.
Gordon, *Introduction to Old Testament Times*, p. 76, n. 2; and W. F.
Albright, "The Smaller Beth-Shan Stele of Sethos I (1309–1290 B.C.),"
BASOR, No. 125 (February 1952), pp. 24–32.

extra-Biblical records in understanding the origins of the Hebrew people.

The problem of the identification is linguistic, sociological, and historical, and the literature connected with it contains all degrees of optimism and pessimism in approaching these aspects of the problem. A final answer that will allow complete identification in every respect is not yet to be had, but the following discussion aims to show the limits of genuine plausibility.

The ramifications of the philological aspect of the problem go beyond the limits of our immediate concern, but the question is essentially one of different forms and meanings of otherwise comparable names in Biblical Hebrew and its cognate Semitic languages. The names to be dealt with are:

Akkadian: ḫābiru, or ḫāpiru. (Often written ideographically, SA.GAZ.)
Egyptian: ꜥpr.w, or ꜥāpiru.
Ugaritic: ꜥprm, perhaps ꜥapirim.
Hebrew: ꜥibrîm.

While the vowels are not negligible, the primary differences to be explained are those of the first two consonants, for the different names contain consonants that are distinct sounds to the Semitic, if not to the Western, ear. If a common root is to be sought for the names, the changes in the first two consonants must be justified. There are two principal possibilities for deriving the respective names from a common supposed Proto-Semitic root; see the excursus at the end of this chapter.

The linguistic argument proves nothing in its own right and can properly be used only as part of a cumulative mass of evidence for demonstrating the general equivalence of the Habiru and the Biblical Hebrews. For itself the argument from philology is beset with several difficulties that are as yet without solution. The derivation that most

41

neatly fits the social status of the Habiru depends upon a root that is difficult to locate in West Semitic. The readily available and well-known Semitic root that would go well with the idea of a semi-nomadic people does not accord with the fact that there is some evidence that the Habiru were relatively settled members of the population. Perhaps the hardest problem is to explain how a descriptive adjective became a proper noun and adjective—or at least took on such "gentilic" form. In Hebrew, the word *Hebrew* has the same gentilic form as many other similar words: *Hittite, Canaanite,* and *Judahite* are easy examples. Actual usage of the word in Genesis is difficult to characterize: despite its form, it is not unmistakably or consistently gentilic in usage, as even Greenberg allows.[9] In fact, the discussion below of the occurrences of *Hebrew* in Genesis represents the writer's conviction that the usage of the word in the legends is just as easily understood as a designation of a social class as of a discrete nationality. When the changeover actually took place is something we do not know: perhaps the Biblical writers themselves unconsciously made the transformation,[10] but that is rather late. The best summary of the philological aspect of the identification of Habiru and Hebrews is that of Rowley, who concludes that philology has no serious objection to the equation but does not prove it.[11] Etymological argument is intricate and often vexing, but it is still worthy of pursuit for whatever final results it may be able to produce. For our purposes here it is most important to recognize that etymology at its best and most conclusive can demonstrate nothing more than the *origin* of a word. It rightly does not attempt to explain the development of associated and derivative meanings that attach

9. Greenberg, pp. 92–93.
10. *Ibid.,* p. 93.
11. Rowley, *From Joseph to Joshua,* p. 52.

themselves to the word, once it comes into existence, and can greatly obscure the original denotation. Even if rigorously scientific research could wholly explain the origin of the term, our principal attention would still have to be given to the way it came to be used by those unaware of its linguistic history.

Greenberg's complete survey of all the appearances of the SA.GAZ-Habiru has quite conclusively demonstrated the sociological nature of the names. They first appear at the time of the Amorite invasions; so they may have constituted the economically depressed element of western Semites who moved eastward at that time.[12] A court deposition from the eighth year of Bur-Sin of the Third Dynasty of Ur (1965) declares, "An-zi-KA, the SA.GAZ, is not my man."[13] This is probably to be interpreted as meaning a vagrant status for the man thus mentioned.

The Habiru men whose redemption is discussed in an Alishar source are taken by Gelb as "foreign captives."[14]

At Mari they appear in a double role; *i.e.*, both as mercenary soldiers in the royal forces and as marauders.[15] We find in one letter the statement that "Yapah-Adad has made ready the settlement Zallul on this side of the bank of the Euphrates River, and with two thousand troops of the Hapiru of the land, is dwelling in that city."[16] Other letters, among those received by Zimri-lim of Mari, tell how some Habiru raided and took a town under cover of night, and two other less readily read texts complain of their warlike activity.[17]

The same ready availability of Habiru for any type of employer is later shown in the Amarna letters, where they

12. Greenberg, p. 88.
13. *Ibid.*, p. 15.
14. Ignace J. Gelb, *Inscriptions from Alishar and Vicinity*, p. 24.
15. Greenberg, p. 63.
16. James Pritchard (ed.), *Ancient Near Eastern Texts Relating to the Old Testament* (hereafter cited as *ANET*), p. 483.
17. Dhorme, *RHR*, CXVIII (1938), pp. 175–176.

are distinct from both loyalists and enemies of the Egyptian governors but are found in both loyalist and rebel armies as irregular auxiliaries.[18] Typical mention of the Habiru as threatening the established order is the appeal to the king, "Let the king, my lord, protect his land from the hand of the Apiru."[19] Even clearer is the longer account:

> The chief of the Apiru has risen in arms against the lands which the god of the king, my lord, gave me; but I have smitten him. Also let the king, my lord, know that all my brethren have abandoned me, and it is I and Abdu-Heba who fight against the chief of the Apiru. And Zurata, prince of Accho, and Indaruta, prince of Achshaph, it was they who hastened with fifty chariots—for I had been robbed by the Apiru—to my help; but behold, they are fighting against me.[20]

On the other side of the conflict, we find a GAZ as a messenger between the king and Rib-Addi,[21] and a commander lists his forces in this order: "army, chariots, brothers, SA.GAZ . . ."[22] It is to be observed that each side in the Amarna troubles associates its enemies with the SA.GAZ.[23]

There are possibly two different strata of SA.GAZ distinguished by Greenberg at Alalakh,[24] and some of them appear to have done fairly well for themselves. Alalakh documents from the eighteenth and fifteenth centuries speak of them as both soldiers and shepherds, though most of them appear to have been state-supported soldiers.

18. Greenberg, p. 27.

19. *ANET*, p. 486.

20. *Ibid.* Other such passages occur on the following several pages in Pritchard.

21. J. A. Knudtzon, Otto Weber, and Erich Ebeling, *Die El-Amarna-Tafeln*, Vol. I, p. 493.

22. *Ibid.*, p. 723.

23. Greenberg, p. 45.

24. *Ibid.*, p. 65.

Their names, interestingly enough, indicate mostly Hurrian stock with some Semites.[25]

At Nuzi, in the same years early in the Amarna Age, the Habiru are the "predominant, if not the sole, element in a class of indigent dependent persons."[26] This is borne out by the record of the following contracts: "Mar-Idiglat, a Hebrew from the land of Assyria, on his own initiative has entered the house of Tehiptilla, the son of Puhi-Shenni, as a slave";[27] again, "Sin-balti, a Hebrew woman, on her own initiative has entered the house of Tehiptilla as a slave."[28] A wealthy lady at Nuzi had trouble with one of her slaves: "Amar-sha-ili the Habiru . . . as slave to Tulpunnaya had come but later withdrew."[29]

While the Habiru were so notorious for their anarchy in Syria and Palestine in the Amarna Age that their name was synonymous for all troublemakers and insurgents,[30] and "to become a Habiru" meant to become a disgraced outcast,[31] elsewhere they were relatively peaceful, submissive workers who entered servitude voluntarily and apparently fulfilled their duties satisfactorily. Some contracts seem to specify a definite time of service, and others do not, but we have only the one record just cited of a Habiru who ran away from slavery once having been committed to it.[32] Yet at least once in the Amarna correspondence we find

25. *Ibid.,* pp. 20–22.

26. *Ibid.,* p. 69.

27. *ANET,* p. 220.

28. *Ibid.* The *ANET* translator (T. J. Meek) skips a step in directly translating the *ḫabiru* of the original as "Hebrew" in both this and the immediately preceding passage. The earlier translation of Chiera and Speiser in *JAOS,* XLVII (1927), p. 44, simply reads it *ḫabiru.*

29. Robert H. Pfeiffer and E. A. Speiser, "One Hundred New Selected Nuzi Texts," *AASOR,* XVI (1935–1936), p. 95. Speiser calls attention to the Semitic name of the slave.

30. *ANET,* pp. 486–489.

31. Greenberg, pp. 73–75. *Cf. ANET,* pp. 488–489.

32. In view of the great amount of material we have from Nuzi it hardly seems too bold to speak of this as an isolated instance.

"slaves who had become Apiru."[33] Of this last more later.

Among the Hittites, according to Goetze,[34] the Habiru seem to have enjoyed some special status as dependent directly upon the nobility, after whom they are named before commoners. The levels of society are listed in descending order: the king, palace officials, the clergy, the army, free-born citizens, offspring of the nobles, and the Habiru; then come the lower classes.[35] The mention of "Habiri gods" in Hittite treaties[36] points to the recognized legitimacy of the Habiru as distinct elements in Hittite society.

Of interest because of its utter uniqueness is the one case we have of thoroughly settled Habiru. A Ugaritic tax list, which can be taken as contemporaneous with the early Amarna time, four times speaks of "Aleppo of the SA.GAZ" (twice in that form, twice employing the term "Aleppo of the Apirim").[37] At least there was one locality where the Habiru were so well settled as to give it their name, but this is a great rarity.

Such a sampling of the complete tabulation is sufficient to show some of the spread of connotations for Habiru-SA.GAZ. They turn up as slaves, as for instance at Nuzi: Tehiptilla and Tulpunnaya, prominent citizens and wealthy property owners there, have left several contracts behind which record their acquisition of Habiru slaves. This subjection of the Habiru to slavery is not apparently required by law or custom but is entered into voluntarily, according to the contracts themselves. Perhaps it was

33. *ANET*, pp. 488–489.

34. Greenberg, p. 77, not to my knowledge published separately.

35. *Ibid.*, p. 52.

36. *ANET*, pp. 205, 206.

37. C. Virolleaud, "Les Villes et les Corporations du Royaume d'Ugarit," *Syria*, XXI (1940), pp. 123–151; Greenberg, p 78. *Cf.* Albrecht Goetze, "The City Khalbi and the Khapiru People," *BASOR*, No. 79 (October 1940), pp. 32–34.

wholly a matter of economic pressure. They also are found as soldiers at Mari, where the record occurs of large numbers of them under the command of one of the officers. In Hammurabi's Babylon the Habiru appear to have been entitled to some kind of dole from the state[38] and perhaps occupied some dependent status there like that recorded for them among the Hittites.

Habiru are not thought of as having any nationality of their own. Sometimes they are clearly Semitic in their names; also, Lewy finds evidence of Hurrian as well as of western Semitic nomenclature.[39] Even if they were not nomads but members of the settled population, as Greenberg thinks,[40] the signs of their origin usually point to some locality other than that in which they appear as slaves, soldiers, wards of the state, or whatever. Furthermore, the manifold variety of origins indicated by their names and other signs of their previous residence or association makes it impossible to think of them as all one homogeneous group with even the most rudimentary tribal organization, or any single racial or ethnic connection. The distribution of the Habiru throughout the Fertile Crescent in the first half of the second millennium shown by the texts demands that they be characterized as follows.

The Habiru were a depressed element of the population wherever we find record of them. The economic nature of their status is indicated by the kind of work they did: it was the kind of work reserved for those who, by reason of their poverty or alien background or both, could not own property and thereby live as free citizens. Instances where Habiru reached relatively high positions lie out-

38. L. W. King, *Letters and Inscriptions of Hammurabi*, Vol. III, p. 93. The fully transcribed text is given by Greenberg, filling in blanks not deciphered by King.
39. Lewy, *HUCA*, XIV (1939), pp. 622–623.
40. Greenberg, p. 86f.

side the limits set earlier for the patriarchal period. The supposition that Habiru worked as interpreters, a higher than usual position and important function in business, appeals to Lewy[41] but is rejected by Greenberg,[42] and impressively so, as a misreading of the language of the contracts. The Habiru, however, do not appear to have been the lowest level of society; they do menial work, but not because there is any sign of their having been born to it: the contracts often emphasize the free choice of the Habiru in binding himself over to the master in servitude. Lewy[43] makes much of the fact that some contracts take pains to state the exact date of the beginning of the term, as if only a specific time of service were being agreed upon. This would indicate that the Habiru had some standing from which to bargain, however little.

If we take seriously the Amarna reference to "slaves who had become Apiru" cited above and can allow in general that runaway slaves leave their masters in order to seek some greater degree of personal freedom for themselves even if the nature of their work does not change, we are well on the way to capturing much of the sense of Habiru. This word stands for a group so designated, not because of the place they came from, for the texts indicate either that they were settled among the many scattered populations where they are found or that they came there from a number of other places; not because of their allegiance to a single, eponymous god, for that implies a tribal organization for which no definite proof exists;[44] but because of their sociological and economic status: "the kind of people" they were and their work. Settled people looked on the Habiru with scorn because they were mi-

41. Lewy, *HUCA*, XIV (1939), p. 599f.
42. Greenberg, p. 23.
43. Lewy, *HUCA*, XIV (1939), p. 609. He suggests comparison with Exodus xxi.2f.
44. Greenberg, pp. 79–80.

grant workers, did work unbecoming free citizens, were mysterious and unpredictable foreigners, or some combination of these.

In short, no single meaning can be everywhere read into Habiru. The generally pejorative sense of the term in the mouths of others is agreed to on all sides,[45] but it represents a state of life to which slaves escaped with what seems to be a transparent motivation of seeking something better and at least a little freer than they had as slaves. This writer suggests the parallel term "tramp" in English, with its many associated meanings. A tramp moves about at his own will, and his life consequently appeals to those with unsatisfied *Wanderlust*. He may be supported by doing odd jobs from city to city, or he may become the restless soldier of fortune ready to fight for anybody—though this role has been romanticized by our fiction and motion pictures. A tramp may never move outside the borders of his native land but is still always someone apart, and the word itself serves to distinguish him from the settled, property-owning population. This is more than suggestive illustration, since each characteristic of the "tramp" in English named here is a trait of the Habiru. It could be that the life of the Habiru, the tramp, is still much the same as always, considering them as a class of people, a kind of life, even though the names change.

The suggestion from Bottéro[46] that we read Habiru as *refugee* is an attractive one, though here again, the contemporary frequency of our encounter with that term causes it to have reverberations of meaning for us that do not really help our understanding of the ancient word.

45. De Vaux, *RB*, LV (1948), p. 338; H. H. Rowley, "Habiru and Hebrews," *PEQ*, LXXIV (1942), p. 52, where he cautiously agrees with Meek on this point; Gerhard von Rad, *Das erste Buch Mose*, p. 322. (Von Rad's volume is hereafter cited as *ATD*.)

46. Jean Bottéro, *Le Problème des Ḥabiru à la 4ᵉ Rencontre Assyriologique Internationale*, p. 195f.

More striking for this writer is a fine modern example of how an adjective descriptive of sociological status has become a gentilic title; namely, the choice of the name for the state of Liberia. There, in Latinic form, the identification of the sociological status of the founders of the country, with all its memories of former slave status, has become the proudly borne national identification.

Mention of the Apiru in Egypt begins just before the Amarna Age and continues into the era of the Ramessids. They appear first shortly after 1500, in the last years of Hatshepsut or the early reign of Tutmose III, in two tomb inscriptions, which show them working on a wine press.[47] Later in that century they were among the captives of Amenophis II, who claims to have captured 3,600 of them.[48] The records of Seti I show them as troublemaking marauders near Beth-Shan.[49] Finally within the period that concerns us, a tale from the period of Seti I, whose scene is laid in the time of Tutmose III,[50] describes how horses had to be guarded carefully against possible theft by an "apir."

The career of the Apiru goes rapidly downward, and their lot is simple to describe: they became slave laborers. It was so rare for a foreigner to become anything but a slave in Egypt that, when it did happen that a foreigner bettered himself, the record of it left by the Egyptians shudders with horror. One thinks of the Egyptians' own description of what it was like to have the foreign Hyksos take over the rule of their country: "The land of Egypt was in distress. . . . Distress was in the town of the Asiatics, for Prince Apophis . . . was in Avaris, and the entire land was subject to him with their dues."[51] Green-

47. Greenberg, pp. 55–56.
48. *ANET,* p. 247.
49. *Ibid.,* p. 255.
50. *Ibid.,* p. 22.
51. *Ibid.,* p. 231.

berg submits that the slave status of the Apiru in Egypt was the result of their having been captured and not necessarily a direct reflection of their pre-Egyptian status,[52] and it is clear from the records that they fared better in Mesopotamia and Syria than they did in Egypt. In Egypt their name would *a fortiori* be one spoken with condescension and scorn.

We have only one record of a time or place when Habiru was in the name of a locality, the Aleppo of the Habiru spoken of before. If Habiru ever was a racial or local name apart from this, as Rowley is cautiously willing to allow,[53] then, as he further states, it sank into an occupational title of opprobrium till anyone of that class of society was known as Habiru, with the end result that the name lost all national or local denotation.

Alongside the references to Habiru that are found in extra-Biblical sources, the Biblical mention of Hebrews stands as strikingly similar. There are markedly few uses of the word in Genesis, and all of them stand in the earliest form of the tradition. De Vaux concludes from this[54] that the Hebrews themselves in the literary age thought of *Hebrew* as an ancient name, associated with the times before the consolidation of the united nation of Israel. A count of appearances is indicative of this. The first mention is in xiv.13, where Abram is described as "the Hebrew" in the account of his martial activities, the only time that he departs significantly from the character of quiet, peace-loving master of flocks attributed to him by the rest of the tradition. All the remaining uses of *Hebrew* in the patriarchal chapters come in the story of Joseph. In xxxix.14 and 17 the term is positively spat out by Potiphar's wife in her false accusation of Joseph. In xli.12 the Pharaoh's but-

52. Greenberg, p. 82.
53. H. H. Rowley, "Recent Discovery and the Patriarchal Age," *BJRL*, XXXII (September 1949), p. 62.
54. De Vaux, *RB*, LV (1948), p. 338.

ler tells the Pharaoh of the Hebrew man who interpreted his dream in prison, and the appositional relationship of this in the sentence with the description of Joseph's being a servant helps to equate the two phrases. Further on, in XLIII.32, the separation of the Egyptians from the Hebrews at mealtime, by the choice of the Egyptians, shows the distinction of position between them. Finally, Joseph himself, in XL.15, tells how he was stolen away from the "land of the Hebrews." All of these appearances of *Hebrew* without exception are in the JE stratum of tradition; the word does not occur in P.

Hebrew, then, is used by a Biblical author to describe the military activity of Abram, and it is hard to think it accidental that this is confined to the one time that Abram is very much out of character. With one exception, the term is used in the Joseph story by Egyptians or in the description of an Egyptian attitude, and this in no complimentary way. The exceptional use of the word by Joseph himself poses two problems, that of the significance of the "land" of the Hebrews and of the unexpectedness of "Hebrew" on Hebrew lips. With both these problems this writer is at a loss for a satisfactory explanation. "The land of the Hebrews" is a rather grandiose way of referring to the small holdings of Joseph's family in Palestine, even in view of the sense of ultimate possession of the whole country that the authors of the tradition attribute to the patriarchs. Likewise, one is surprised to find Joseph using a word that was tantamount to an insult in the mouth of his Egyptian masters; such self-deprecation, even if in a servile attempt to be disarming, is out of character for Joseph. This author recalls more than once being approached on the street by a colored person who asked for "help fo' an ole niggah," but that is hardly the posture of Joseph in the prison scene. Perhaps it is an inadvertent,

unwitting use of the word, as de Vaux suggests.[55] Apart
from this, though, the Biblical use of Hebrew parallels
quite closely the non-Biblical use of Habiru. Potiphar's
wife is determined to make quite clear the enormity of
the crime of which she accuses Joseph, and so she makes
it explicit by referring to his station in life as rendering
his alleged advances most abhorrent. Similarly, although
the ritualistic purity of the later Egyptians in regard to
their food is attested by Herodotus[56] as a general habit of
theirs, we can still sense the implied insult it was for the
Egyptians to refuse to eat with the Hebrews, who were
of such an inferior social standing as to be unfit for table
companions. Nothing can thus far be made of the interpretation of dreams by a Hebrew, at least as indicative of
social position, but one does think at this point of the
fortune-telling, dream-reading gypsies of later centuries.

It can be concluded, then, that the Biblical authors
were reluctant to use the word *Hebrew* and did so only
when a distinction of social rank or occupation had to
be indicated in the story. In these connections the word
is used ordinarily by non-Hebrews, and this serves to
identify Hebrew as a sociological term and probably as
one not of Hebrew manufacture: they would hardly use
gladly or often a word indicative of inferior social status,[57]
whereas a racial tag would in all probability be used
proudly. Even if Genesis supplies us with little useful
material for a demonstration of an etymological, linguistic relationship between the words Habiru and Hebrew,
the use of the word in Genesis is strikingly close to that
of Habiru and Apiru. Even in places where the Hebrews
are not so spoken of by the tradition, the similar social

55. *Ibid.*
56. II, 41.
57. *Cf.* Greenberg, p. 91.

53

position and activity can be noticed. De Vaux argues[58] this by comparing the warlike Habiru with Abraham the Hebrew in Genesis xiv and the barbarous Simeon and Levi of Genesis xxxiv; the mercenary Habiru soldiers of Amarna times and elsewhere with the (later) Hebrews in the Philistine army (1 Samuel xiv.21, xxix.3); and the Habiru servants and slaves with the mention of Hebrews at hard labor in Egypt under the oppression (Exodus i and v) and the Hebrew slaves of the Law (Exodus xxi). Due allowance must be made, of course, for de Vaux's instancing post-patriarchal parallels.

It can be seen thus far that Habiru and its equivalents are the linguistic kin of Hebrew; even if evidence is lacking for an outright and categorical identification of them or derivation of the latter from the former, they are nevertheless too close to have no connection with each other. In the matter of usage of the words in their respective contexts, not all uses of the one directly correspond to all uses of the other, to be sure. It is not until after the end of the patriarchal period, for instance, that Hebrews in the Bible become slaves in any great number, since even Joseph spent only a short time in servitude, and Jacob served Laban not as a slave but as a relative.[59] Violence of the Habiru type is not a prevailing characteristic of the patriarchs, either. We cannot, in short, make a total identification of all the associated meanings of Habiru and Hebrew,[60] but there is an area of common meaning where the usages do overlap. Arguments from time and place help to reinforce this general similarity.

Most points at which the Habiru manifest the traits of the Biblical Hebrews fall within the general limits of the patriarchal period previously fixed. Greenberg's

58. De Vaux, *RB*, LV (1948), pp. 342–343.
59. *ATD*, p. 253.
60. *Cf.* Rowley, *PEQ*, LXXIV (1942), p. 51.

chart of the Habiru is the most complete listing of the record we have of the people, and it shows in detail the place and time of Habiru activity, along with the nature of their life and work at each. Joining and slightly simplifying his findings with the listing of Meek,[61] we find this spread for the Habiru and Apiru:

The Habiru

In the middle of the twentieth century at Ur.

In the nineteenth century at Alishar.

In Babylon under Hammurabi at the end of the eighteenth century.

At Mari in the Hammurabi period.

At Nuzi in the fifteenth century.

Among the Hittites of Boghazköy in the fifteenth and fourteenth centuries.

In the Amarna letters of the fifteenth century and after.

In a Ugaritic text of the same Amarna time.

Later occurrences of Habiru in Mesopotamia in the twelfth and eleventh centuries are too late for our purposes here.

The Apiru in Egypt

Tomb inscriptions from the time of Tutmose III in the early fifteenth century.

The stela of Amenophis II at Memphis in the late fifteenth century.

The stela of Seti I at Beisan in the late fourteenth century.

Harris Papyrus 55, also from the time of Seti I.

Papyri and an inscription from the time of the second, third, and fourth Ramesses mention the Apiru as late as the middle of the twelfth century, too late to be of help with the patriarchal period, though they have bearing on the problems of dating the Exodus.

It is apparent on the face of it that the Hebrews of Genesis are, so to speak, enclosed both in time and in place within the Habiru of extra-Biblical records. The Habiru were a phenomenon of the whole of the second millennium, as we might expect in an age of such unset-

61. Greenberg, p. 85; Meek, *HO*, pp. 8, 12.

tled *Völkerwanderungen*; they disappear at the end of that time with the advent of more stable sociological and political conditions, the "relative equilibrium" of the early years of the first millennium.[62] As it is, Habiru are mentioned outside the Bible later than the time of the last appearance of Hebrews by that name in the patriarchal period; that is, if we allow a time in the thirteenth century for the Mosaic Exodus, which banded together a group of people for whom, as they moved to final settlement, the name of Hebrew became increasingly inapplicable in its larger and former sense. Likewise, the Habiru lived in parts of the world with which no contact is ever claimed for the Biblical Hebrews. The Hebrews of Genesis are taken no farther north in that account than Haran, but Habiru were numerous enough in population centers of Asia Minor to be given a recognized position in Hittite records. Furthermore, long after the latest possible time for the excursion of Abraham and his family from Mesopotamia, there is clearly a number of Habiru individuals or families still resident there—a fact that the Genesis account itself seems to recall. The chronological and geographical distribution of Habiru does not allow us to make a direct identification of them and their travels and settlement with those of the line of Abraham in Genesis. Instead, the former provides a context for the latter; the journey westward of the Biblical Hebrews is to this writer the story of the larger group of Habiru in miniature, a sample of the experience of the whole class throughout their entire period in history and in the same part of the world.

The writer insists that this conclusion must be maintained even in the face of Greenberg's partial denial of it. The difference in interpretation of the evidence lies in reading the record of the Habiru "from east to west"

62. Greenberg, p. 88.

through the years from 2000 to 1000. Greenberg acknowledges, as all must now, that the Habiru were recognized
members of society, if inferior, as far as from Sumer to
Alalakh by the eighteenth century, while there is no evidence for their having made their way into Palestine and
Egypt before 1500.[63] The early mentions of the Habiru,
down to the end of the First Dynasty of Babylon, show
them to have been spread out from southern Mesopotamia
as far as northern Syria: Ur, Larsa, Alishar, Mari, Haran,
Alalakh. This, to Greenberg, does not point to a gradual
migration, despite the arguments earlier advanced for it
by Jirku.[64] The chances are that that is a proper conclusion,
as far as it goes, since it would be despicably trivial to
measure the comparative longitudes east to west of those
cities along the line to the northwest from Ur. That does
not, however, contradict the westward pattern of the
Habiru occurrences after that early period. The great
bulk of references to the Habiru in the northern and
eastern portions of the Fertile Crescent lies before those
which show Habiru farther south and west in Palestine
and Egypt, and Mesopotamian references to Habiru
become less frequent after Egyptian references begin to
appear. The first reference to Apiru in Egypt is roughly
contemporaneous with the Nuzi mentions of them,
which show many Habiru still in Mesopotamia, but it is
also contemporaneous with the Ugaritic and Amarna
references, which show that Habiru must be dealt with in
Syria and in Palestine in significant numbers. It should
not be forgotten that these Amarna letters are the first
record we have of Habiru that far west and south.

Lack of evidence, then, for a gradual migration in the
eastern territory in the early part of our period is not such

63. *Ibid.*, p. 85.
64. *Ibid.*, p. 64; Greenberg recapitulates Jirku's discussion, "Die Wan-
derungen der Hebräer," *AO*, XXIV (1924), on his own, p. 7.

an important conclusion from the record—sound as that conclusion probably is—as is the conclusion that the broad pattern of Habiru records throughout the whole period as far west as Egypt does point to a westward migration over all. This is not to argue for a total departure of all Habiru from each successive settlement, but it is to suggest that, the times being as troubled and unsure as they were, the younger generations could conceivably have moved on farther westward in search of a better life, leaving behind in the former settlement those already comfortable or lacking in adventurous spirit.[65] In connection with this conjectural migration of the younger Habiru we can well remind ourselves there is no need to claim that all Habiru migration was inevitably westward. Jacob's trip to Haran from Palestine was an eastward one in search of fortune and a wife, and indeed travel must have been just as easy in one direction as in the other. The general tendency was still to the west.

On the basis of the kinship between Habiru and Hebrew as words sharing similar and kindred stems; of the similarity between the use of the respective words to indicate a certain sociological type of people; and of the presence of the Biblical Hebrews in many of the places and in the sort of times in which the Habiru lived—on these bases the writer concludes that both similarities and dissimilarities between Hebrews and Habiru are best accounted for by recognizing the line of Abraham, Isaac, Jacob, and Joseph as some segment of the great mass of Habiru in the world of the Fertile Crescent during the first half of the second millennium.[66] There is the possibility, as Greenberg suggests, that the Biblical writers themselves were the ones who changed the sociological

65. *Cf.* Böhl's dating of Abraham's migration in the aftermath of the Hurrian invasions: F. M. Th. Böhl, "Das Zeitalter Abrahams," *Opera Minora* (hereafter cited as *Zeitalter*), p. 36.
66. *Cf.* the conclusion of de Vaux, *RB*, LV (1948), p. 344f.

term into a family name,[67] but it seems more likely that we are here dealing with an instance of the coalescing, simplifying, schematizing tendency of legend, which recalls certain facts dimly and preserves them in some degree of their essential meaning, without, however, doing so with detailed accuracy. It is rather a matter of the unconscious conservatism of a people preserving their ancient tradition with a certain tenacity for fact not quite obscured by their naïveté.

One can view with greater respect the essential truthfulness of the "hymn" of Hebrew origins in Deuteronomy xxvi.5,

> A wandering Aramean was my father,
> And he went down to Egypt,

or that of the similar passage in Ezekiel xvi.3,

> Your father was an Amorite, and your mother a Hittite.

If these passages reflect a liturgical recitation of the humble background of the Hebrews, we have in them parallel examples of the essential trustworthiness of the traditional.

Social Status and Way of Life

The received traditions of Genesis are not unanimous in their description of the social position and occupations of the Hebrews, just as there is no clear-cut picture of their origins and travels. A survey of the way the Genesis folk are represented is instructive.

When Abram and his family depart from Haran, they do so as people who own property, although there is no mention of land: Abram's holdings are represented as only movable property and persons (Genesis xii.5), and this would fit well with the nomadic mode of travel and

---

67. Greenberg, p. 93.

temporary dwelling of XII.8. The Pharaoh's handling of Sarai probably has little to show of the social standing of her and her husband, but we might observe that, after the experience in Egypt, Abram emerges as a well-supplied man (XII.16, XIII.2). In fact, Abram is a wealthy rancher upon his return to Palestine from Egypt, and Lot shares his prosperity (XIII.5). They do sound like the prosperous men found in Retenu by Sinuhe in his travels.[68]

The fourteenth chapter of Genesis, so troublesome in its apparent nearness to an historical tie but tantalizing distance from it, alters the picture of Abram remarkably. Suddenly he emerges as a military man, a right successful commander at that. In his defense of the family honor he is specifically called a Hebrew, as we have had occasion to notice before, and he has allies, *ba'ale berith* (XIV.13). Perhaps we try to make too much of this acquisition of "allies" and Abram's other "military" traits in this story. One does wonder if any arrangement describable as *berith* at this time could afford not to have at least implied military provisions. Likewise, the trained servants of XIV.14 need not have been trained specifically as soldiers;[69] again, one wonders whether any man except one infirm with age could long live in the household if unable to carry his share of whatever fighting needed doing. Have the commentators and most of the rest of us been wise in looking upon this chapter as an abrupt change to military life on the part of Abram? Is it so indicative of quasi-professional or outright soldiering as a first reading makes it appear? The concluding scene of the episode, for instance, is demonstrative of great magnanimity on Abram's

68. *ANET*, pp. 19–20.
69. There is, however, the use at Taanach of a kindred word in a military sense: W. F. Albright, "A Prince of Taanach in the Fifteenth Century," *BASOR*, No. 94 (1944), pp. 12–27. *Cf.* de Vaux, *RB*, LV (1948), p. 328.

part (xiv.23–24) but hardly fits in well with a supposedly soldierly character—at least by the standards of ancient warfare.

Some of Abram's family become settled before he himself does. In xix.2, Lot has turned into a full-fledged city-dweller with a stationary home, and there is no surprise in this in view of his having moved into the civilized and wicked city of Sodom. Abram, however, remains a semi-nomad and in xxiv.67 is still living in tents. He is not averse to owning fixed property, though, and patiently goes through the intricacies of Oriental business etiquette in order to purchase a grave for his wife (xxiii). Whatever else is to be made out of the all-but-unclassifiable story of the purchase of Machpelah, it does point to a tendency to become more closely associated with a particular locality. Perhaps the Hittites' soaring reference to Abraham as a "mighty prince" (xxiii.6) is no more than an example of the expansive manners of business in the Levant, but it is not out of keeping with the gradually increasing wealth and prominence of Abraham spoken of elsewhere in his story.

The tendency toward settling more and more continues through the lifetime of Isaac. It is true that he himself continues to be the tent-dwelling semi-nomad, according to the idealized pattern of the authors of the tradition, but the contrast between Jacob and Esau in xv.27 makes Jacob appear to be much the more settled of the two brothers. In this case, at least, Esau sounds more like the typical Habiru than does Isaac or Jacob. At any rate, in xxvi.12, Isaac becomes a farmer, and this turn in the story deserves careful attention as the first instance of patriarchal agriculture. The patriarchal families do not abandon the keeping of flocks, but from this point on they have taken the step that fixes them, ties them to the ground: they have become farmers who raise both animals

61

and field crops. There are further references to the farming activity of the patriarchs in xxx.14 and xxxvii.7. We should probably observe that, as soon as the family of Abraham are well enough settled in their new homeland, they take up farming, thus reproducing the form of livelihood attributed to their relatives still settled in Mesopotamia. They prosper at it, too, thanks to Jacob's intriguing devices of animal husbandry (xxx.31ff.), among other things. Apart from the large numbers of the animals in Jacob's reconciliation gift for Esau, we can see that both farm and ranch animals are included in the group (xxxii. 14–15). Jacob goes so far as to build a house after the return to Palestine (xxxiii.17) and buys land (xxxiii.19), thus continuing the trend toward settled farm life. This last passage, coming from the JE tradition, should be noticed as lacking the hostility or cynicism of the earlier J tradition toward settled, agricultural civilization—as, for instance, in iv.1–16. Jacob settles down in what had once been the kind of life scorned by the author of the earlier tradition, and with that we reach the opposite position: when Jacob and Esau separate (xxxvi.6–7), it is Esau, the one who comes off second best, who goes off to the free and open life of the plains with the flocks, and Jacob who becomes the sedentary farmer, keeping both small and large animals and raising crops.

Because with the beginning of the adventures of Joseph the patriarchal legend becomes for a time narrowed to the consideration of just one man, it is of use to consider at this point what the life and status of the family of Abraham have been up to the youth of Joseph. It has been one of semi-nomadic moving about through the countryside when necessary, but of settled, more or less permanent residence whenever possible. In a sense, the animals of the flocks have been the determining factor in the moves, for Abraham and Isaac are represented as having moved out of the "promised" land when famine conditions made it necessary to do so in order to keep the animals of the flocks alive. Once the step is taken of leaving Haran, the patriarchal wanderings are within a constantly decreasing radius, and there is a marked tendency toward settled life. The little bit of agriculture, which originally served the semi-nomads as a kind of side line or secondary means to the greater end of supplying food for man and beast, has, by the time of Joseph's younger years, become a co-equal occupation for his family. The picture of Jacob's home life with his family is in a way the very opposite of that of Abraham. Since it parallels the kind of life described on Laban's property in Haran, however, the writer takes it as the way of life toward which the Hebrews were working, having left it behind in Mesopotamia and taking it up again in their new home as soon as conditions allowed. Joseph and his brethren worked in the fields (xxxvii.7) and tended the flocks (xxxvii.12), just as their settled relatives in Mesopotamia did (xxx.14, 40). It is true that, in xlvii.33ff., Joseph's family represent themselves as "shepherds" pure and simple, but this has about it the look of a ruse. For that matter, Skinner considers it an interpolation into the story.[70]

This should teach us to be more careful than we customarily are in speaking of the Hebrews as "nomads" or even "semi-nomads." In so doing we tend to place too much emphasis on the footloose aspect of nomadic life, as if it were that which constituted its main characteristic, as if the nomad were the man who simply could not stay long in any one place without growing uncomfortable with the confining ties of sedentary life. That there is something of this about the nomad cannot be denied, but this writer submits that, for all his enthusiastic comparison of the patriarchs with modern tramps, it is not merely a desire

70. *ICC,* p. 496.

for travel that made nomads of the patriarchs. What caused them to live nomadic lives was their occupation, which, dependent as it was on good grazing ground, forced them to pull up stakes and move somewhere else when the natural grasses and grains turned out to be insufficient for the men and their beasts. The semi-nomadic life attributed to the Hebrews by the Biblical authors themselves, as just now surveyed, seems to indicate that they were nomads perforce, who would gladly have settled down to stay, and did so as soon as they had the opportunity.

Joseph alone of the Biblical Hebrews of the patriarchal period did not manage to escape the servitude that so characterized the Habiru. He is also the only one of them who reached any great pinnacle of worldly success. The family is represented as gradually increasing in prosperity from Abraham on, but there is no suggestion that their life ever became one of splendor or luxury, just as none of them except Joseph ever lost, even for a time, the freedom of his person and labor. Joseph, in short, sank lower for a time and ultimately rose higher than any of the rest of his family.

After having been sold into Egypt, Joseph began to capitalize on the good aspects of his imagination and his drive to excel that, in their other form, had aroused the angry jealousy of his brothers (xxxvii.8,19). It was these qualities of person which enabled him to rise to his position of trust in Potiphar's house (xxxix.4) and later in the court of the Pharaoh (xli.39ff.), after his ingenuity and insight in the interpretation of dreams secured his release from prison. Although he started in Egypt in the employ of the captain of the guard (xxxix.1), at no point in his subsequent career did Joseph play any military role. Likewise, although he came from a family of farmers and promulgated a large-scale crop conservation program in Egypt during the productive years against the coming famine (XLI.48), Joseph himself never engaged in farming. All his efforts and energies were directed toward the administrative duties of his office as vizier. Both in the depths and in the heights that he reached, Joseph is the exception among the Biblical Hebrews. After his family moved to Egypt, they were unable to share in Joseph's good fortune except in the indirect way of being placed by him in favorable territory where they could make a good living: they continued for their part as the shepherds and farmers they were when they arrived, sharing in the general welfare of the country (XLVII.27), even though never accepted as really belonging by the Egyptians.

If we put alongside each other the traits of social status and occupation that we can deduce from the records about the Biblical Hebrews and the Habiru, we find a not-too-congruent set of data:

The Hebrews

Semi-nomads with slowly settling tendency.
Small-scale but increasingly prosperous farmers.
Semi-professional soldiers.
The exception: Joseph.

The Habiru

Vagrants.
Prisoners.
Mercenary soldiers.
Slaves, or ex-slaves.
Marauders, rarely settled when free.

Clearly the Hebrew tradition represents its ancestors as occupying a higher position than that of the people with whom those ancestors appear to have had the most affinity. This in itself should be no surprise to us, unless it is exclusively a contemporary habit to exaggerate the prominence of past heroes, but perhaps there is not so much exaggeration on the part of the Hebrew tradition as there might appear to be; at least, whatever exaggeration there is, is not anywhere near so extreme as it might be.

The highest position occupied by the Hebrews or the Habiru as a whole is roughly the same: if one is a small landowner, he is in no position to look down on a herdsman with a fairly good living from his flocks or on a professional soldier; and the other way around. These represent the best that can be said for the Hebrews and the Habiru, as a whole. The legends of Genesis make it clear that they consider Joseph by far the exception, the one who did much better than the rest of his family. The best that Genesis claims for the Hebrews as a whole is the best that can be said for the Habiru. What is lacking in the Genesis tradition is evidence that the Hebrews as a whole ever occupied such a low position in society as it would appear the bulk of the Habiru did.

There are the occasional, rare similarities on the lower level of society. Joseph was clearly a captive foreigner sold into slavery, but he is the only one of the patriarchs to suffer that fate—and for only a short time, at that. Abram once carried on a rather far-reaching campaign of fighting, and he is called a Hebrew at that point, but this incident is impressively *sui generis* in the tradition. Other instances, previously cited as indicative of the sociological status of the Hebrews, can be recalled here. The most important observation to be made on the relative social position of the Hebrews is that they occur in Genesis most often as occupying that status which the Habiru least often have: gradually settling down, while free and propertied. The Habiru of Mesopotamia and the Apiru of Egypt knew a settled life, all right, but it was the settled life of slaves, by and large. When free, the Habiru were more often troublemakers than not, or at the best undependable in their loyalty to authority.

This is to say, then, that the Biblical Hebrews and the Habiru of extra-Biblical records occupy the same general class, but the Hebrews seem gradually to rise to its upper limit, without going beyond it as a whole. Such modern terms as "middle class" and "working class" are quite out of place in the ancient Near East, but, *mutatis mutandis,* it would appear that Genesis shows the Hebrews as "lower class" people who gradually reach a prosperous and settled life that others of that general class did not know to any great extent. The Habiru probably indicate the social and economic stratum out of which the Hebrews came, then, but there is little similarity in specific occupations.

The ultimate conclusion of this aspect of our study needs to be anticipated now enough to remark that the authors of the Genesis traditions are probably not guilty of exaggerating the social or economic station of their forebears, at least in any conscious way. Perhaps the generations of Hebrews themselves simply forgot, as the years went by, the specific details of how low on the social scale they began. However, even if we imagine that the line of Abraham had actually enjoyed the relative prosperity attributed to them in the patriarchal period, we need not be too shocked by the simple fact that it does not accord with the bulk of what we know about the Habiru. Perhaps it is simply a matter of our lacking the same kind of documentation of Hebrew life as we have for the Habiru. After all, if the Hebrew farmers and herdsmen largely avoided urban centers, we should not expect them to turn up so often in government and business documents as the Habiru, who, as slaves, soldiers, and the like, often had their names in official records.

Contact with Other Known Peoples and Places

Up till now the writer has demonstrated his conviction that the Hebrews of Genesis are to be understood as one group within the heterogeneous type of people known in the second millennium as Habiru. How the Biblical group developed into the Hebrew "nation" lies beyond the scope of this study, though a later chapter will deal with the arrival and settlement of the patriarchs in Egypt, out of which the nucleus of the Hebrew nation was led by Moses. Within the agreed limits of the patriarchal age, however, the Hebrews are shown in the legends as having contact, either direct or indirect, with other peoples, many of whom are known to history now through the material remains of their life that Biblical archaeology has studied. Identification of these peoples, then, and a survey of what is known of their civilizations will be useful in determining the significance of the Hebrews' contact with them, especially if it should be that some influence or similarity might be shown to have existed between the religion and life of the Hebrews and their neighbors. Chief among these other peoples of the Fertile Crescent in our period were the Hurrians, the Hittites, and the Hyksos, although there are other smaller groups and some individuals to be dealt with, also. Some, indeed, may be nothing but names in the erudite imagination of a Biblical author, and the Hyksos, one of the most important peoples in ancient history, are never mentioned in the Bible. A fair degree of identification is possible, though.

The Hurrians

Shortly after 2000 there appeared in northern Mesopotamia a people whose origin remains to this date unspecified, the Hurrians. Though they were not the indigenous inhabitants of Nuzi and Tell Billah, by 1900 they were well settled and dominant there, and even before 2000 Hurrian names can be found in Babylonia and Cappadocia.[71] In the movement of peoples that went on in the first half of the second millennium the Hurrians moved

71. Robert H. Pfeiffer, "Nuzi and the Hurrians," *Smithsonian Report for 1935*, p. 551.

southward and westward, and by the middle of the millennium they were the principal element in the kingdom of Mitanni on the upper Euphrates, in which, however, they were not the ruling class. The control of the kingdom was in the hands of an Indo-Iranian minority,[72] although the Hurrian tongue of the majority of the population was the nation's language. Racial and linguistic identification of the Hurrians is still not to be had; they were not Semites, but they do not fit into any other category known to us at present, either.

It would appear that the Hurrians no more had single, over-all leadership at the beginning of their wanderings than did the Habiru, for the Hurrian settlement at Nuzi enjoyed a period of relative independence until it became a part of the Mitannian empire around 1500.[73] Other Hurrians did not hesitate long in northern Mesopotamia but proceeded farther west through Syria and Palestine: their presence there is attested not long after 1900.[74] Gelb further suggests that they went on to enter Egypt as part of the Hyksos invasion in the eighteenth century.[75]

There is real attractiveness in the idea of connecting the migrations of the Hurrians with several other movements of the time. Gelb allows that they may have invaded Assyria at the time that a break of two hundred years appears in Assyrian records after the death of Shamshi-Adad I in 1718.[76] This would have driven before them the Kassites, who put an end to the Old Babylonian Kingdom.[77] There might also be some connection between the Hurrian movement and the decline of the Old Hittite Kingdom,[78] for Goetze calls attention to the fact that nothing is heard of

72. *Ibid.*, p. 552.
73. *Ibid.*, p. 553.
74. *Ibid.*, p. 552.
75. Ignace J. Gelb, *Hurrians and Subarians*, p. 70.
76. *Ibid.*, pp. 65–66. *Cf.* also Meek's remarks in *Haverford Symposium*, pp. 175–176.
77. Finegan, *Light from the Ancient Past*, p. 164.
78. Gelb, *Hurrians and Subarians*, p. 68.

the Hittites between 1650 and 1400, the very time of the spread of the Hurrians.[79]

Most of our knowledge of the Hurrians comes from the remains at Nuzi.[80] The kingdom was bilingual, with Hurrian as the vernacular and Akkadian as the literary and official language. Largely lacking in artistic skills, the Hurrians were, however, good governors and set up a relatively efficient feudal system, in which economic pressures bit by bit forced the amalgamation of small landholdings into great estates presided over by the wealthy few. The great bulk of the population thus became virtual or actual slaves. Land could not be transferred outright, however, for other Orientals seem to have shared the Old Testament notion of the inalienability of family and land. The legal fiction of adoption of the creditor by the debtor made the transaction possible and satisfactory to both traditional law and the existing financial situation. The adoption contracts from Nuzi have preserved for us the actual wording of these transactions, and they will be quoted at the relevant point in the later discussion of patriarchal family life. Family life was polygamous and allowed for concubinage, and the husband and father exercised absolute control over his family and property. The Mesopotamian Ishtar and the Hittite Teshub were the chief deities.

The Hurrians were thus the dominant cultural element in that northern Mesopotamian area to which the Biblical Hebrews looked as their homeland and at the time most plausible for the patriarchal sojourn there. Even if Nuzi is almost the eastern outpost of the Hurrian sphere of influence, what we find there is fairly to be taken as representative of other Hurrians, in the midst of whose territory

79. *Haverford Symposium,* p. 148.

80. The following paragraph is summarized from Pfeiffer, *Smithsonian Report for 1935,* p. 553f.

was (and still is) Haran, the starting point for Abram's journey of faith to Canaan. In view of that, when we find parallels between Hurrian and patriarchal practices, we have a significant opportunity for illuminating the Biblical narrative. Not only in northern Mesopotamia but farther west, also, the Hurrians were found frequently enough throughout the western half of the Fertile Crescent for the Egyptians to refer to that region in general as that of the Hurrians: "Hurru" in Egyptian records is to be taken as meaning "Syria."[81] Since the Hurrians were living that far west, and the Egyptians took such notice of them as to apply their name to the whole territory even though it was not under the political control of the Hurrians, we should not be surprised if we find both the name of the Hurrians and signs of contact with their culture in the patriarchal legends. The time, the place, and the significance of the Hurrians all point in this direction.

In Genesis the Hurrians appear as the Horites; it is an easy linguistic identification. Although the received text of Genesis x does not contain the Horites in the listing of the Table of Nations, they are probably there just the same, albeit in disguise, as will be shown just below. The passages in which the Horites *are* named, however, are these: xiv.6, and xxxvi.20, 21, 29, 30, the four verses in xxvi being doublets of each other. All these passages locate the Horites in Edom, and it should be noticed that xxxvi is assigned to the P author; the literary source of xiv remains as uncertain as ever.

That exhausts the mention of the Horites under that name in Genesis, but chances are good that, where Genesis speaks of the Hivites, the text represents a careless copying of Horites. Lexicons call attention to the hint of this in the Septuagint, and anyone who has ever learned Hebrew or marked the examination papers of those who are learning

81. *ANET,* pp. 258, 260.

Hebrew knows how easily *waw* and *resh* can be mistaken for each other when the characters are quickly read or carelessly written. The Hivites are mentioned just about as often as the Horites: we find them in x.17, xxxiv.2, and xxxvi.2. Again the authorship of all but the last of these instances is P, and there is even a fair probability that P is the source of xxxvi.2. The most important mention of the Hivites is that in x.17, which gives them a place in the Table of Nations: there the Hivites are made the descendants of Canaan, and this in the genealogical table that goes to such an extent to be complete but omits the Horites. Again, the connection of the Hivites is more directly with Edom than with any other territory.

Either nothing at all is to be made out of this coincidence, or it is to be taken as demonstration of the identity of the Horites and the Hivites. Furthermore, one cannot but be struck by the fact that the vast bulk of the references to these people is of Priestly authorship. It is possible to be cynical about the reliability of P: if we wish to assume that lateness of composition is indicative of factual unreliability because of the distance between the time of the event and that of the author, then we can doubt the accuracy of P and attribute to him only a splendid memory for ancient proper names like Horite. That hardly seems just toward P, in view of the archaeological evidence about the Hurrians. It is not really a matter of whether the Hebrews actually made contact with real, living Horites in Palestine as they moved through the land, though there is certainly nothing about the archaeological data to make that impossible. What counts is the aptness of the Biblical author's use of the names for pre-Israelite inhabitants of Palestine. Horites had passed through Palestine in their migrations, and, even if they had all gone on the rest of the way into Egypt, they still left their name behind them as associated with the territory they once occupied.[82] In the light of present knowledge of the Hurrians, there is nothing inaccurate about describing an early inhabitant of Palestine as a Horite. Perhaps we may prefer to take it as some sort of generic name for those who lived there before the Israelites, in some such way as the Egyptians spoke of Hurru, or we may prefer to understand it as more closely limited to the early inhabitants of Edom.[83] In either case the Biblical account of Hebrew contact with Horites in Palestine cannot be discounted purely on the basis of the lateness of P; if anything, this should possibly teach us to have more respect for the accuracy of P's sources and his erudition than we often allow him.

It is relatively unimportant to prove actual contact between the Hebrews and the Hurrians in Palestine, so far as illuminating Hebrew practice by that of the Hurrians, for the Hebrews would probably have acquired all that they could of Hurrian influence during their residence in Mitannian lands. It is enough here simply to point out the plausibility of the use of the name of the people as it occurs in Genesis.

The Hittites

Lost to history almost as long as the Hurrians were the Hittites, who like them, for many centuries existed in the memory of man only as names in long, seldom-read lists in Genesis. With the opening up of the past that has come about with the excavations at Boghazköy and the deciphering of the Hittite language, it has come to be recognized now that the Hittites were no mere insignificant tribe of the early Biblical period. Far from that, theirs was a great

82. *Cf. ATD*, p. 289.
83. *Ibid.*, pp. 149, 303.

empire reaching out from central Asia Minor at the height of its power as far as the northern Euphrates and into Syria and the northernmost part of Palestine. The Hittites knew two periods of flourishing power, the first of which, the Old Kingdom, came to an end at the time of the Hurrian migrations, as has previously been mentioned. The Old Kingdom went into a decline soon after 1700, but the resurgence of Hittite power in the New Kingdom of Suppilu-liumas, Mursilis, Muwatallis, and Hattusilis (1400–1200) brought the Hittite hegemony to its greatest extent, as described above, and made the Hittites an empire unafraid to deal with the powerful Egypt of the Ramessids on equal terms. Ramesses II of Egypt, as a matter of fact, almost lost out to the Hittites at Kadesh[84] and was probably quite happy to conclude the famous nonagression treaty with Hattusilis.[85] The Hittites finally fell from power at the time of the invasions of the Sea Peoples in the thirteenth century, and with that they virtually disappeared from history. Only their name remained, as a standard title for the western half of the Fertile Crescent: long years after the Hittite kingdom fell to ruins, Syria, Palestine, and eastern Asia Minor were still known as Hatti-land.[86]

The Hittites are classified by P in the Table of Nations as belonging to the Hamitic family (Genesis x.15), with descent traced from Ham to Canaan to Heth, the father of the Hittites. This is, of course, not a scientific genealogy, but it is no worse than any other, for the racial and linguistic affiliations of the Hittites are yet to be worked out satisfactorily. There is, however, aptness in P's placing the Hittites in the Hamitic line, in the same family of nations as Mizraim (x.6), as we realize when we recall the two great powers of Hatti and Egypt linking arms across

84. Finegan, *Light from the Ancient Past,* p. 167.
85. *ANET*, p. 199f.
86. *E.g., ANET*, pp. 275, 277, 279, 283, 287, 290. The usage runs as late as the time of Esarhaddon of Assyria in the seventh century.

the eastern end of the Mediterranean in the days when the Hittites were as strong as the Egyptians. For all its nature as a political and military necessity, this was an alliance between powers important enough to allow for a folk memory in later centuries of some sort of relationship between Heth and Mizraim, Hatti and Egypt.

Once in the pre-exilic tradition the Hittites are mentioned by the JE material in the list of peoples whose lands are promised to Abram in the establishment of the covenant with Yahweh (Genesis xvi.20). Other appearances of the Hittites in Genesis are in the Priestly tradition: xxiii, in which Abraham acquires Machpelah through purchase from Ephron the Hittite, and in later references to the same event, xxv.9, xlix.29, 30, and l.13. In two other passages the Hittites are mentioned as the source of the wives of Esau resented by his family, xxvi.34 (twice) and xxxvi.2. We can see from this that both early and late traditions are unanimous in considering Hittites among the peoples of Canaan in its broadest, most general sense, but the uniqueness of P is in thinking of them as having a definite settlement in the South. Again, the lateness of P is in itself no argument against the reliability of what he records. There is still something more to be said about the way the authors of tradition make use of this word.

The JE tradition seems to regard the Hittites as one of the peoples of Canaan in a clear-cut way, one of several distinct groups. This connotation for the word is in the P references, too, but P contains an additional sense for the word that is not found in the earlier tradition; namely, a generic name for anyone who lived in Palestine before the Hebrews settled there. While P does contain the peculiar notion of a settlement of Hittites far south in Palestine at Hebron, his use of Hittite also indicates that he considers it a name that has largely lost specific national or ethnic meaning and has become an antiquarian's synonym for "Canaanite."[87] While P may be off his base in designating the people Abraham found at Hebron as Hittites specifically, he thereby only reproduced the error of JE in considering the Hittites as present among the components of the early population of Palestine. On the other hand, there is nothing at all wrong with P's using that title in the vague, general sense. If it is in the latter sense that P generally uses the word—it seems so to this writer—then he is in line with the prevailing custom of referring to that part of the world in general as Hatti-land.

It is impossible to claim that Palestine as far south as Hebron was ever part of the Hittite Empire, or even more than the most northern part of Palestine; when a foreign empire controlled Palestine as a whole during the patriarchal period at all, it was Egypt. We know from the Amarna letters how much trouble the Egyptians had controlling territory so far from their home base, and we may be sure that the Hittites would have found it similarly difficult to hold the mastery over lands so far from their seat of power. Forrer is quite definite in his fixing of the limit of the Hittite rule: *"At no time did any district south of the northern ends of Lebanon and anti-Lebanon belong to the Hatti-empire, either as a federal or a dependent state."*[88] The chances for a Hittite outpost or colony as far south as Hebron are slim, although there is a hint of an expedition of settlers who left Hittite territory in the north and moved southward. Forrer suggests that they were fugitives from Hittite rule who moved eventually into the areas of Jerusalem, Hebron, and Beersheba, and were thus called Hittites by their new neighbors in Palestine.[89] Gurney likewise considers these Hittites from Kurstamma in northern Hatti, who moved into the land of Amka, the

---

87. *ATD*, p. 210f.

88. E. O. Forrer, "The Hittites in Palestine," *PEQ*, LXVIII (1936), p. 194. The italics and the diction are both in the original.

89. *Ibid.*, LXIX (1937), p. 112.

Biqa valley near Lebanon in Egyptian territory, as the possible source of the Hittites found later by the Hebrews in the hill country, although he considers them an official colony instead of fugitives.[90] Both Forrer and Gurney date this expedition in the reign of Suppiluliumas in the middle of the fourteenth century, and we must admit that this is too late to be of much help in accounting for contact with the Hittites in Palestine in the patriarchal centuries. The Habiru who are mentioned at Boghazköy in the fifteenth and fourteenth centuries are of no help in solving this particular aspect of the question, since they tie in with no part of the Biblical account. It might be possible to argue that, because an expedition of Hittites took place in Suppiluliumas's time, a similar group could have migrated earlier, but this seems to be spinning the yarn too fine. The excavation of Mamre throws little light on the subject, since it finds the earliest settlement there simply in the Bronze Age.[91] If we had more precise identification of the first stratum at Mamre in a particular portion of the Bronze Age, we might reckon more accurately who were the first settlers there, but in the absence of such data we cannot go very far.

Genesis xxiii may be based on some earlier tradition, as Gurney allows,[92] and its possible reflection of Hittite real estate procedure, to be discussed in a later chapter, may indicate that. Even with all that proven, which it is not, we still do not have adequate evidence from either the Bible or archaeology for the presence of Hittites as such in Palestine during the patriarchal period. The most that we can say for either the early or the late tradition is that it uses the name Hittite as loosely as the later Assyrian chronicles, and thus with no more accuracy or precision.

90. O. R. Gurney, *The Hittites,* p. 59f.
91. *ATD,* p. 145.
92. Gurney, p. 59f.

The Hyksos

The Hyksos who dominated lower Egypt and parts of Palestine and Syria in the second quarter of the second millennium are never once mentioned in the Bible; in fact, their name is seldom found anywhere, yet they have left their definite mark on history. They would not have their identity as Hyksos if the Egyptians whom they mastered for a little over a century had not given them the name. The title is a pejorative one with the meaning of *foreigners* or *shepherds;* the second element of the name, *shos,* is a general term in Egyptian for bedouin[93] and could be taken to refer to the occupation of the people or to their alien status in Egypt—the effect is much the same. Like Habiru, Hyksos has no definite or national significance except a negative one: they were not Egyptians.

We identify with the Hyksos the southwestward movement of tribes of unknown origin from the north toward Egypt in the eighteenth century and afterward. Up through most of the nineteenth century Egypt had been able to maintain her domination in Palestine and Syria as far as Ugarit and Qatna, but after 1800 it was impossible for the Egyptian control to be kept up so far north; it was then that Northwest Semites and others were able to develop economic and military strength on their own.[94] The composition of the Hyksos was a bit of everything: Albright speaks of Indo-Aryans and Hurrians,[95] and Rowley declares that with "no uncertainty" there were Semites among them.[96] Between 1700 and 1500 the move was at its height, and those who swarmed into Egypt became known there as Hyksos. They moved the capital northward from its tradi-

93. H. H. Rowley, "Israel's Sojourn in Egypt," *BJRL*, XXII (1938), p. 247.
94. W. F. Albright, *The Archaeology of Palestine,* p. 85.
95. *Ibid.,* p. 86.
96. Rowley, *BJRL*, XXII (1938), p. 247.

tional location to Avaris in the Delta[97] because of the northern center of gravity of their rule. Earthwork fortifications in the Asiatic part of their kingdom were thrown up with greater strength than had been known before,[98] and Albright points to the Hyksos period as one of relative prosperity for Palestine,[99] probably from commerce. He continues that the signs of wealth found at Palestinian sites at this time are of Egyptian style: weapons and ornaments, particularly scarabs, more at this period than at any other. On that basis he suggests that they were brought back to Palestine by those who had fought for the Hyksos in their invasion of Egypt. This prosperous Hyksos empire was organized as a loose federation in which chariot-warriors formed the aristocracy.[100] It was not, however, a peaceful kingdom, for the wealth of Palestine in the Middle Bronze Age was accompanied by great unrest, with almost constant chieftains' wars;[101] the strife of the Amarna Age in Palestine was thus no new thing in the outer reaches of the empire. The Hyksos were finally expelled from Egypt in 1580, and affairs were settled once again in native Egyptian hands.

For themselves the Hyksos are principally important as an example of the movement of peoples through the area of Palestine and Syria during the restless second millennium, or perhaps as the only foreign overlords of Egypt before the arrival of the empires of the next millennium. In connection with the patriarchal traditions, however, they take on considerably more importance. The Hyksos represent the successfully military side, so to speak, of that westward migration of many peoples in the patriarchal period, that migration which included the Hebrews of

97. *ANET*, p. 231.
98. Albright, *Archaeology of Palestine*, p. 90.
99. *Ibid*, p. 86f.
100. Albright, in *Haverford Symposium*, p. 17.
101. Albright, *Archaeology of Palestine*, p. 90.

Genesis. If the Hebrews were the relatively peaceful men they are shown to be in Genesis, then they followed along behind the fighters as gradually-settling shepherds, and they shared bit by bit in the growing prosperity of the age in Palestine. Finally, as the chapter on the patriarchs in Egypt will show, the Hyksos period of rule in Egypt offers a most plausible time for a Hebrew to reach such eminent position there as is attributed by the patriarchal legends to Joseph.

The Philistines

Moving slowly through the eastern part of the Mediterranean world in the second half of the second millennium, the Peoples from the Sea came, within the course of a couple of centuries, to displace or absorb many of the existing peoples and cultures there. They put an end to the Minoan Age in Crete; they appear to have been the chief cause for the downfall of the New Kingdom of the Hittites; although repelled from Egypt, they dealt a blow to the Ramessid establishment that hastened its loss of power; and one group of them entered Palestine at the same time as the Exodus Hebrews were probably making their way there from Egypt. The struggle between the Philistines and the Hebrews of the period of the Judges and early monarchy was to be seen in many cases as a contest between two invaders for possession of the same territory. Although the Philistines never attained permanent possession of more than a section of the coastal region of southwestern Palestine, they gave their name to the whole country. It is one of the great ironies of history that, though their culture was materially much higher and more advanced than that of the Hebrews, the Hebrew attitude toward them has caused the name of Philistine to become synonymous with uncultivated boorishness.

The records of Ramesses III tell of his efforts that withstood the invading Sea Peoples and kept them from entering the homeland of Egypt,[102] but it is plain from later Biblical history that the once-powerful Egyptian control over Palestine was unable to keep them from settling there. It is fortunate that an absolute date for the account of Ramesses III and the Sea Peoples is relatively easy to fix; *viz.*, the eighth year of his reign, 1188.

It is this very clarity and exactness of the dating of the Egyptian record which throw into a suspicious light the two mentions of Philistines in Genesis: xxi.32, 34 speak of a sojourn of Abraham among the Philistines, and xxvi.1ff. also briefly associate Isaac with the Philistines. The fact that both these passages mention the Philistine king is of literary critical interest but is of no further concern for us here. That Philistines should be in Palestine at all at the time of Abraham and Isaac is difficult to account for if we are going to take seriously the record from the age of Ramesses III and also avoid arbitrarily narrowing the patriarchal period to a specific, single century. To be sure, Gordon can avoid the scandal of an anachronism here, but he does so only by settling on the Amarna Age, and no earlier, as the patriarchal period.[103] One can easily understand this conclusion of Gordon in the light of his zeal to concentrate attention on the "international" age of Amarna and Ugarit, with Ugarit as the connecting point that explains many parallels (found by Gordon) between the Hebrew patriarchal tradition and the heroic tales of the Greek Homeric Age.[104] With all due respect to Gordon for his zeal and undeniable originality, this writer finds it impossible to accept this line of reasoning, at least as an ex-

102. *ANET*, pp. 262–263.
103. Gordon, *Introduction to Old Testament Times*, p. 108f.
104. *E.g.*, his "The Patriarchal Age," *JBR*, XXI (1953), pp. 238–243; "The Patriarchal Narratives," *JNES*, XIII (1954), pp. 56–59; "Homer and Bible," *HUCA*, XXVI (1955), pp. 43–108.

planation for Abraham's and Isaac's meeting Philistines in Palestine in their day.

Perhaps it is wisest simply to admit that, if it is ever correct to speak of archaeological evidence as contradicting Biblical material or as proving it anachronistic, the case of the Philistines in Genesis is one instance of it.

Other Names of the Patriarchal Period

The point of view of the historian, or, for that matter, of the author of tradition, determines which names are importantly and frequently mentioned in his composition. Since the court recorders of ancient Near Eastern monarchs were supposed to glorify their kings and other great leaders, we search in vain in what we have left of their records for any mention of the men who are the central characters in the family chronicle of the Hebrews in Genesis. Likewise, at only one point does Genesis provide information of the type that one finds in the annals of rulers, and that point is the fourteenth chapter, whose interpretation remains still beyond us.

The most that we can fairly expect of the two bodies of Biblical and extra-Biblical material is that they incline toward each other, even if we cannot ask that they provide us with cross-references to each other. In all this following section we need to hold in mind that there is not one extra-Biblical reference to any person mentioned in Genesis, and there is not one name in Genesis that can be proved to be a specific, historical person.

The cognate of Abraham's name has been located in Mesopotamian documents of the patriarchal period, albeit late. A Babylonian receipt-contract from the reign of Amizadugga (*ca.* 1550) mentions one Aba-rama.[105] The revision of the chronology of Babylonian kings since the

---

105. George A. Barton, *Archaeology and the Bible,* p. 344.

publication of Barton's work requires this downward dating of what Barton placed earlier in the patriarchal period. Likewise from Babylonian territory and records comes the record of an Abam-rama who leased land and paid his rent at Dilbat, a populous settlement to the south of Babylon.[106] Whether the etymology of this name determines its origin or not is a matter of conjecture. De Vaux[107] thinks that the root contained in Abam-rama is one probably not known in West Semitic and thereby properly considered Babylonian. Albright,[108] on the other hand, allows the name to be interpreted in West Semitic as meaning "he is exalted as to father," also adding that, if it is Akkadian, it is probably to be read as coming from the root *ra' amu*, "to love." What we have in this name, then, is not the Abraham of the Bible or even necessarily the same name; rather, it is a name whose etymology can be traced in the Semitic family of languages, possibly even West Semitic, and whose meaning can be taken as parallel to that given by the folk etymology of Genesis xvii.5. There is probably nothing to be gained by taking Abram as a theophorous name, "Ram is father," although this suggestion has Lewy's prestige behind it.[109]

As yet there is no equivalent of the name of Isaac that has come to light in extra-Biblical material.[110] A number of Jacob-type names, however, have come to light in both Mesopotamia and Egypt. Barton[111] cites a Yakub-ilu from the reign of Apil-Sin in the First Dynasty of Babylon, but this seems to this writer unimpressive. If the transliteration is to be trusted, then this name lacks a consonant of the root of Jacob: Yakub-ilu has nothing to correspond to the *ayin* of Jacob in Hebrew. Much more to the point are the

---

106. *Ibid.*, p. 345.
107. De Vaux, *RB*, LIII (1946), p. 323.
108. W. F. Albright, "The Names *Shaddai* and *Abram*," *JBL*, LIV (1935), p. 202.
109. Lewy, *RHR*, CIX (1934), pp. 58–59.
110. *Cf.* de Vaux, *RB*, LIII (1946), p. 324.
111. Barton, p. 364.

names *Ia-aḥ-qu-ub-el*, from the eighteenth century at Chagar Bazar,[112] and *Ya'k-b'-ra*, from the captive city list of Tutmose III (1478–1446), who lists this Egyptian equivalent of Jacob-El.[113] Barton reports the occurrence of the name of Israel in the first half of the third millennium at Agade,[114] although, of course, there is no connection of this name with a Jacob-type name. From the time of the Hyksos, though, scarabs have been found with the name *Ya-'qob-har*,[115] and we could hardly ask for a more helpful tie of the name Jacob with the patriarchal period.

The name of Joseph has its extra-Biblical parallels, too. *Yashub-ilu* has been found at the time of the First Dynasty of Babylon,[116] and Tutmose III captured a *Ya-sha-p'ra*, the Egyptian equivalent of Joseph-El,[117] as *Yashub-ilu* is in Akkadian.

We can notice, if only in passing, the occurrence in the records of Asshur-bani-pal of a Nuhuru, a personal name possibly the same as the town mentioned in Mari letters and a conceivable equivalent of the Nahor of Genesis.[118] Also, the appearance of Benjamites (*Bene Yamina*) in the Mari correspondence[119] needs to be recorded because of the striking similarity of the name to that of the Biblical tribe. If there was any connection between them, then the Biblical group will have to be seen as a small offshoot who went south, leaving behind the larger group of bedouins in northern Mesopotamia,[120] but the chances are that de Vaux is right in denying that there is any direct relationship.[121]

---

112. De Vaux, *RB*, LIII (1946), p. 324.
113. *ANET*, p. 242.
114. Barton, p. 365.
115. Burrows, *What Mean These Stones?*, p. 71.
116. Barton, p. 365.
117. *ANET*, p. 242.
118. *Ibid.*, p. 300.
119. *Ibid.*, p. 482.
120. *ATD*, p. 298.
121. De Vaux, *RB*, LIII (1946), p. 344.

These are not all the names of the patriarchal legends that have equivalents in non-Biblical sources; the others will be mentioned at those points in the succeeding chapters where it will be relevant to do so. We shall have cause to observe this again, but it should still be stated here: what we seek to find in this searching of name lists is not necessarily individuals or even tribes bearing the names of the Hebrew patriarchs—although we do find just that in some cases. What we do seek to establish is that names containing the elements of the patriarchal names in linguistically recognizable form did exist in the patriarchal period in areas where the Hebrews are supposed to have lived.

The seeming completeness of detail given by the author of Genesis xiv has impelled most modern students of Genesis to try to identify the kings and nations mentioned there with those known from sources outside the Bible. Everyone who sets his hand to this task soon realizes the difficulty of avoiding both literal-mindedness and cynicism about the value of the material presented in the troublesome chapter. Much of this difficulty can be obviated by the simple recollection that by and large the best we can expect from archaeological data is the illustration or illumination of the tradition, not outright substantiation or refutation of it.

Skinner's classic discussion of Genesis xiv.1 should be enough to convince all that the attempt to identify Amraphel of Shinar with Hammurabi of Babylon introduces far more problems than it solves. Barton likewise warns, with great caution, that if Amraphel is Hammurabi, then the name is corrupted badly—so badly, he seems to imply, as to make the identification profitless.[122] Perhaps de Vaux is wiser in suggesting that Amraphel need not be Hammurabi and Shinar need not be Babylonia: indeed, he sub-

122. Barton, p. 348.

85

mits that Amraphel strikes him as a northern Mesopotamian name and that Shinar could be that *Sha-an-ḥar* to the
east of the Euphrates.[123] Böhl suggests some such name as
Amarpiel, on the analogy of Mari names like Iturpiel and
Ibalpiel, and locates the kingdom not far east of Ugarit
and Alalakh.[124] Cornelius insists on the identification with
Hammurabi of Babylon, however, and speaks of the battle
in Genesis XIV as one in the same campaign as that in which
Egypt finally fell to the Hyksos; thus Babylonian power,
either late in the days of Hammurabi or early in the time
of his immediate successor, was involved in hostilities that
sought to wrest Palestine from Egyptian control.[125]

As for the other kings and nations, Airoch is reminiscent
or Arriwuku, son of Zimri-lim of Mari, a contemporary
of Hammurabi; Tidal recalls Tudhalias, the name of
several kings of the Hittites, and we might think specifically
of Tudhalias I, also a contemporary of Hammurabi;[126]
Elam we know; Ellasar seems to parallel Ilanzura, known
from Hittite records and from Mari.[127] Chedorlaomer presents another problem: the components of the name recall
the Elamite Kudur and Lagamar, both well attested and
apparently simply transcribed by the Hebrew. What we do
not have, however, from Elamite records is an Elamite
name comprising both these elements.[128] It can already be
seen that it is not so much the names that cause the trouble

123. De Vaux, *RB*, LV (1948), pp. 331–333.

124. *Zeitalter*, p. 45f.

125. Friedrich Cornelius, "Genesis XIV," *ZAW*, LXXII (1960), p. 4.

126. Gurney, p. 216. Specifically so named in Böhl, *Zeitalter*, p. 45f., and
"King Hammurabi of Babylon in the Setting of His Time," *Mededeelingen
der Koninklijke Nederlandsche Akademie van Wetenschappen afd. Letterkunde*, Nieuwe Reeks, IX, 10 (1946), p. 357.

127. Georges Dossin, "Les Archives Economiques du Palais de Mari,"
Syria, XX, (1939), p. 109. *Cf.* Böhl's *al Assuri* near Carchemish, *Zeitalter*,
p. 45f. Similar identifications of the kings and lands are given by de Vaux,
RB, LV (1948), pp. 331–333, and von Rad, *ATD*, p. 149.

128. De Vaux, *RB*, LV (1948), p. 334. Böhl suggests Kuter-Nahhunte
(*ca.* 1680), the forerunner of the Cassite invaders; *cf. Zeitalter*, p. 45f.

as it is their supposed contemporaneity and alliance with each other.

The nature of the campaign on which the kings are represented as going is problematical. De Vaux[129] finds the places of combat in Genesis xiv all along the main route between Syria and the Red Sea and speculates that the excursion was one with the purpose of keeping the route open for travel and trade. It is a matter of fact known from the work of Albright and Glueck that Transjordanian towns from Damascus south to Moab through Gilead were settled in the years of the early patriarchal period but were suddenly abandoned somewhere between 2000 and 1800, not to be resettled until the thirteenth or twelfth century.[130] Perhaps this abrupt cessation of urban life across the Jordan in the Middle Bronze Age can best be explained by some such military outburst as the campaign of the kings.[131] In that case, Genesis xiv shows only that aspect of the greater expedition which directly affected Abram and his family. This cannot be pressed too closely, however, for the towns of the region were abandoned something more than a century before the time of the kings suggested above. However, there must have been several such excursions to keep the trade routes open, especially after the disappearance of safe, settled towns. Böhl insists that the historicity of Genesis xiv cannot be doubted,[132] and, if this writer cannot share Böhl's certainty, he at least agrees to the point of allowing that the Biblical authors came very close to identifying the personages in the story.

The implications of this comparison of the Biblical account of patriarchal encounter with other peoples and the archaeological record of those other peoples should already be apparent, and the concluding chapter will draw them

129. *RB*, LV (1948), p. 329–330. *Cf.* Böhl, *Zeitalter*, p. 48.
130. Burrows, *What Mean These Stones?*, p. 71.
131. De Vaux, *RB*, LV (1948), p. 335.
132. *Zeitalter*, p. 48; also in *Mededeelingen* . . . , IX, 10 (1940), p. 356.

out fully. Even now, though, we must admit that the Biblical authors, even the late P author, did not create this aspect of their narrative out of imaginative fancy but rather drew upon traditional material that we can now recognize as gratifyingly trustworthy in many essential details, although its dependability does not allow us to claim that we have pinpointed any direct identification.

❧ EXCURSUS

ON THE PHILOLOGICAL PROBLEM

I F WE ASSUME a Proto-Semitic root ʿbr, "to cross, to move about," the verbal adjective form derived from that stem would be ʿābiru (pl. -ū), "one on the move, a transient."[1] That this could underlie the cuneiform ḫabiru is explained by the ambiguity of cuneiform characters, which were unable to distinguish clearly between ḫ and ʿ.[2] No such confusion between the consonants existed in Egyptian.[3] As for the second consonant, a b/p ambiguity is observable in both Egyptian and cuneiform and does not present an insurmountable obstacle.[4] A similar process would produce the Ugaritic ʿprm. The corresponding verbal adjective form in Proto-Hebrew would have been ʿābir, whence possibly ʿēber and ʿibrî in Biblical Hebrew.[5] The end product of such a succession as this is the derivation of a gentilic from a verbal adjective, and that is difficult to explain, but not impossible, if both go back to the same base.[6]

Alternatively, if we assume a Proto-Semitic root ʿpr,

1. E. A. Speiser, "Ethnic Movements in the Near East in the Second Millenium B.C.," *AASOR*, XIII (1933), pp. 40–41. *Cf.* Greenberg, p. 90. I am particularly indebted to Professor J. Philip Hyatt for his help in organizing the linguistic detail of this excursus.

2. Speiser, *AASOR*, XIII (1933), p. 39. *Cf.* also H. H. Rowley, *From Joseph to Joshua: Biblical Traditions in the Light of Archaeology*, p. 50.

3. Speiser, *AASOR*, XIII (1933), p. 39. *Cf.* also John A. Wilson, "The 'ʿEperu' of the Egyptian Inscriptions," *AJSL*, XLIX (1933), p. 280.

4. Speiser, *AASOR*, XIII (1933), p. 40, and T. J. Meek, *Hebrew Origins* (hereafter cited as Meek, *HO*), p. 11. See also Rowley, *From Joseph to Joshua*, p. 50.

5. Speiser, *AASOR*, XIII (1933), p. 40; Greenberg, p. 91; Meek, *HO*, p. 7.

6. *Cf.* Greenberg, p. 91, especially n. 27.

"to provide for," the verbal adjective would be *ʿāpiru,* which read as a passive would mean "one provided for."[7] This proposal has the advantage of immediately visible relationship with the Egyptian *ʿāpiru* and the Ugaritic *ʿprm,* while the ambiguity of cuneiform characters would produce the Akkadian form. The Biblical Hebrew words then proceed, as before, from the Proto-Hebrew verbal adjective. This proposal is linguistically simple and has fewer changes to explain, and it has a certain sociological aptness if the Habiru were a settled and indigent part of the population. The great difficulty of this theory is that the root *ʿpr* is known at present almost entirely from East Semitic sources, as in the Akkadian *ʿepēru,* whereas the available evidence points to a West Semitic origin for *ḥābiru,* which made its way eastward, it appears, as a loan word.[8]

There are those who have long resisted identification of the Habiru and the Hebrews and have maintained that *ḥābiru* and *ʿibrî* must be derived from separate roots.[9] It is characteristic of this point of view to emphasize the gentilic form of *ʿibrî* as derivative from *ʿēber,* which does occur as a proper name in Genesis x but whose meaning is essentially that of "place on the other side." By this interpretation *ʿibrî* becomes simply the designation of those who lived on the other side of a river—either the Jordan or the Euphrates, as one may wish to take it.[10] If *ʿābir* and *ʿibrî* can be derived from the same base, however, the gentilic derivation of *ʿibrî* is no serious obstacle to its kinship with *ḥābiru.*

7. Greenberg, p. 91, citing unpublished notes of Goetze.

8. Greenberg, p. 91; A. Leo Oppenheim (ed.) *et al., The Assyrian Dictionary of the Oriental Institute of the University of Chicago,* Vol. VI, p. 84. However, for *ʿpr,* "to provide," in Egyptian, see John A. Wilson, review of Moshe Greenberg's *The Hab/piru,* in *JNES,* XVI (1957), pp. 139–141.

9. *E.g.,* E. G. Kraeling, *Aram and Israel,* p. 31f.; most recently in his *Rand McNally Bible Atlas,* pp. 50, 97.

10. The same view is that of the standard grammar, E. Kautzsch (ed.), *Gesenius' Hebrew Grammar,* pp. 8–9.

✑ III

PATRIARCHAL FAMILY LIFE

W HEN WE seek to use the patriarchal legends of Genesis
for the reconstruction of the external history of the
events of the age, we constantly find ourselves drawn up
short because of the lack of appropriate material in the
legends for such purposes. No such disappointment meets
the effort to learn quite intimately of the personalities in
the legends, as individual persons and as members of
families, for the accounts of the patriarchs are full of
remembered details of family life and relationships and
true-to-life personality sketches. We have at hand much
material in Genesis for reconstructing satisfactorily fully
the structure and life of the Hebrew families of the patriarchal period. Much of it has about it that self-substantiat-
ing quality of being true to human nature as we know it
and consequently requires no further comment; other aspects of patriarchal family life are helpfully illuminated by
the archaeological remains of the period. In fact, so many
actions, practices, and customs shown in the patriarchal
legends are now to be seen through archaeological study
as reflecting those of the people with whom the Hebrews
had close cultural contact that we can feel entirely safe in
accounting the picture of family life in the legends largely
true, not only in the general, human sense, but in the
specific period and place of the patriarchal age. These are
stories of real men and women with real family problems,[1]
as the arresting number of parallels shows.

1. *Cf.* von Rad, *ATD,* pp. 258–259.

No one would have had to tell the patriarchal Hebrews that the family is the fundamental unit of human society. They had naïvely taken this particular truth for granted. The patriarchs knew no other society than the family, even when family is taken in the broadest sense to include the whole clan with all its many relations by blood and by marriage and its associated servants of various classes. Lacking any sort of intertribal organization of their own, once the Hebrews departed from the Mesopotamian homeland, they lived on in Palestine without participating to any great extent in the larger society of a state or national group. Neither Egypt nor any other of the great powers was able to exert steady control over Palestine in this period, and this, with the freewheeling independence of the nomadic occupation, kept the Hebrews from becoming citizens of any state until the time that they formed their own. Thus it is that in the patriarchal legends we find that the family was all the "society" its members knew. In the absence of any strong demand for loyalty in other directions, the Hebrews of the patriarchal age devoted their whole effort toward the family and its work. Even if the time of the literary fixation of the patriarchal legends was an age in which family life was breaking down in a later civilization, we need not conclude on that basis that the authors of the tradition colored it with an idealized picture of peaceful, close-knit family life. Rather, it seems to be a simple reflection of the way the patriarchal families actually lived: their occupation made for this kind of life, and there was no strong external power to compete with the family unit.

Husbands, Wives, and Children

The patriarchs have left no statement of their "doctrine" of marriage but make it reasonably plain by their actions

92

that they looked on it as the means for the establishment and continuation of the family. The parent felt it part of his responsibility to arrange for the marriage of his children, either by taking action on his own (Genesis xxiv.4) or by sending a son off to find his own wife (xxviii.2). The son could, of course, act on his own initiative in the matter, as Esau did (xxvi.34), but the results were not completely satisfactory. The ordinary procedure was for the father to arrange for the marriage of the son, at least for his first wife; subsequent arrangements for additional wives or concubines seem to have been left to the son himself. In the unusual circumstances in which Hagar and her son Ishmael found themselves, it was the mother and not the father who arranged for the young man's marriage (xxi.21); apparently Hagar had suffered so much at the hands of her master and mistress that she despaired of their showing further attention to her son.

Although the patriarchs were kind and considerate toward their women, romance played little part in the arrangement of marriages. The woman could be consulted as to her willingness to marry a certain man, as was Rebekah (xxiv.57), but this is a rarity in the story. Marriage was more often agreed upon by the suitor and the prospective father-in-law, as between Jacob and Laban (xxix.18), and the woman's brothers as well as the man's father might also enter the discussion (xxiv.50, xxxiv.6f.). As numerous passages in Genesis show, the patriarchs were not devoid of tender sentiments, but marriage was looked upon as something which involved more than just the bride and groom, so that the making of a match called for a certain amount of what might strike us, in a different civilization, as unromantic bargaining and dealing. This is, of course, simply to say that the patriarchs did not think of marriage as a private affair.

Patriarchal marriages were untroubled by modern notions of limited childbearing; indeed, the classic picture of patriarchal blessedness is that of the large household of many children. The economic and sociological basis for this, with so much work to be done by so few, is too obvious to require discussion. It was in this context that a man would take more than one wife and beget children even after having begotten children by his first wife, like Abraham (xxv.1), or at the very beginning of his married life, like Esau (xxvi.34) and Jacob (xxix.28). As a further preventive of childless marriage, a wife who had failed to bear children would present one of her maids to her husband as a concubine, so as to provide a substitute mother in something similar to the way that levirate marriage provided a substitute father, as is discussed below. This was the pattern of behavior of Sarai when she gave Hagar to Abram (xvi.2) and of Rachel when she sent Jacob to Bilhah (xxx.4). Concern for continuation and increase of the family as vitally important gave this polygamous practice a character totally distinct from adultery or any other sexual license outside the permitted limit. Jacobson, in fact, considers one wife a sign of poverty because of the Semitic desire for many children.[2]

The institution of levirate marriage is a further instance of the patriarchal care to assure the family's growth. Since it would be the most tragic end of all for a man to die without leaving children behind him, it was felt to be the duty of the dead man's brother to take the widow as his own wife. By this means his brother's wife still bore children as descendants of her husband, with the brother-in-law substituting as sire. While the most celebrated Biblical levirate marriage is that of Ruth, the assignment of Tamar to Onan, the brother of her dead husband Er, is a clear-cut instance of the custom in the patriarchal legends (xxxviii.8). Further, although the narrative does not take us that far,

2. David Jacobson, *The Social Background of the Old Testament*, p. 40.

Tamar was promised to the next son in line after the death of Onan (XXXVIII.11). It should be obvious from such an extreme case as this that once a woman became a member of a family by marriage to one of its men, she was expected to bear children to increase and strengthen that family. Perhaps it is for the very reason that it is such an extreme instance of the necessity for family continuation that the bizarre story of Tamar, Onan, and Judah is recorded.

Because marriage was of such significance for everyone in the two families concerned, the formation of the marriage contract called for serious discussion of the sort that, as has previously been remarked, seems unromantic if considered outside the circumstances of the patriarchal period. Marriage was, however, the affair of the whole family and not just of the contracting parties, even when the latter were adults, for women had value in their own families before marriage as workers and potential mothers and after marriage, of course, in the husband's family as both in fact; in either case they could also be, in some cases, owners of property.[3] The transfer of a woman from her father's family to that of her husband meant the loss of someone valuable to the former and the acquisition of her by the latter, just as nowadays one hears grooms' mothers being consoled at weddings by the reminder that they are "not losing a son but gaining a daughter"—though this was a matter of hard fact for the patriarchal families and not a sentimental platitude. It is on this basis that patriarchal marriages typically involved the exchange of something of value given to the bride's family in return for the work and children she would bring to her husband's. Abraham's servant paid well for Rebekah (XXIV.53), and there are other references to this bridal price in XXXI.15 and XXXIV.12. Although the dealings between Jacob and Laban were hardly ever honorable on either side, one

3 Millar Burrows, *The Basis of Israelite Marriage,* pp. 9–10.

would say that the years of work that Jacob contributed to the household of Laban constituted some sort of substitute for the bridal price. Some ambiguity is introduced here by the peculiar phrasing of the complaint of Leah and Rachel in xxxi.15, but Laban had received compensation of a sort for his daughters, even if with a currency debased by fraud and trickery.

Burrows may well be right in insisting that this notion of compensation to the bride's family is an older one than the idea of sale and barter for a wife,[4] but that is not of immediate importance for us here. What is significant about Burrows's discussion is his statement that marriage involved an "alliance" between the two families: they had to be brought close enough to each other to permit the transfer of a daughter from the one to the other in exchange for whatever recompense was suitable for the work, children, and property she would bring to her new family.[5] Burrows's actual words of summation are worth reproducing:

The basis of Israelite marriage was the continuance of the husband's family. This required . . . a wife from another family, who had to be induced to give her up, . . . by a gift, creating an obligation, sealing a contract, and establishing a family alliance. Other gifts were exchanged and feasts . . . partaken.[6]

For all the jollity that would naturally surround a wedding, it was nevertheless a solemn family occasion as well.

One cannot argue that all the marriages in the patriarchal legends were contracted in such an atmosphere or with such full form, for the great bulk of the couples mentioned are simply recorded as getting married: "So-and-so took Such-and-such to wife." Nevertheless, Burrows argues

4. *Ibid.*, p. 14. *Cf.* Jacobson's views on marriage by purchase, *The Social Background of the Old Testament*, p. 40f.
5. *The Basis of Israelite Marriage*, pp. 10–13.
6. *Ibid.*, p. 15.

his point convincingly, and a careful reading of Genesis at those places where we are told in some detail about the nuptial contract appears to bear him out. Suffice it to say that the difference between marriage among the Hebrews and the picture of it to be gained from the Code of Hammurabi is worthy of note, inasmuch as the latter represents probably the highest point of legal development among Fertile Crescent peoples till much later and did serve as something of a general basis for the laws of those directly or indirectly influenced by Babylonian civilization. Fortunately, we also have Hammurabi's laws almost intact. Sections 155 and 159 designate as the essential condition of a marriage contract an agreement between the fathers or between the groom and the bride's father. Burrows's argument strikes this writer as slightly tenuous at this juncture,[7] but it cannot be denied that Section 128 designates a document signed by the groom guaranteeing the bride's status as the *sine qua non* of a valid marriage arrangement. No consistent mention is made of compensation given the bride's father in all marriages, and it is clear that Section 139 envisions some marriages without the payment of any marriage price.[8]

The significance of this difference may be manifold: one could argue that either the Hebrew or the Babylonian arrangement was superior to the other, or that the Babylonian laws indicate a more complicatedly developed social order than the simple, family-style life of the Hebrews. The writer hopes not to be begging the question when he suggests that the casuistic law of Hammurabi's Code, representing areas of litigation, does not show us the same side of marriage arrangements that we find in the patriarchal legends. A law is a device for settling disputes that arise; a legend is meant to edify or entertain. Conceivably

7. *Ibid.*, p. 31.
8. *Cf.* the texts, *ANET*, p. 171f.

we should not try to make too much out of such comparison, but the difference is plain to see.

The patriarchal Hebrews were simple and unsophisticated people; so their marriages showed remarkable stability, but they did have their problems. The running battle over several years between Jacob and his father-in-law is the sort of controversy that has afflicted many another family where there is a considerable amount of property to be divided and neither party to the dispute is transparently honest or fair with the other.[9] While this struggle had many ramifications, as is usually the case, the way in which it touches upon this discussion is its raising of the question of the terms on which Jacob entered Laban's household and married Laban's daughters.

It is clear that Jacob was received not as a slave or even as a laborer but as a kinsman, a member of the family (xxix.15).[10] This status he had by virtue of blood relationship on his mother's side of the family to begin with, and it would have given him all the position he might have needed in Laban's house without any further establishment of relationship. His fourteen years of labor may, as previously suggested, have been in place of payment of bridal compensation to Laban, but one does not read the Old Testament for very long before acquiring a slight suspicion of any phrase containing the number seven; perhaps the work that Jacob did was simply that expected of him as an able-bodied man in the household, in which case the terms of the marriages to Leah and Rachel would be different. Not all the details are congruent with each other so as to allow a clear-cut decision as to whether Jacob made some sort of bridal payment at the time that he was married to Leah and Rachel. If we are to take literally the complaint

9. For the view that Jacob was largely honest and just see Finegan, *In the Beginning*, p. 128.
10. *Cf.* von Rad, *ATD*, p. 253.

of the daughters of Laban in xxxi.15, then some sort of payment had been made, and the women condemn their father for having misappropriated it in some way. That the Nuzi practice allowed the father to use the bridal price at his will is made clear by Burrows's discussion,[11] but, while refusing to dogmatize, Burrows seems to favor the conclusion that what was legal and proper at Nuzi was not so among the Aramaeans. It would seem that Laban's people considered the bridal payment a sort of trust fund for the bride's future needs, a fund that the father was not allowed to use for other purposes.[12] This writer would further suggest that it might be a simple matter of Leah's and Rachel's decision on their own that their father was not entitled to spend whatever had been given him in exchange for them.

Jacob does appear to have held, at least in the first few years, some additional status over and above that which he had when he arrived. The following discussion will show the writer's belief that Jacob was adopted by Laban into a special kind of sonship, which involved his marriage to the daughters of Laban and his becoming heir presumptive to Laban's holdings. Whatever the status of Jacob may have been, though, it needs to be remarked here that, as Burrows shows,[13] Laban's deception of Jacob in regard to the marriage to Leah first was illegal, or at the best not customary; women were not mere chattels in Haran any more than in Palestine. For the slight relevance that it has to this matter, Burrows refers to Section 31 of the Assyrian Code, which allows that in the case of the death of the promised bride the suitor might,

---

11. Millar Burrows, "The Complaint of Laban's Daughters," *JAOS,* LVII (1937), pp. 259–276. *Cf.* also Jacobson, p. 40, and Cyrus H. Gordon, "Parallèles Nouziens aux Lois et Coutumes de l'Ancien Testament," *RB,* XLIV (1935), p. 36.

12. Burrows, *JAOS,* LVII (1937), p. 270.

13. *The Basis of Israelite Marriage,* p. 25.

at the father-in-law's discretion, take another of his daughters to wife or even leave, taking the money part of the bridal gift with him.[14]

An argument from silence is always a dangerous one, but it is still true that there is no mention of Laban's having any sons until Jacob has been in the household for some years (xxx.1), and with the first mention of the sons the story adds the further detail that relations were not the same between Jacob and his father-in-law as they had been at the first (xxx.2). This might be explained as an indication that, when Jacob arrived, there was no son to inherit Laban's property, so that Laban adopted him; as years went by, though, Laban could have become the father of sons, and this would cause a radical change in the relationship.

If such an adoption took place when Laban could foresee no other male heir, then probably Jacob entered Laban's household on the terms of an *erebu* marriage, by which a husband was taken for the daughter of a sonless man in order to continue the family.[15] The antiquity of this custom in Mesopotamian lands may be shown by what appears to be a reference to it in the Lipt-Ishtar Code, Section 29 of which speaks of a young man who enters the house of his father-in-law.[16] The continuation of the custom into patriarchal times is demonstrated by the adoption contract between Wullu and Nashwi at Nuzi.[17] In this contract Nashwi adopts Wullu, and in return for Wullu's taking care of Nashwi during his lifetime Wullu will be the heir at Nashwi's death. As part of the agreement Wullu will marry Nashwi's daughter, and no other if all goes well and she bears him children. Nashwi apparently has no son of his own at the time of

14. *ANET*, p. 182.
15. Burrows, *JAOS*, LVII (1937), p. 261.
16. *ANET*, p. 160.
17. The full text is in Pritchard, *ANET*, pp. 219–220.

this adoption, but, if he should have one, then the son will inherit half the estate and take the father's gods. It is so close a parallel that we could almost substitute Laban and Jacob for Nashwi and Wullu throughout, as Gordon suggests.[18]

This would explain the cordial reception given Jacob by Laban, the extended time of Jacob's residence in Laban's house, and in part Jacob's marriage; there is evidently no explanation of Laban's deceit other than his being as much a trickster as Jacob. It would also explain and even justify the complaints of Laban and of his sons. As soon as the sons grew old enough to recognize what Jacob was doing with their father's wealth, half of which would rightly be theirs after Laban's death, they had every good reason to protest. Likewise, if Jacob entered the household as an adopted heir, he had no right to take with him all that he did when he decided to leave, and Laban's complaint (xxxi.43) is completely understandable and legitimate. Daughters, grandchildren, cattle, and all the rest that Jacob had with him were Laban's, because Jacob had come into the family by adoption, a condition of which was the marriage; Rachel and Leah had no right to leave; above all, the gods (xxxi.30f.) were by no right Jacob's, now that there were sons in Laban's house to receive them. Von Rad argues, not too impressively, that as a nonlandholding foreigner, Jacob had no status that would allow him possession even of his wives and children;[19] this does not really penetrate the heart of the matter.

It is difficult, and not really necessary, to feel sympathy for either Jacob or Laban in their charges and counter-charges, and one can readily agree with them (xxxi.52)

18. Cyrus H. Gordon, "The Story of Jacob and Laban in the Light of the Nuzi Tablets," *BASOR*, No. 66 (April 1937), pp. 25–27. *Cf.* the overcautious mention of this parallel by Jacobson, p. 99f.

19. *ATD,* p. 261.

that they would do well simply to avoid each other from that time on. The fact remains that, if Laban transgressed the standards of fair play in marrying off his daughters, both Jacob and the daughters committed a serious breach of the contract that had originally brought them together.

Further illumination of the relationship between Jacob and Laban, or at least a supplementary example like it, would be the situation described in Section 25 of the Code of Eshnunna,[20] where the beginning clause of the law speaks of a man who "calls at the house of his father-in-law" and whose father-in-law *"accepts* him *in servitude."*[21] Care must be exercised in the use of this particular law, however, for Goetze italicizes *accepts . . . in servitude* in his translation, evidently as uncertain in the original, and that is the key idea of the clause. Also, as previously argued, Jacob does not appear to have entered servitude, in its ordinary sense, in the household of Laban. The similarity can still be conjecturally pointed out.

Several interesting parallels can be found for the custom of a man's taking a maid of his wife's as a concubine. In this practice the patriarchs followed the pattern prevalent among their Mesopotamian neighbors; the detailed intricacy of the wording of the laws governing this practice would probably be a sign of the wide practice of such concubinage. Humanly speaking, also, the delicacy of the relationship in the family brought about by the practice can be seen in the care taken in the laws to protect the rights of all concerned. Section 146 of Hammurabi's Code deals with the problem of a slave girl thus given as concubine to her master; if she later became arrogant toward her mistress because the concubine had borne children, appropriate punishment is provided: she was to be returned to mere slavery again.[22] We should observe that

20. *ANET*, p. 162.
21. Italics in the original.
22. *ANET*, p. 172.

this law is probably more gentle than it might appear; certainly it is kinder than the treatment given Hagar. The law specifically protects the slave from being sold in such a case, yet wifely jealousy, as humanly understandable as the pride of the concubine, caused Sarah to treat poor Hagar harshly and finally to cast her out (Genesis XVI.4f., XXI.10). The illegality of thus casting out the bondwoman is clear, and the Biblical writer must have been aware of it, for he mentions specific intervention by God at this point: only after this assurance from God Himself that he may break the law with impunity does Abraham proceed with the actual expulsion of Hagar (XXI.12).[23]

The function of Hammurabi's laws regarding children of concubines must surely have been to protect their position and prevent their being victimized. They were thus assured a place in society and in their own household, and at least could not end up worse off than before. Sections 170 and 191 of the Code[24] make this clear; concubines' children who had been fully recognized as his children by the father received an almost equal share in his estate at his death, the son of the first wife obviously receiving a preferential share of the estate. Even if they had not been so recognized and could not share in the goods of the estate, they received their freedom, as did the concubine, at the death of the master. In view of this we should have to say that Jacob dealt more legally and humanely with the children of his concubines than did Abraham; no discrimination was made by Jacob between children of Leah and Rachel and children of their maids (XXX.4f.).[25] However, Abraham followed the right pattern to some extent (XXV.6).

The extension of a widow's childbearing usefulness through levirate marriage has already been referred to in

23. Von Rad, *ATD,* pp. 162, 198f.
24. *ANET,* p. 173.
25. *Cf.* Jacobson, p. 90, for the same conclusion.

the case of Tamar (xxxviii.6f.). Her unique behavior in xxxviii.14f. can probably be explained somewhat by citation of the custom envisioned in the Middle Assyrian Laws, which may go back as far as the patriarchal period. Section 33 of the Law provided that a childless widow might be married by her father-in-law to another of his sons, or that the father-in-law himself might marry her.[26] It would appear that Tamar, twice widowed and with no prospect of remarriage in sight, simply took the initiative in carrying out the intention of the custom in regard to widows without children.[27] Successive remarriage of the widow was clearly taken for granted; one set of contracts from the records of Tulpunnaya of Nuzi[28] describes the way that hard-bargaining businesswoman took a girl, Kisaya, into her household as an adoptive daughter, or daughter-servant, in return for which Tulpunnaya was to marry her off to anyone she pleased and, as the contract specifically and somewhat emphatically states, would keep her married in the event of the death of her spouse, no matter how many marriages this might entail. The transactions between Tulpunnaya and Kisaya are a singular bright spot in cuneiform literature, since they relate how Kisaya, having made this bargain with Tulpunnaya, objected to the husband whom her guardian-mistress had picked for her and successfully insisted on legal divorce from him and remarriage to the man of her liking. We cannot claim that this provision in Tulpunnaya's contracts represents true levirate marriage, for it does not, even if it achieves the same effect. However, we do know that Section 193 of the Hittite Code provided for levirate marriage.[29]

It is truly difficult to say with any precision whether Hebrew women enjoyed a higher and better position

26. *ANET*, p. 182.
27. Von Rad, *ATD*, p. 314. *Cf.* also Lewy, *RHR*, CIX (1934), pp. 30–31.
28. Pfeiffer and Speiser, *AASOR*, XVI (1935–1936), pp. 88–89.
29. *ANET*, p. 196.

than their Mesopotamian sisters. Jacobson thinks they did not.[30] One wishes it were possible to make a clear comparison and relative evaluation, for the position of women is an important consideration in the understanding of the nature of the family. The information we have about the women of Genesis, though, is not the same kind of record we have about the Mesopotamian women of the time. For all the assertiveness and initiative shown by such women as Tamar, Hagar, Leah, and Rachel, there is no counterpart in the patriarchal legends for Tulpunnaya of Nuzi: the story of Genesis would have been a different one indeed had there been. This Tulpunnaya was much more important than her husband: evidently she brought the money to the wedding in the first place, for in the records of her dealings the husband's name is mentioned only twice; otherwise she is known as her mother's daughter.[31] In her long career she showed a head for business that would be outstanding in any age, but we have nothing to guide us in estimating what the internal life of her own family was. It is exclusively the latter type of material that we have about the women of Genesis. As cited immediately above, Speiser concludes, on the basis of this and of other evidence that he displays in full, that women enjoyed a remarkably prominent and independent position at Nuzi. To be sure, Tulpunnaya quite dominated the scene in any transaction, showing great financial and personal independence, but perhaps she was unique even in a society where women played a great part in the family's business affairs. However that may be, we meet the domestic type of woman in the patriarchal legends, for the scene of the legends is the family, the only social group of any real stature the patriarchs knew. In such a context as this women enjoy a high

30. Jacobson, pp. 74, 78.
31. Pfeiffer and Speiser, *AASOR*, XVI (1935–1936), p. 76.

position of affection and respect, if not of financial independence,[32] and the power wielded by the women of the legends through the exercise of the proverbial quiet influence of the woman might well be said to be just as real and as efficient as that of the Nuzi women, for all their business acumen.

The Structure of Family Organization

We may describe the structure of the Hebrew patriarchal family as simple, if we remember that the word is not just the negative, opposite idea from complex; simplicity can actually be quite intricate if all the parts fit harmoniously and effectively together. In this sense, then, the simple family life of the patriarchs had a well-defined structure, in which each individual member had a position and function.[33] Not all tasks were performed by all members of the family, although there appears to have been a certain amount of communal sharing of the work; for instance, sons and even daughters worked in the fields and pastures (Genesis XXIX.9, XXXVII.2, and elsewhere), sharing the tasks that a more aristocratic society would consider appropriate only to servants. None could be idle, though, except the young children, the aged, and the sick. While it is not a full handling of the matter to show structure purely in terms of function and authority, this nevertheless provides a convenient outline for understanding the organization of the family.

The ultimate, decisive authority in the family was that of the father. The once popular idea of matriarchal organization appears to have been largely abandoned, as Jacobson's summary of the arguments shows.[34] There was no

32. Burrows, *The Basis of Israelite Marriage*, pp. 32–33.
33. Jacobson, p. 69.
34. Jacobson, p. 23f.

legitimate appeal beyond the father's will, and his word was the final one. His wish or decision might be disobeyed, as by Rachel and Leah, or he might be made the victim of deceit, as were Isaac and Laban, but there was no question of his essential right to will as he might. The decision to leave Haran was Abram's (xii.5), and he directed the course of the journey and its stops. A man was free to expose his wife to the danger of adultery by having her pass as his sister (xii.13 and parallels), and he could offer his daughters for prostitution, as Lot did (xix.8).

The role of the father as frequently the dominant one in the arrangement of marriages has already been discussed in the preceding section. He was likewise the dispenser of hospitality (xviii.3, xix.2, xxix.13). If we should take Genesis xxii quite literally, we might assume that the father actually had the power of life and death over his children, but literary criticism has taught us to read this chapter as a moral fable on the themes of faith and obedience,[35] and Woolley's now famous attempt to draw a connection between this story and a statue of a goat in, or more likely eating from, a bush, found at Ur, has made us wary of taking the tale and its fine points too seriously.[36] In his old age the father made disposition of his goods through the blessings bestowed by him on each of the children, blessings held to be irrevocable even when given mistakenly and vastly powerful in shaping the future careers of the children (xxvii.28f., 39f., xlviii.9f., xl). All this paternal authority was in general exercised with wisdom and benevolence, even if tainted occasionally with favoritism, as in Jacob's case in dealing with Joseph (xxxvii.3), but it was for all practical purposes unchallengeable.

35. Cf. the commentaries ad loc. As we might expect, Kaufmann approaches Genesis xxii from a different direction, giving serious attention to the motif of human sacrifice, in The Religion of Israel, p. 137.

36. Cf. Finegan, Light from the Ancient Past, p. 35.

The discussion of the position of women in the preceding section has shown that the Hebrews of patriarchal times thought of woman's place as in the home with the children. Although the wives did not usually assert their power in a direct way, they could often secure their wishes by complaint, as Sarah did, or by a bit of feminine intrigue, as Rebekah did (xxvii.6f.).

Male children, whether by birth or by adoption, stood next below the father in authority, somehow shared it with him, as will be shown below, and received it from him at his death, with the preference going to the son who was either the first-born or the recipient of the superior blessing from the father. Except in the case of Ishmael, there appears to have been no other distinction in this between the children of wives and those of concubines.

The servants of the household, whether the "trained" servants of Genesis xiv or the general class of workers, lacked any real authority by virtue of their status, but their function as household and field servants and, as the need arose, fighters assured them a living and occasionally the opportunity for rising to a position of importance. Women servants could become concubines of the master and mothers of his children, and a man servant could become a trusted overseer of the property and emissary on an important and responsible task (xxiv.2f.).

Because the patriarchal legends are written, so to speak, from within the family, the picture of the Hebrew father that we find in the legends is a more benevolent and lovable one than what we find in the legal documents of Mesopotamia that speak of the actions of fathers toward their children. Although the legal records do occasionally drop their impersonal formality and display human tenderness and affection in recognizable shape, it is not to legal papers that we turn as a rule to find examples of such. If we hold this in mind when comparing examples

108

of paternal authority in the two types of source, we can avoid assuming that Mesopotamian fathers were coldly cruel toward their children. Legal records and business documents seldom disclose the warm and loving side of people.

One place where the court records do, however, show us that the love and concern of a father for his son are very much the same wherever we find them, is in the Nuzi litigation about the right of a young man to his wife, a former slave of his father.[37] The testimony of the man, Tarmiya, relates how his father, in old age and in what must have been his terminal illness, took the son's hand and spoke tenderly to him about his not yet having found a wife; to fulfil his fatherly duty before his death, the old man gave his slave-girl Zululi-Ishtar to Tarmiya, and, we may assume, he died happy in the knowledge that he had at last made arrangements for the marriage of all his sons. Speiser singles this passage out as unique in cuneiform literature for its homeliness and appeal and speaks of it as "a worthy forerunner of the Benjamin episodes in the Old Testament." One can readily agree with Speiser here, for he obviously thinks, as we do, of the anxiety of the aged Jacob for the welfare of his youngest, Benjamin, in Genesis XLII. We also think of the blessings and death-bed scenes of Genesis.

Other records from Nuzi lack the personal appeal of this incident but still illustrate the nature of the paternal authority. Two different fathers gave their sons to Tulpunnaya in slavery, evidently as security for the payment of debts owed to her.[38] Hanatu entered her service for ten years, and Taena for six years. On the face of it this might appear reasonable enough, since a definite end was set for the period of service, but we can sympathize with

37. Pfeiffer and Speiser, *AASOR*, XVI (1935–1936), p. 107.
38. *Ibid.,* pp. 85, 87.

both fathers and both sons and also be reminded again of the hard bargain that Tulpunnaya drove, when we compare the length of these sons' servitude with that allowed in such a case in the Code of Hammurabi. The latter in Section 117 permitted a man to sell the services of his wife or children for the payment of debts—their services only, and not their persons[39]—but specifically fixed the term of service at only three years.[40] Such a system at its best has much to be said against it, of course, even if it would appear that the cruelty of it lay more in the harsh use of it by such as Tulpunnaya in her amassing of wealth. The Hebrews never had to resort to this in the patriarchal age, so far as our knowledge of it goes, and their manner of life probably helped them to keep their children out of such servitude. It is nevertheless illustrative of the notion of a parent's authority over his family among the people who were the Hebrews' neighbors. The extreme examples of the authority of the head of the house in Genesis are without extra-Biblical parallel, and this much should be said about them as they stand: the exposure of a wife to the chance of adultery is in a story that has as its principal theme the craftiness of the patriarch and not the weight of his power; and Lot's offer of his daughters for prostitution has about it the mark of a move of desperation described in detail by the narrator in order to make it clear beyond mistake that the men of Sodom had designs only upon the male occupants of the house. The closest approximation to this in actual, legitimate practice was the Babylonian father's offer of his daughter as a sacred prostitute, provided for in Section 181 of Hammurabi's Code,[41] but sacred prostitution was a totally different thing and a recognized institution of the society. It is true that

39. Burrows, *The Basis of Israelite Marriage*, p. 34.
40. Pritchard, *ANET*, p. 170.
41. *Ibid.*, p. 174.

110

the contract by which one Shitanka gave herself to Tul-punnaya states that Tulpunnaya could make her a harlot if she so wished, but this statement occurs in a list of several things Tulpunnaya could do with Shitanka, as evidence, it would seem, of the completeness of the mistress's control over her but not of her actual intention.[42]

One aspect of authority in the patriarchal family has been given insufficient attention by previous writers on Genesis; this writer finds no mention in the classic critical commentaries of the manner in which brothers exercised a kind of fratriarchal authority over their siblings. This is, however, no fault in Gunkel, Driver, or Skinner, for one does not look for such a custom until he has discovered the existence of such a system of authority in the records from Nuzi; the great critical works on Genesis were published, of course, and their authors dead before the Nuzi material was made available to students of the Bible. Von Rad, who has written the best major commentary on Genesis since Nuzi material came to light, makes use of it frequently, but not on this subject.

We observe in the wooing of Rebekah for Isaac by Abraham's servant in Genesis xxiv that the whole family are involved in the discussion of the arrangement for Rebekah to go with the servant to Palestine. In the light of the foregoing discussion about the concern of the entire family in such cases, we are not surprised at this. A closer reading of xxiv.50–60, however, focuses our attention on the important part played by Laban in the engagement. As a matter of fact, Laban is the dominant member of Rebekah's family throughout the chapter; Bethuel, the father, is mentioned by name frequently, but he speaks only once (xxiv.50), and then in concert with Laban. The

42. Pfeiffer and Speiser, *AASOR*, XVI (1935–1936), p. 84. Not too great a stigma was attached to prostitution at Nuzi, however; *cf.* Cyrus H. Gordon, "The Status of Women Reflected in the Nuzi Tablets," *ZfA*, N.F. IX (1936), p. 148.

question as to departure is put to Rebekah by her mother and her brother. The verse that describes her departure speaks of Rebekah as "their sister," and the benediction that sends her on her way blesses her as "our sister." Clearly these are words from the standpoint of a brother.

In a later episode, after Dinah has been deflowered by Shechem, he deals not only with Jacob, her father, in his attempts to win her in honest marriage, but the narrative makes it a point to state that Jacob took no action on the matter until his sons, Dinah's brothers, arrived to join the discussion (XXIV.5). Shechem addresses himself to both father and brothers in his plea, as we should expect, but again clearly it is Dinah's brothers who take the dominant part in the arrangement; they set the terms on which Shechem may have Dinah to wife (XXXIV.14f.). It is true that they deal deceitfully, as the author takes pains to state in so many words, but there is no question of their having the authority to act so, albeit treacherously.

A third instance is the sale of Joseph by his brothers to the Ishmaelites who passed by (XXXVII.27). It is true, of course, that in one of its most successful analyses literary criticism has separated this episode into its component accounts, in one of which the unfortunate Joseph is simply left in the pit, where he is found by Midianites. In the parallel account, however, which is interwoven with the other, the brothers sell Joseph outright. Though without parallel in the patriarchal legends, such dealings with a brother or a sister are well attested at Nuzi, as shown below.

These three incidents are unrelated with each other as they stand; in each one a different situation obtains, with a different outcome in each case. What links all of them together, though, is the common theme of the action of brothers on an authority that appears to be theirs on their own. In the cases of Rebekah and Dinah, the brothers

112

actually make the decision in the matter that regards the family as a whole. In the case of Joseph, though the action of the brothers is motivated by spite and hatred, it is still clear that they have the power to dispose of their arrogant brother by selling him.

This fratriarchal authority was no unique trait of Hebrew family structure but was part of their shared culture with the Hurrians we know from Nuzi, where fratriarchy, according to Speiser, is amply attested.[43] A most interesting document from Nuzi is the record of how one Akiya in a public act assumed guardianship over his sister, Kunyashu.[44] She had previously been married off by another guardian, who had since died, and now her husband too was dead. Speiser thinks that the previous guardian who arranged her first marriage was also a brother, although there is nothing said directly in the text to prove it positively. In this document Akiya assumes fratriarchal guardianship over his widowed sister, and he is to marry her to another husband at the bridal price specified in the document.

Speiser admits the difficulty of making precise statements about the nature of fratriarchy because of the linguistic difficulty of translating the pertinent texts. We might add further that, since the texts take the institution for granted, they do not take the trouble to explain it. Its essential import is plain, though, even if the details escape us. It represents a type of shared authority within the family circle and not simply a succession of brothers to the authority of the parents after their death. There is nothing in the Nuzi material above to indicate that the father is dead, so that the brothers in turn have taken over authority as head of the family; fairness, of course, compels us to admit that likewise there is nothing to prove

43. Pfeiffer and Speiser, *AASOR*, XVI (1935–1936), p. 84.
44. *Ibid.*, p. 104.

that the father is not dead, either. Nevertheless, the institution of fratriarchy would have no separate status if it were merely a matter of the son's taking the place of the deceased father.[45] Consequently, the parallel with Hebrew fratriarchy is closer still, for in both cases it would appear that the father, while still alive, shared his authority as head of the family with the sons of the family. We cannot but be struck by the fact that in the two clearest instances of it among the Hebrews and in the Nuzi material the exercise of this fratriarchy characterizes arrangements for marriages of women of the family.

An inverse kind of fratriarchy can be observed in Nuzi records, and for the sake of general interest in the subject of family authority it needs to be mentioned here. A most peculiar contract among the archives of Tulpunnaya tells, it seems, how a woman, Shitanka, gave herself over into the service of our lady tycoon and likewise gave her brother, Hanatu, into Tulpunnaya's power, too.[46] The key sentence in this contract is unfortunately obscure because of the carelessness of its syntax: the verb is in the masculine form, which would indicate that the father of both Shitanka and Hanatu was the one who made this disposition of his children, but the direct object of the verb is the reflexive feminine form of the pronoun, which would indicate that, true enough, the initiative was Shitanka's. If this latter is the correct reading of the sentence, then we have in this a unique example of what, for want of a more felicitous term, must be called *sororate*,[47] a turning of the tables on fratriarchy in which the sister gives her brother into service. Such a thing is unique at Nuzi, and the argument for its being the subject matter of this con-

45. Speiser, however, thinks fratriarchy did not operate at full force until after the father's death: E. A. Speiser, "New Kirkuk Documents Relating to Family Laws," *AASOR*, X (1930), p. 21.
46. Pfeiffer and Speiser, *AASOR*, XVI (1935–1936), p. 84.
47. *Ibid.*, p. 85.

tract eventually must be reduced to the principle of *lectio difficilior*. Nevertheless, that is what the text seems to say, and it deserves notice for its own peculiarity and as a variation from ordinary custom so rare at Nuzi that we should not be amazed to find no parallel to it among the Hebrews, who followed the more usual pattern.

The elaborateness of Oriental etiquette, to this day a source of wonder to bustling Occidentals, makes its presence felt in both Biblical and extra-Biblical materials of the patriarchal age. What reader of Genesis has not been fascinated and even entertained by the careful attention to courtesy and the expansive manners shown by the characters in its pages? Abram obsequiously falls all over himself making his heavenly guests welcome (xviii.2f.). The purchase of Machpelah (xxiii) is a celebrated glimpse of the niceties of polite business. When asked by Abraham's servant for a little drink of water, Rebekah serves him forthwith and proceeds unasked to water the camels, too (xxiv.18f.). Examples can be multiplied. The truthfulness of the Biblical narrative in the recording of such details is remarkably shown by their similarity to passages found outside the Bible. It was no figment of the writer's imagination, for instance, that Isaac should send his son out to prepare and bring him a meal (xxvii.3f.), nor was it merely a fretful bid for attention on the part of the senile Isaac. Such deference of son toward father must have been standard custom, for we find in Ugaritic literature the same sort of behavior expected of a son: he must humbly wait upon his father at table and even support him and take care of him when he got drunk, if it came to that.[48]

Respect of a different sort was shown by the abject bowing before one to whom obeisance was due. The fundamental principle of Oriental manners must be, "When in doubt, overdo it," if we are to believe Biblical and extra-

48. Pritchard, *ANET,* p. 150.

Biblical references to it; the author has not forgotten his own observation of Arab customs in our own age, either. When Genesis tells us that Jacob, on meeting his estranged brother, bowed himself low seven times (xxxiii.3), it is a sign not of the author's predilection for the sacred number but of his accurate knowledge of custom. Throughout the Amarna correspondence the governors begin their pleas to the pharaoh for help in this wise: "Beneath the feet of the king, my lord, seven times, and seven times I fall." Or, as the ultimate even by Oriental standards, "At the two feet of the king, my lord, the Sun-god from heaven, seven times, seven times I fall, both prone and supine."[49]

Not a facet of the organization of the patriarchal family, to be sure, but an aspect of their life, just the same, is the mode of their transportation. The most intriguing aspect of this subject is the mention, in xxiv.10 and elsewhere, of the use of camels. To this Albright objects that there is no evidence of the domestication of camels in Palestine before 1100, and it would thus appear that their mention in the time of the patriarchs is patently anachronistic; Free counters with evidence from figurines, skeletons, carvings, and even a camel's hair rope that camels were known and domesticated in every Egyptian period from the predynastic on.[50] De Vaux approaches the subject differently.[51] He acknowledges that camels are in general associated with full-fledged nomads, which the patriarchs were not. Furthermore, camels are represented in Mesopotamian drawings as early as the Obeid Age and in Egyptian art as early as the first dynasty, but they then apparently fall into disuse until the end of the second millennium. In between we do not know about the use of camels, but it is worthy

49. *Ibid.*, pp. 483–485.
50. The opposing arguments are Albright, *The Archaeology of Palestine*, pp. 206–207, and Joseph P. Free, "Abraham's Camels," *JNES*, III (1944), pp. 187–193.
51. De Vaux, *RB*, LVI (1949), p. 8f.

of note that the representations of camels from the earlier age all come from settled sites. Nomads and seminomads do not leave behind them the records and evidences that settled peoples do, so it might be that they continued to use them right along. This would not disprove the anachronism of the mention of camels in Genesis, but it prevents our being positive that it is an anachronism. The latest written on the subject known to this writer agrees essentially with Albright but acknowledges that the question is still open.[52]

Property Ownership and Management

Although the patriarchal Hebrews were never poor in this world's goods, as represented in Genesis, they never were people of spectacular wealth, either. They prospered with their flocks and their fields, but they never suffered from the embarrassment of riches. The kind of property they owned—servants, ranch and farm animals, farm land, temporary and permanent dwellings, household furniture, and a family cemetery—was not extensive enough or complicated enough to make for involved procedures of procurement or supervision. The head of the family in each generation could manage his property by direct oversight on his own, or he could make a trusted servant his overseer, responsible directly to him, as Abraham did (xxiv.2).

Ownership of property is not made specific in the patriarchal legends, since they are not real estate records, but in a direct and elementary way the actual owner of property was the head of the family. Whether this could be considered a case of his ownership by virtue of his own right or one of his being the head of the family that owned the

---

52. Jozef M. A. Janssen, "Egyptological Remarks on the Story of Joseph in Genesis," *Jaarbericht van Het Vooraziatisch-Egyptisch Genootschap,* XIV (1955–1956), p. 63.

property in common[53] is a question never raised in the legends. The right of the head of the family to use and speak of the property as "his" was never questioned except in the unusual controversy between Jacob and Laban, in which, as we have seen, the argument was over the division of the estate between father and (presumably) adoptive son, not over Laban's original ownership.

Three principles of legitimate property acquisition apply to the patriarchs: squatter's rights, inheritance, and purchase. When Abram and Lot decided to part (xiii.12), Abram simply settled where he could find room and no one to contest his moving in. Isaac and Jacob in turn settled as they could, set up their tents or houses, and took possession of such land as they needed and could manage. Isaac was his father's sole heir (xxv.5), and Jacob secured the bulk of his property by taking advantage of the law of the land, his brother, his father-in-law, and everyone else in sight. The purchase of Machpelah is the one instance of the patriarchs' actually paying out money for land (xxiii). The Hebrews' attitude toward their land, with the exception of the family burying ground, was a nomadic "easy come, easy go," for they made no serious attempt, for instance, to retain ownership of their Palestinian land when they went to Egypt. With the rest of the property, though, there was real concern that the family's holdings remain in the family, and steps were taken to assure that there would be a proper heir: we see this most clearly in the case of Abraham.

The pathos and irony of the situation of Abram and Sarai are touchingly but unsentimentally told in the early chapters of the legend: with a sense of vocation to establish a new people (xii.2, xv.5, xviii.2f.), Abram finds himself without an heir of his own and with a wife who is past childbearing (xvii.11). Attention has already been given

53. *Cf.* Jacobson's discussion of communal ownership, pp. 71–72.

118

to the step taken to provide an heir for Abram's property through his taking Hagar as his concubine. Even before that, though, the childless man had moved to provide himself with an heir for his property that would satisfy the sense of propriety of the time: he had made Eliezer of Damascus, one "born in the house," his heir (xv.2f.). This would mean that this Eliezer was one of Abram's servants, not only because of the obvious sense of "born in the house" in Hebrew, but also because of the parallel usage among the Babylonians.[54] Whether this Eliezer was the eldest of the servants selected to find a bride for Isaac, we are not told in so many words, but it seems plausible to assume that, if the man was trustworthy enough to have been made an heir at one time, he could surely be trusted to find a suitable wife for the son when the time came.

Genesis xv.2 does not describe the manner by which one of the servants was made the heir; in fact, the verse is probably corrupt in the Hebrew at the crucial point and, as it stands, not satisfactorily translatable. Nevertheless, the sense of it can now be made clear through comparison with similar situations shown in the Nuzi contracts, despite the difficulty of translation.[55] If there is any single instance that by itself can prove the value of archaeological study for the clarification of difficult or uncertain passages in the Bible, it is this one—perhaps even more so than in the case of the relationship between Jacob and Laban.

The feudal society of Nuzi holds the key to the understanding of Abram's situation and action. In such a society every landholder had his property ultimately from the king, and, since the land was held in such terms, it could not properly be passed to any but the legitimate heir of the holder. Sale or even mortgage of the property outside the family line of succession would be improper, even

54. Cf. de Vaux, RB, LV (1948), p. 328.
55. Cf. von Rad, ATD, p. 154.

illegal, for the land was held in trust by the "owner" from the king. Such a strict rule fails to take account of the inevitable needs of people, and the Hurrians had to resort to a legal fiction in order to meet their financial problems while maintaining outward compliance with the law. This brought about the custom of adoption of a creditor or would-be purchaser, so as to bring him within the family and thereby sufficiently legitimize his taking over some part of one's property. So universal was this custom at Nuzi that thus far no document of outright sale, rent, or loan of real estate has come to light.[56] Among the many adoption contracts found at Nuzi two classes emerge: those of real adoption and those of sale adoption. In the former a share of the inheritance is gained by the one adopted, and provision is made for natural heirs, if any, and a division of duties among natural and adopted heirs. In the latter, property that is being "transferred" is minutely described, and a "gift" in return is specified, this representing probably the fair market price.[57] The first of these two types of adoption would apply to the situation of Abram, just as to that of Laban, though we can see a kinship between the two kinds of procedure that shows their common derivation from the same notion of property holding and disposition. Both are amply represented in standard sources.[58]

Study of the Nuzi contracts has yet to produce one that is a direct parallel in every detail to the situation of Abram; none is so strikingly analogous as what can be found for the action of Laban. Abram has not adopted the servant in terms of an *erebu* marriage to a daughter, since there are no daughters, and Abram's holdings of real estate must have been negligible. What we have here is rather Abram's deliberate action on the basis of his background in Hur-

56. Frances Rue Steele, *Nuzi Real Estate Transactions*, p. 14.
57. *Ibid.*, pp. 15–18.
58. *E.g.*, Pritchard, *ANET*, pp. 219–220; Speiser, *AASOR*, X (1930), pp. 1–73; and Pfeiffer and Speiser, *AASOR*, XVI (1935–1936), p. 82f.

rian culture. The property, real or movable, that he had he viewed as inalienable from his family line. In the absence of a natural heir, not even a child by a concubine at this time, there was only one thing that a man could do; that he had done it is reflected in his remarks in xv.2f. We know of no other way in which "one born in the house" could become an heir.

We cannot say what the terms of the servant's adoption were, since we are not told any more than that he had been made the heir. If the adoption was according to the standard pattern, however, we might wonder what the ultimate fortune of the man was. He disappears from the story after having completed his bridal mission to Haran; if still alive at the time of Abraham's death, he should have received his share, as the sons of the concubines did (xxv.6). Perhaps he had already died, though, so that Abraham's memory is spared the embarrassment of a second transgression of the law of the time.

Abraham's purchase of Machpelah stands in Genesis xxiii as a unique tale. It is, as already noted, the single instance of the patriarchs' actual purchase of land and, also, a most charming and lifelike portrayal of the extreme politeness of Orientals in even the most pedestrian transaction. From the point of view of literary criticism, it is one of the longest single contributions of the P writer to Genesis. The main theme of the story is plain to see: Abraham bought and paid for (and dearly: four hundred shekels!) a plot of ground near Hebron, and it became the burying ground for himself and most of his immediate descendants. The significance of this otherwise negligible event is a bit harder to fix, and the standard commentaries all have their suggestions, though the most attractive is that of von Rad,[59] who sees a guiding theme of "promise and fulfilment" in the patriarchal legends and conse-

59. *ATD*, p. 213.

121

quently interprets the purchase of Machpelah as a fulfilment, in Abraham's own lifetime, of the divine promise that he would possess the land; a small fulfilment, to be sure, but a legitimate earnest.

There is more to be said about the story than that, as Lehmann has shown.[60] Quite apart from whatever theological motivation P may have had in telling the story in such detail, the minutiae themselves are more than literary filler. The progress of the delicate maneuvering between Abraham and Ephron shows that, beneath the genteel conduct of the business, Ephron wishes to dispose of the whole field, not just the cave at the end of it, while Abraham wishes to buy only the cave (xxiii.9, 11). Ephron and the other inhabitants of the neighborhood are described as Hittites, and we have seen in the preceding chapter that one must not take that too literally in the patriarchal age that far south in Palestine. We are therefore intrigued to find that whether Abraham bought the whole field or just a part of it would make a considerable difference in the nature of the transaction according to provisions of the Hittites' own laws.

Sections 39, 46, and 47 of the Hittite Code provide that, if one acquires the whole of a field, he must render the "service" due from that field to the king, whereas one is not liable for such service if he holds only a part of the property.[61] Evidently the service due was some sort of feudal obligation by way of taxes or manpower for the lord's army, though this is not specified in detail. By contrast with the Babylonian theory of law, the Hittites looked on the land itself as producing service to the king, not to the owner;[62] thus the possessor of the whole of the

60. Manfred R. Lehmann, "Abraham's Purchase of Machpelah and Hittite Law," *BASOR*, No. 129 (February 1953), pp. 15–18.
61. Pritchard, *ANET*, pp. 190–191.
62. Lehmann, *BASOR*, No. 129 (February 1953), p. 17.

land was responsible for seeing to it that the land performed its duty. This could well explain why Ephron was so eager to sell the whole field—in fact insisted on it—and why Abraham began optimistically by trying to purchase only a small portion of the land: both wished to avoid the service due from the field.

Lehmann also calls our attention to the fact that Hittite documents of sale often list trees on the property, just as is described in xxiii.17.[63] We can readily understand how it would be an aid to precise establishment of property lines to have as a sort of double check the mention of the number or type of trees enclosed within the boundaries, and this would further serve to emphasize total purchase of the land and everything in or on it.

This does not prove that the account of the purchase of Machpelah is factual, or that the people with whom Abraham dealt were true Hittites in the strict sense, or that the story should be assigned to an earlier literary source than P. The similarities in the story to Hittite law and practice are possible coincidences, but we have too much earlier evidence of the accuracy with which the Priestly writer manipulates details of the patriarchal period to permit that. There is really no reason why we should not assume that P had access here, as elsewhere, to an independent body of tradition not used by earlier authors or that he substituted for their cursory account his own full and detailed version, which would more adequately illustrate his theological formula. What the comparison with archaeological data shows us in this area is, as before, the great erudition of P and the need for readier respect on our part for his general dependability.

Few transfers of property in the patriarchal legends, or in the Old Testament as a whole, are more amazing to the

63. *Ibid.*, p. 18.

reader than that strange one in which Jacob acquired
Esau's birthright. One may share the thinly veiled scorn of
the Biblical author for the stupidity of the rustic Esau, who
had so little sense of value for his inheritance as elder of the
twins (xxv.34), or one may feel sorry for the slow-witted
Esau when he is thus victimized by his crafty brother. In
any event, this transfer of the birthright from elder to
younger brother deserves attention because of its uniqueness in the Genesis tradition and its somewhat more frequent occurrence in extra-Biblical sources. This is, of
course, not the only case in which a younger brother out-
stripped his elders. Joseph fared much more prosperously
than any of his brothers, who remained mere shepherds
while he became the vizier of Egypt. What is unique about
the Esau-Jacob transaction is the actual transfer of the
birthright from the former to the latter.

It has previously been pointed out that both among the
Hebrews and among their Mesopotamian cousins it was
taken for granted that, in the division of the father's estate,
a preferential share was reserved to the eldest son. This,
along with the superior blessing he could expect from his
father on his deathbed, constituted the greater fortune of
the eldest son. The story of Esau and Jacob shows how
Esau was tricked out of both advantages he could otherwise have enjoyed as the first-born of Isaac (xxvii.36).

Other sons, first-born or not, must have found themselves
in Esau's predicament, but we may assume that they had
been hungry or threatened with hunger longer and made a
better bargain for themselves. We have from Nuzi the contract of adoption in which Ehelteshup adopted Uthaptae.
Whether Ehelteshup was the first-born of his family is not
stated, but we observe that he specifies that property which
he is going to give up under the terms of the adoption as
his "inheritance-share."[64] The Akkadian for this, *zitti*,

64. Pfeiffer and Speiser, *AASOR*, XVI (1935–1936), p. 108.

124

found in other contracts,[65] is the specific term for one's share in an inheritance, while the word for "share" in the general sense, *ka-az-zu-um*, turns up in other contracts;[66] so something special is obviously meant by *zitti* in such a context. Gordon has also called attention to the purchasable birthright at Nuzi.[67]

The absence of a direct coincidence of detail here does not mitigate the usefulness of the Nuzi material for illustrating the Biblical story. Probably the specific mention of "inheritance-share" in the contract cited above serves to lend a bit of pathos to the situation: poor Ehelteshup must have been at the end of his rope in order to part with his share of his father's inheritance, if we can assume that he would hold on to that last of all his property, like the modern beneficiary of a fixed income who tries to avoid "going into principal." By the same token, we could say that Esau had nothing with which to bargain, since Jacob insisted upon payment, except his share in the inheritance. Esau was not the only man who ever had to part with his inheritance-share, but he probably deserves to be sympathetically recorded as the one who received least in return for it.

The final conclusions to be drawn from this comparison of the picture of patriarchal family life and the archaeological record of family life in general at that time must be reserved to the closing chapter. For the present, however, it should be remarked that such a comparison as the foregoing enables us to see why practically every alert reader of Genesis observes that the patriarchal legends have much to show of human nature and the inner workings of family relationships and dealings. This comes about because the legends, with the peculiar tenacity for the

65. *Ibid.*, p. 84: Pritchard, *ANET*, p. 219.
66. *Cf.* the "share of Arteya," Pfeiffer and Speiser, *AASOR*, XVI (1935–1936), p. 113.
67. Cyrus H. Gordon, "The Patriarchal Age," *JBR*, XXI (1953), p. 240.

nucleus of fact previously observed, are in general true to the everyday life of people of their time: comparison with pertinent archaeological data serves only to heighten our awareness of this.

IV

PATRIARCHAL RELIGION

EVEN the most thorough-going opponents of "relation-ship theology" must admit that the adherents of this popular approach to religion have hold of one of the perennial truths about religion as such, namely, that among other things religion truly is a relationship, a binding together, as the etymology of the word suggests, of deity and man. As something larger than the ethics by which the believing worshiper governs his life in order to make it acceptable to his deity, religion is the whole active relationship between a man and the person or near-person he considers the most important point of reference in his life. This can be discerned as essentially true of patriarchal religion, early in the development of Biblical religion, just as in the Judaism and Christianity that grow out of patriarchal religion.

However, the patriarchal legends, as they now stand, are stories told in a religious context with a religious purpose, and there rests much of the difficulty of the following discussion. There are two levels of religion to be recognized in the present form of the legends of the patriarchs: the one is the actual religion of the patriarchs themselves in their own time; the other is that of the later authors and editors of the legends. The latter is often superimposed on the former, sometimes accidentally and inevitably, sometimes with transparently conscious intention. We can often see the obvious signs of religion of detail in an early story that a later, more developed revision found offensive or unedifying; almost as often we suspect that aspects of the earlier which were not too useful or meaningful to the later were minimized or passed over lightly as not contributory to the author's purpose in retelling the old tradition. The J author, for instance, goes to great lengths to insist that the worship of Yahweh goes back to time immemorial, to the days of Enosh (Genesis iv.26), although the J tradition itself is not entirely consistent about this. The E and P documents are equally doctrinaire in maintaining that Yahweh was not known by that name until the definitive revelation was given to Moses at Sinai.[1] In each of these cases we have an author-editor in possession of ancient lore that he is not content simply to record and pass on but uses in such a way as to demonstrate his theological lesson. We thus have on the one hand a reading back of a later situation into a much earlier time, which leaves little room for development or growth; on the other hand we have a clearly developmental account, which for its very neatness arouses suspicion in the critical mind.

The task here, then, is to seek out the remaining material that can show us something about patriarchal religion as the patriarchs themselves lived it and thought about it, how they themselves conceived of the relationship between themselves and their God. If the legends contained formal statements of faith or clear rubrics of worship, the investigation would be much easier, but creedal statements and outlines of worship are lacking. What we have are legends that can only reflect patterns of belief and practices of worship. Comparison with the archaeological remains of the time helps in the evaluation of the details in the legends, even if we are in a sense on less sure ground here than in other areas of patriarchal life, because of the

---

1. Kaufmann does not separate the J and E material and thus finds a unanimous assertion that Yahwism was known before Moses: *The Religion of Israel*, p. 222.

special bias with which each author approached the material as he passed it on.

Ideas of God

To Juliet's famous question, "What's in a name?" the patriarchs—the Biblical Hebrews as a whole—would have had a ready answer, "Very much indeed!" The name of a person, divine or human, was conceived of in the Semitic mind as a surrogate for the person with a real power of itself and as a summary of his nature and person. An important change in one's status called for a new name, as with Abraham and Jacob, and attaching a significant and appropriate name to a newborn child was a matter of real concern for parents. Even the name of a place was understood as having to do with the character of the locality or some event that had happened there; for instance, Beersheba, Bethel, Zoar, Jehovah-jireh—the list can be carried on. Since the Hebrews took names so seriously, we must with something near their attention to such matters look at the divine names that occur in the patriarchal legends. In the absence of any formal theological definitions or statements in the legends, the content of the names is probably the safest approach to the question of the patriarchal "doctrine of God."

The actual occurrences show that neither the scheme of J nor that of E and P is wholly faithful to the received traditions, for the names do not suggest either a single, unified notion of deity among the patriarchs or, for that matter, an undiscriminating indifference that made them embrace gods or notions of deity at will. The names that we find in the legends can be conveniently classified as representing three main types of form: the general word for deity, "God," with or without qualifying attribute; an epithet for "God" used in place of an actual name; and the tribal or ancestral god. Standing somewhat apart from each of these categories is "Yahweh," a name whose uncertain meaning causes it to defy ready classification, as will be seen below. Exhaustive tabulation of each name is satisfactorily done in standard concordances; the writer lists in the following paragraphs the most representative occurrences of each that most helpfully indicate its meaning and usage.

The general word for deity, *Elohim,* is the usual choice of the E writer in Genesis, though this usage is by no means limited to that document. Standing by itself, it is of little value for the present investigation, since its lack of special coloration or association makes it an all-inclusive term: while this makes for greater theological dignity, it keeps us from fixing on any clear connotation for it. It shares with other divine names in Genesis a certain idea of *power* as a root meaning,[2] but the etymology is so uncertain that we must admit that the attempt to state it as sure is overoptimistic; a glance at the lexicon shows this clearly. Even so, the notion of power itself is so inclusive that we are really no farther along if we accept this as its meaning. It is when some attribute or epithet accompanies the word for God that we can grasp hold of something more specific.

Perhaps akin to *Elohim* by common derivation from the same root is the divine name *El.* This is the name that turns up with the greatest variety of forms among the divine names in Genesis. If not the most frequently found, it is nevertheless the name that occurs with the greatest number of accompanying epithets. El, both with and without other titles, is known from Ugaritic literature as the chief deity and father of gods and men in Canaanite religion,[3] and the name occurs in three E passages in Genesis: xxxi.13, xxxv.1, 3, and xlvi.3. In xxxi and xxxv, however, it should be observed that the name is that of the

2. Meek, *HO,* pp. 84–85.
3. Pritchard, *ANET,* p. 129f.

deity of Bethel; in XLVI, a paternal deity at Beersheba. This kind of overlapping prevents us from making a thorough identification, but, in general, it is apparent that the patriarchs knew the El-type of deity described in Ugaritic mythology.

El Elyon, "God Most High," occurs in the blessing scene of Abram by Melchizedek in XIV.18f. In this episode Melchizedek is directly identified as the priest of God Most High at Salem; so we assume that the author wishes us to understand El Elyon as the God of Salem in the days before the Hebrews captured the city.[4] To this deity Abram made an offering, but no one else besides Melchizedek pronounces a blessing or otherwise refers to God Most High in Genesis; so this is a singular reference to the Salem deity. The theological connotation of Elyon is still reasonably clear, despite its infrequent appearance: the presence of the root, "to be high," in the word makes its meaning accessible. One might speculate about the appropriateness of such a name for God in a city in the hills of Judah, but from the strictly religious standpoint it is the name of a god who keeps his distance from people, much above and beyond them. No other Salem deities are mentioned, but, on the assumption that the people of the city had other gods, too, it seems not too fanciful to read in Elyon an assertion of this god's superiority to other gods as well as to men. If the chapter is from P, we can also look on the mention of El Elyon as an instance of the antiquarian interest of the P author in giving his narrative at least the appearance of authenticity by the mention of such ancient names.

Another case of P's flair for the long-ago is his frequent mention of *El Shaddai,* which is usually translated "God Almighty." El Shaddai is found in XVII.1, XXVIII.3, XXXV.11,

---

4. *Cf.* Lewy, *RHR,* CIX (1934), p. 64.

XLIII.14, XLVIII.3, and XLIX.25. Probably very little can be made out of the last cited passage, since it is in poetry that is undeniably late. Of the various mentions of El Shaddai, only two connect the deity with a particular place: in xxv and XLVIII El Shaddai is associated with Bethel; otherwise El Shaddai is without any definite geographical association. A definite association is made, however, between El Shaddai and the establishment or renewal of or reference to the covenant relationship between God and the line of Abraham. Clearly the author thinks of El Shaddai as the covenanting aspect of God, for when the covenant is first made with Abraham, when it is renewed with his descendants, and when a blessing is given that more or less takes the covenant promise for granted, it is El Shaddai that is mentioned in the story. This can hardly be accidental, for few things are in P. *Shaddai* cannot be too easily explained in Hebrew, for it cannot be definitely derived from any known Hebrew root. Even Albright, who is often willing to assert a relationship that others are hesitant to allow, frankly admits that the meaning of the word in patriarchal times "quite escapes us."[5] He does insist, however, that El Shaddai cannot be considered a subordinate member of a pantheon, in view of the Biblical evidence, which allows so important a position to this deity. An equivalent can be found in the Akkadian *shadda'u*, which occurs as an archaism in texts from the time of Sargon III and Esarhaddon and has the meaning of "mountaineer."[6] This opens the way to speculation about the possibility of a reminiscence of some sort of a mountain god brought from Northwest Mesopotamia by the Hebrews who once lived there, but we have little to go on here. El Shaddai lacks a traceable origin among the Hebrews' one-time neighbors as well as a definite geographical association in Palestine, so that we

5. *JBL*, LIV (1935), p. 191.
6. *Ibid.*, p. 184f.

are left with only the idea of covenant-god as a clear significance for this deity. Perhaps that is exactly what P intended when he chose an archaic name whose original meaning had been lost even in his day.

El Bethel, "God of Bethel" or "the God, Bethel," is twice mentioned in the E material, xxxi.13 and xxxv.7. This comes as no great surprise in view of the supposedly Northern provenience of E, since Bethel was the principal shrine of the Northern Kingdom at the time of the composition of E, as commonly accepted. The author thus underscores the dignity of the Bethel shrine as the site of an important revelation of deity to the patriarch Jacob. However, the Genesis tradition is explicit in telling us that Bethel was so named only after the patriarchal time (xxviii.19), though we know that the site has been occupied since Middle Bronze times.[7] This raises the possibility that the place was named for a deity, Bethel—just as conceivable a procedure as that the deity was named for the place. On the basis of the Ugaritic occurrence of Bethel as a proper name,[8] Hyatt suggests that the god Bethel may have come to be so recognized by the process of virtual, and then outright, deification of the personified temple, possibly through loose usage of what was at first only a circumlocution for El. This process is not without Mesopotamian parallels.[9] The worship of Bethel, originating in Syria early in the second millennium, could have spread southward to Palestine by the middle of the period of the patriarchs. In this Hyatt follows some of the implications of the hypothesis of Eissfeldt,[10] who assumes that a pre-Israelite deity, Bethel, was worshipped there and was

7. *Cf.* von Rad, *ATD,* pp. 249–250.

8. Bethel is not the only divine name of Genesis thus attested by Canaanite sources. *Cf.* Albright, *From the Stone Age to Christianity* (hereafter cited as *FSAC*), p. 188.

9. J. P. Hyatt, "The Deity Bethel and the Old Testament," *JAOS,* LIX (1939), pp. 81–98.

10. Otto Eissfeldt, "Der Gott Bethel," *AfR,* XXVIII (1930), p. 22.

133

taken over by the arriving Hebrews, who remembered this cult as originally non-Yahwist. The evidence is not conclusive either way, and we cannot therefore assert positively that the god's name was Bethel or that the origin of the cultus was Palestinian or Syrian. If the name Bethel was taken at all literally by the patriarchs, though, it points to an established cult of an enshrined deity, who let himself be approached by men at a particular holy place.

El Roi, "God of Seeing," or "God Seen," is referred to in the episode of the expulsion of Hagar (XVI.13) in a text whose corrupt state in the Hebrew makes precise translation difficult, if not impossible. This writer feels that the sense of the words in the passage is made clear by the context and particularly by the mood of exclamation that seems to pervade Hagar's words as she reacts to her experience. Her astonishment is the result of having seen the god who saw her, of having had a face-to-face experience of the presence of deity and having survived it. This is of the same mood as the terror of Jacob at having discovered the divine presence at Bethel (XXVIII.16) and having confronted deity quite intimately at Peniel (XXXI.30). We might remark parenthetically that here is a marked difference between patriarchal and later religion. At this point it is the revealed presence of God that causes wonderment and consternation in men; in later, more highly developed religion (for instance in Second Isaiah), it is the concealment of God that causes men to cry out in amazement. Of more direct importance is the observation that this appearance of El Roi marks the beginning of the sacred association of Beer-lahai-roi and thus deserves attention as the only instance of a divine name as the central element in an aetiological story of the sort in which Genesis abounds. We seen that it is uncertain whether this is the case with Bethel, but there can be little doubt of it here in the naming of the well for "the one who lives and sees." As a matter of fact, the Hebrew is telegraphic enough to allow the interpretation of it as a commemoration of Hagar's experience there, "the one who (still) lived, having seen (God)." In either event the stress in the idea of God contained in the name El Roi is on the self-revelation of the all-seeing God, and on the unpredictability and potential danger of that revelation.

El Olam, "Everlasting God," like El Roi, is mentioned only once (xxi.33) and is likewise found in the early J material. Associated with Beersheba and Abraham's residence there, El Olam would appear to articulate the attribute of eternity or agelessness in the divine person. To the mind that insists on thinking of religious growth completely in developmental terms, the idea of eternity in primitive religion probably seems too advanced, just like its correlate idea of universal sovereignty. Perhaps this is why von Rad bristles at Abraham's oath by the "God of heaven and earth" in xxiv.3 and interprets it as a sign of late development,[11] and translates El Olam into German, not as "Gott der Ewigkeit," which one might expect, but as "Gott der Urzeit."[12] To take the name thus is surely not contrary to the Hebrew, but "God of Old" or "God of Antiquity" does not cover all the range of time suggested in the Hebrew. Since the ideas of everlastingness and universality are closely correlative, and since, further, the latter appears well developed in the religion of the patriarchs' Mesopotamian background,[13] we shall do well not to deny to patriarchal religion the basic idea of divine eternity. It may be that it is made explicit only in this one name, which occurs only once, but that is not to say that the idea was not naïvely understood and accepted.

It appears that in a few passages of Genesis we have epi-

11. *ATD,* p. 218.
12. *Ibid.,* p. 202.
13. Albright, *FSAC,* p. 143.

135

thets of divinity used as euphemisms for the divine name. Here we can mention the "Shield of Abraham" of xv.1 and the "Mighty One of Jacob" paralleled by the "shepherd, the Rock of Israel" of xlix.24. The occurrence of these terms in lyrical passages keeps us from being too sure of them, though. But clearly the "Fear of Isaac" of xxxi.42, 53 is used as a substitute for a divine name; not only its position in the verses, as a parallel for other divine names in the one and as the guarantee of an oath in the other, demonstrates this. We also have the suggestion of the lexicon that Elohim may have its root in the idea of "fear," in which case "Fear of Isaac" is a direct parallel for "God of Isaac." This interpretation of the name is opposed by Albright, however, who renders the Hebrew as "kinsman" rather than "fear."[14] To find this phrase on the lips of Isaac's son Jacob is to alert our attention to something else about it: namely, that if it is a substitute for a divine name at all, then more than an epithet or euphemism, it is the name of a paternal deity.

It has been asserted repeatedly in the preceding pages that the only society that the patriarchal Hebrews knew and thought in terms of was the family. This basic sociological structure is also reflected in an idea of God which is far from being the only one mentioned in the legends and cannot with any certainty be shown to have been the chief one, but which plays an increasingly important part in patriarchal religion from the time of Isaac on, as the story now stands. When God appears to Isaac after the death of his father to renew the covenant promise made earlier to Abraham (xxvi.24), he identifies himself in a manner that is new to the legends; that is, as the "God of your father." No one referred so to any deity before, not even Abraham himself, who is represented by the J writer as exacting an oath of obedience from his servant simply in the name of

14. *Ibid.*, p. 189.

Yahweh, "the God of heaven and earth" (xxiv.3). There thus appears in the time of Isaac a new kind of idea of the relationship between God and man, that of the continuation of the faith of one's father. Isaac and then Jacob are represented as having the inaugural religious experience that makes for their own submission, but it is made in terms of continuing the loyalty of the father, and then the grandfather. At one point it goes so far as to reckon back to the grandfather and the great-uncle and then to the great-grandfather (xxxi.53), when Jacob and Laban swear by the God of their grandfathers, "the God of their father." This is unique in Genesis, however; the ordinary formula is to address or refer to God as "the God of my (your, his) father," e.g., in xxviii.13, xxxi.5, 29, 42, xxxii.9, xliii.23, xlvi.1, 3, and l.17. This manner of speaking is found in the speech of both God and man, and we might observe that most of the occurrences of it are in the cycle of stories dealing with Jacob, and usually in a conversation (including prayer) to which Jacob himself is party; this latter may simply be a result of the great number of chapters over which the life of Jacob extends, however. At one point, xlix.25, the God of your father is equated with El Shaddai by the parallelism of the poetic line, but the context is a poem of late composition that probably reflects the identification thus made in Exodus iii.

This paternal deity is not spoken of in Genesis by the same formula as is found in later Hebrew religion, "the God of Abraham, Isaac, and Jacob," for it is obvious on the face of it that the later formula speaks in terms of the same God as the God of all three. Patriarchal references do not regularly make that identification: as a matter of fact, about half the occurrences together of "the God of Abraham" and "the God of Isaac" in Genesis are open to the interpretation that these were not the same deity to those patriarchs but were so identified by later generations,

137

later even than Jacob and his children, possibly. This distinction between the early "God of my father" and the later "God of the fathers" has been noticed by May.[15] It needs also to be remarked here that there is no regular association of the God of one's father with a particular site. The aged Jacob's journey to Beersheba to worship the God of his father is unique in this respect (XLVI.1); it may be that Beersheba was chosen only because of its association with Isaac.[16] Otherwise the paternal deity is conceived of as following the family wherever each generation might go: Jacob and Laban, for instance, both speak of Jacob's paternal God as being with him in Haran (XXXI.29, 42). Undeniable ambiguity is introduced into this latter, however, by the appearance of El Bethel to Jacob, inciting him to leave his father-in-law (XXXI.13), and the neatest documentary analysis does not remove the confusion. Perhaps the E author simply did not care to be precise.

On the basis of Genesis as received, one would not be justified in concluding that the patriarchs were polytheists, pure and simple, for the Genesis narrative takes some trouble to avoid giving that impression. If we had no record of patriarchal times but the legends themselves and were to pay no heed to critical analysis of their component documents, we would have to note that, for all the different names of God that appear, each one appears on a more or less one-at-a-time basis. The only clear reference to outright polytheistic practice is in XXXV.2, though von Rad takes the whole episode as slightly anachronistic.[17] If it were objected that the stolen gods of Laban in XXXI indicated polytheism, one could answer that they undoubtedly stood for that for Laban himself, but for Jacob their significance would be something other than that: since he was leaving Haran, the adoptive father's gods no

---

15. H. G. May, "The God of My Father—A Study of Patriarchal Religion," *JBR*, IX (1941), pp. 155–158, 200.

16. *Cf.* von Rad, *ATD*, pp. 351–352.

17. *Ibid.*, p. 294.

longer had even the standing of guaranteeing property rights and were thus probably taken simply as a sign of prestige. In any event, Jacob's interest in the gods of Laban was not a religious matter.[18] Thus one could argue, with something close to a fundamentalist reading of Genesis, that, for all the primitive vagueness and uncertainty about the identity of God among the patriarchs, the single deity Yahweh predominated as chief god, becoming more and more prominent up to the time of Moses, who finally demanded absolute and unique loyalty to Yahweh. This is close to the position of Gordon, who maintains that Abraham was a Yahwist, having made the identification between Yahweh and El Elyon.[19]

We have the J writer almost exclusively to thank for the idea that the patriarchs were worshipers of Yahweh. He achieves this in his writing, not by suppressing other divine names, but by the simple expedient of adding the name of Yahweh in the immediate context of each in such a way as to infer, "This was really Yahweh who appeared and spoke." Though Yahweh is not confined to J material, and J does not lack other divine names, the purpose of J is apparent to the careful reader and is easy to understand if we accept the customary dating of the J writer in the days of the kingdom, when the leaders of the official national cult of Yahweh were having difficulty competing with the religion of the Baalim. The absence of this emphasis in E and P serves to heighten its presence in J. Both the J and the E writers appear to have taken it for granted that, whatever the name used, the patriarchs did worship the same God as later Israel knew,[20] but the controversial animus is markedly stronger in the J tradition.

The question of the origin of the cult of Yahweh and

18. *Cf.* Gordon, *Introduction to Old Testament Times,* p. 117. Contrast Kaufmann, p. 145, where the argument sustains their religious value: minor deities were helpful though inferior.

19. *Introduction to Old Testament Times,* p. 104.

20. *Cf.* John Bright, *A History of Israel,* p. 88.

even of the meaning of the name is a whole study in itself. It has vexed the minds of adherents of Biblical religion at least since the time of the J writer, who was almost as much at a loss as we to explain what Yahweh means. The weak attempt of Exodus III to explain the derivation of Yahweh in Hebrew turns our inquiry elsewhere for a root from which the name can legitimately be derived. One may favor the storm god reminiscence contained in the Arabic root *hwy*, "to blow,"[21] or the causative idea of life-giver and -sustainer,[22] or the assertion of pure, essential being, "the One who is."[23] In any choice we are driven to admit that it is strange that the earliest traditions of the Hebrews were unable to explain such an important thing as the name of the God who was supposed to have been theirs, according to J, for so long. The ingenuity of their un-scientific but appropriate folk etymology hardly ever deserted them elsewhere. As long as only J makes Yahweh the patriarchal God, and E and P, so reliable in their handling of tradition equally as ancient as that of J, represent patriarchal religion as being nowhere near so settled in the worship of this chief deity, we shall do well to pardon J for his good purpose in his zealous assertion of the antiquity of Yahwist worship among the Hebrews' ancestors. J had ample reason for trying to add to the prestige of Yahweh, but in doing so he had schematized patriarchal religion in a manner that the whole picture of it will not allow. Attempts to identify as Yahwistic such Old Babylonian names as *Yaum-ilum* and *Yawi-ilum* seem doomed to linguistic impossibility.[24]

If we permit all the documents of Genesis to speak and

21. Meek, *HO*, p. 99.

22. J. P. Hyatt, "Yahweh as 'The God of My Father,'" *VT*, V (1955), p. 136.

23. E. Schild, "On Exodus III.14—'I Am That I Am,'" *VT*, IV (1954), p. 302.

24. W. F. Albright, *Archaeology and the Religion of Israel* (hereafter cited as *ARI*), pp. 63–64.

140

consider the names and ideas of God contained in them, we can come up with the following estimate of patriarchal religion, based simply on a close reading of Genesis, before making any reference to extra-Biblical sources.

The patriarchs may have been on the way to monotheism, but they were practical, if not systematic, polytheists. This is to say, not that they perversely embraced every notion of deity that came within their reach—that is the polemical monotheist's idea of polytheism—but that they in all simplicity of mind continued their traditional family loyalty while sharing in the prevailing religious obedience of the land where they happened to be living. They made no real distinction between differing names or ideas of God and probably saw no serious conflict between them, perhaps even made some kind of naïve identification back and forth between them. In this they would be following the pattern of simplification of a complicated polytheistic heritage that Albright attributes to both Mesopotamian and Egyptian religion by this time.[25] They recognized El, the chief god of Canaan, and knew him under several titles; this El was something of an aloof and majestic deity who from time to time would make his presence known in a frightening way. A more companionable deity was that of the family, the God of one's father, who did not conflict with El but simply operated closer at hand. The understanding of this paternal God and the awareness of a relationship in a definite covenant with him grew alongside each other as the patriarchal generations went on. The patriarchs recognized certain attributes of the divine person: he was superior to man in dignity and power, could do things man could not do, and enjoyed a freedom from the boundaries of time and space. His general attitude toward man was a benevolent one, but he was unpredictable and not to be dealt with lightly. Deity was self-

25. *Ibid.*, p. 33.

141

disclosing and accessible, but it was a terrifying experience for the one to whom the disclosure was made; the form of the self-revelation was more or less anthropomorphic, and one could never tell when an appearance of a god might turn up in a dream or at a well or beneath a tree or atop some stones. It was a religion tinged with the naturism and ancestor worship one often finds in primitive religion,[26] and, while not unethical, it nevertheless lacked the strongly moral tone of later Biblical religion. Thus patriarchal religion is shown by the legends themselves to manifest what Albright defines as (1) a dynamistic belief in a real relationship between a clan and its gods and (2) a recognition of the right of a clan-founder to choose his own god.[27]

It is difficult to gainsay this kind of summary of patriarchal "theology," yet it is equally difficult to catch hold of the hints and traces of it that are imbedded in the later ideas of God of the literary custodians of the traditions. Those hints and traces are there to be seen in the material handed on by each of the documents of Genesis, although in all probability E and P themselves were not aware of the fact that they were handling reminiscences of polytheistic religion in the traditions of their fathers; or it may be that, while quite aware of it, they were not troubled by it because of their emphasis on the true faith as having come only through Moses at the holy mountain. Whatever preceded could not, for them, be expected to have much truth or rightness about it. J, on the other hand, was so sensitive to these polytheistic vestiges that he took great pains to try to level them out to congruence with the national religion of the kingdom of his day. He would hardly have gone to such lengths in asserting the antiquity of Yahwism among the patriarchs if he had not felt very

26. *Cf.* Meek, *HO,* p. 85f.
27. Albright, *FSAC,* p. 189.

142

keenly that the traditional material at his disposal showed something else.

The polytheism of the patriarchs' neighbors is plain in all the records we have from Mesopotamia, Canaan, and Egypt. Its presence in later Hebrew life, long after the Exodus, is attested by the historical books of the Old Testament and the prophetic invective against it almost a thousand years after the patriarchal age. Most of us who profess a faith that claims Biblical basis would like to find something unique and superior in patriarchal religion by contrast with what we know of nearby religions, but we have the foregoing to reckon with if we try to assert that the uniqueness lay in devotion to a single deity.

The religion of the patriarchs must have shared many ideas with the dominant religions of the various peoples with whom they had contact, though the grosser of them have probably been suppressed by the Biblical authors, if not always with complete success; e.g., Genesis xviii.1f., xxxiii.24f., and, of course, the myths of the early chapters. The writer wishes to point out the following similarities and differences, although he is well aware of a certain unfairness in doing so. We have to be careful about such a comparison, because two classes of material not always alike must be put alongside each other: the myths of Ugarit and Babylon are not exactly the same kind of material as the legends of the patriarchs. With no other place to turn, though, we must let the myths show us what they can.

For all practical purposes there were no "little" gods in the pantheon of the Fertile Crescent. If they played any important part in the mythology at all, they were possessed of sweeping power and grandeur. Each one had his own special activity, of course, but within that particular sphere he had universal domain, as Albright argues.[28] In

28. *Ibid.,* p. 143.

his own right each deity was overwhelmingly impressive, like Marduk, so visually splendid.[29] He wielded tremendous power, was "keen in battle" like the Hebrew Yahweh of Hosts,[30] and also the Ugaritic Puissant Baal,[31] and was so majestic that, in the case of Marduk, he had fifty different names.[32]

The gods did not ordinarily mingle very closely with mortals: when Ut-napishtim is given immortality, the story makes much of the fact that he is now going to live "far away,"[33] and the long search that Gilgamesh had to undertake to find him is well known. Even though a god could be conceived of as "settling down" to become the protector and patron of a specific place, accessible there, like Marduk in Babylon,[34] the distance between deity and man was kept quite distinct. The Creation Epic is quite explicit in claiming that men exist simply to serve the needs of the gods.[35]

Gods nevertheless did draw near to men from time to time in order to establish communication with them and to take them under their protection. Their benevolence was seldom unmixed, though: the god Ea who interceded with his fellow-deity Enlil in an attempt to persuade the latter to mitigate the coming flood,[36] and who revealed the counsel of the gods helpfully to Ut-napishtim, so that the latter might escape the death about to overtake the world in that flood, was the same Ea who revealed the divine secret to Ut-napishtim in such a way that only Ut-napishtim could understand it, it being a deliberate trick

29. Pritchard, *ANET*, p. 62.
30. *Ibid.*, p. 64.
31. *Ibid.*, p. 129f.
32. *Ibid.*, p. 69.
33. *Ibid.*, p. 95.
34. *Ibid.*, p. 69.
35. *Ibid.*, p. 68.
36. *Ibid.*, p. 95.

played on the population of the world at large.[37] The good will of the gods could be confounded with thoroughly capricious favoritism and might be damaging at any point. Gilgamesh was well aware of this when, in rejecting the amorous advances of Ishtar, he reminded her that all her previous lovers had come to disastrous ends.[38]

The heavenly courts were no peaceful place, nor was love of peace an attribute of many of their inhabitants. Apsu's rage with his noisy children and the ensuing conflicts between whole armies of gods are told in full and gory detail,[39] as are the struggles of Baal and his rival deities.[40] There is, however, a certain mellowness of old age, even of timelessness, in the Ugaritic El, who is spoken of as "father" and fulfils that role in a benign way, who is described as a quiet old fellow with "gray hair," and one of whose epithets is "King Father Shunem," which may mean "Father of Years."[41]

This kind of anthropomorphism must have had its place in the patriarchs' actual religion, although the Biblical authors have done away with as much of it as they could. For all its crudity, it should be noticed that this Babylonian and Canaanite anthropomorphism is closer to Biblical religion than the Egyptian notion of deity, which tended to identify gods with plants or animals.[42] The distance is still great, though, for there is little in the Hebrews' neighbors' myths to correspond with the God of the Covenant, who made and kept promises and looked after his people with diligent faithfulness and loyalty. In asserting that, however, the writer acknowledges that the comparison cannot

37. *Ibid.*, p. 93.
38. *Ibid.*, p. 84.
39. *Ibid.*, p. 61f.
40. *Ibid.*, p. 129f.
41. *Ibid.*, pp. 129, 130, 133, 137.
42. Albright, *FSAC*, p. 143.

be pushed too far, for the predominating religious tone of the present form of the patriarchal legends is more ethically advanced and theologically consistent than that of Mesopotamian mythology.

Because of the sparsity of detail available to us about the actual religion of the patriarchs and the rather general nature of the parallelism of its ideas with those of neighboring religions, it is next to impossible to point to any aspect of patriarchal religion as definitely borrowed from or influenced by the Hebrews' neighbors. Having seen what we have about the tendency of the patriarchs to keep their distance from the already settled population, we need not be too surprised at this. The patriarchal Hebrews were in general true to type of the Habiru category from which we assume they were derived, in that they kept much to themselves and went about their own way. Thus it is understandable that the "Hapiri gods" of Hittite documents[43] are simply mentioned as that: they were peculiarly the gods of that class of people who kept themselves so distinct that the rest of the population had no clear idea about the identity or nature of their deities. This leaves us next to nothing to go on in evaluating the religion of the people with whom the Hebrews show most affinity; even at Nuzi, whose society and life can be reasonably well reconstructed now, we know very little about the religion of the Habiru: whatever else it may have been, it was far removed from anything known in the earliest layers of Biblical tradition. Gordon states outright, for instance, that the Nuzi Habiru show no sign of Hebrew names or religion,[44] and this cannot but be impressive, coming as it does from an author who seeks to date Yahwism about as far back as the J writer did.[45]

---

43. Pritchard, *ANET*, pp. 205–206.
44. *Introduction to Old Testament Times*, p. 101.
45. *Cf. ibid.*, p. 25; also the same author in *JBR*, XXI (1953), p. 238.

Contact of the Hebrews with the official state gods of the Fertile Crescent must indeed have been slight: there is nothing in the divine names in Genesis and only little in the notions of deity found there to suggest much traffic with Ea, Enlil, Marduk, Teshup, Ishtar, and the others. Where mythological reminiscences are found in Genesis, Yahweh is the hero, as Kaufmann maintains.[46] The best illumination that can be found for patriarchal religious practice lies in the area of the family god, the God of one's father. As the foregoing survey has shown, this deity becomes increasingly important in the patriarchal legends and needs full attention, since patriarchal life was so thoroughly family-bound. The classic, though not the final, word on the subject is that of Albrecht Alt; this writer's dependence on his important essay will be obvious in the following, with its frequent reliance on Alt.[47]

The cult of Yahweh was as important a factor in the unification of the Israelite tribes who eventually became the Hebrew nation as any other; in fact, as the Hebrew historian tells the story of the rise of the united kingdom, it was primarily the centralization of the devotion of the tribes to the new national God that brought them together and held them as one as long as they remained so. In that case, if the worship of Yahweh had already played an essential part in the life of the tribes who came together in Palestine, its creative power in the formation of the union would hardly be understandable.[48] It had the power of a new and freshly vital force for them. Earlier religion must have been centered round a different deity otherwise identified. In the case of the legends of Genesis this is usually El, with some epithet indicative either of place of worship or attribute of the divine personality, and the God

46. *The Religion of Israel,* p. 11.
47. Albrecht Alt, "Der Gott der Väter," *Kleine Schriften zur Geschichte des Volkes Israel* (hereafter cited as *GdV*), p. 178.
48. *Ibid.,* p. 5.

of one's father. Looking a little farther afield, Alt is satisfied that most other Syrian and Palestinian deities lacked proper names of their own; they were known simply as El with some second and identifying part of the name.[49] This accords with von Rad's assertion that the prevailing practice was to speak, not of "God" in general, but of "the God who" appeared somewhere, had done something, or the like.[50] El was often worshiped at a particular holy place, as is apparent even in Genesis. Alongside this kind of localized El, the paternal deity was more independent of place and stood in relationship to people by means of a personal tie to the family line itself. The worship of a paternal deity at a specific place in Genesis XLVI.3 is unique, for usually the family God was thought of as being bound to the people, wherever they might be.[51] Such a God would be specified, not by the name of a shrine, but by the name of the man with whom religious contact was first made. Alt cites the occurrence of such deities in the Semitic areas of Syria.[52]

The short duration of times of settled life known by the patriarchal Hebrews would naturally bring them into contact with the localized Elim of the various places they stayed, as the Genesis account reflects. However, the deity that would mean most by close association with them would be that family God who, having called forth worship from the founder of the cult, would continue to command the loyalty of the founder's descendants and to look out for them and their interests, as he had for the original founder himself.[53] Through the years of this continuing relationship the family God would keep the tie with the family in whatever place they happened to be: man thinks

49. *Ibid.*, p. 6.
50. Von Rad, *ATD*, p. 293.
51. Alt, *GdV*, pp. 18, 21–22.
52. *Ibid.*, p. 33f.
53. *Ibid.*, p. 44.

of God, not so much in his own image, as the cynics would have it, but in terms of his need and actual situation. Thus the patriarchs, displaced as they were, thought of the deity closest to them as being as little bound to a permanent site as they themselves were, even if they did not ignore the chief god of the land where they were. So it is that Bright asserts that each patriarch turned to a new faith in God from whatever his earlier commitment had been, and, with that kind of reinforcement, within each clan "the patron God was worshiped above, if not to the practical exclusion of all other gods."[54]

Parallels to this are available from the patriarchal period. Lewy notes how Assyrian contracts with Amorite settlers are sworn by "Asshur and the god of thy father," and concludes that this means that the contract was made before the national god, Asshur, who is given primacy of mention, and the god of lesser dignity, the ancestral god of the settler. Thus the Amorite settlers in Assyria paid their respects to the existing, established god of the region and at the same time continued their loyalty to their traditional family deity.[55]

The archives of Mari have also preserved in the correspondence of Yasmah-Addu a complaint about insufficient payment for some horses, in which a not thoroughly translatable phrase, *ash-shum ilim sha a-bi-ia,* is taken by Dossin as "à cause du dieu de mon père," and interpreted as indicating the involvement of the writer's whole family. Dossin adds the opinion of Gadd that the latter would interpret the phrase as an oath, "by the name of the god of my father." If the actual force of the mention of the deity is uncertain, the reference to the family deity of the signer is at least clear.[56]

54. Bright, *A History of Israel,* pp. 91–92.
55. Lewy, *RHR,* CIX (1934), pp. 51–53.
56. Georges Dossin, *Correspondance de Iasmah-Addu,* pp. 37, 129.

Not too helpful, because of linguistic difficulty and distance from our period, but still worthy of mention for the sake of illustration, are the possible reference in a late Hittite document to an ancestral god,[57] and also the even later references to a "god of the fathers" mentioned by Alt.[58] With his fondness for making use of Ugaritic material, Gordon submits the possibility of references in Ras Shamra texts to an ancestral god, but there is some doubt of what that evidence actually shows.[59]

Admittedly a clear picture does not emerge from the evidence of either the Bible or archaeology. By comparison with other aspects of patriarchal life this extremely important one is poorly "documented"; the amount of material fit for comparison is slight, and the relationship is often indirect or negative. It appears that the patriarchs' neighbors and associates were polytheists like their ancestors, even if they were simplifying their deities by wholesale identification and assimilation of them. There are those who argue for something close to monotheism in this age: Albright has already been cited, and Gordon, who prefers the Amarna period alone for the patriarchal age, speaks of that period as one characterized by an internationalism and a trend toward a monotheism of El, the chief god of the pantheon if not the only god.[60] Both Albright and Gordon protect their positions with appropriate qualifications, of course. As for the Biblical account, the preceding discussion has already shown how the bias of J, the relative indifference of E, and the erudition of P fail to give a coherent record of patriarchal religion.

Perhaps one can find as much advance toward monotheism or monolatry in the patriarchal legends as he wishes to find. Only recently Finegan has represented the per-

---

57. Hyatt, *VT*, V (1955), pp. 130–136.
58. Alt, *GdV*, p. 36.
59. Gordon, *JBR*, XXI (1953), p. 238.
60. *Ibid.*

sonal, covenant-centered faith of Abraham as on the way toward henotheism, if not quite there,[61] and de Vaux believes that the patriarchs took El Bethel, El Olam, El Shaddai, or whatever deity they knew as local manifestations of the supreme El and as their only God.[62] This writer can only protest that for him the evidence points toward a double-level kind of religious belief and activity among both the patriarchs and the people with whom they had their most important contacts. They recognized a national, or even supranational, deity whose lordship extended over the immediate horizon. This was the faraway God of heaven and earth who presided over other gods as well as men, even if it was thought that this almighty one could be approached, or that he approached men, at certain established places—and sometimes unexpectedly. Of this type of god were Marduk, El, Asshur, and, for the later Hebrews, Yahweh. Alongside this "fluid dynamistic expression for impersonal supernatural power"[63] was the tribal God of one's father, later the God of the fathers, the paternal deity of the whole clan descended from the first progenitor. This was the God of close companionship who was tied to the people directly, and it was with this notion of God that the idea of covenant relationship was most significantly developed. As previously remarked, it hardly seems accidental that the covenanting God of P, El Shaddai, has no shrine but is with the patriarchs as they move along their nomadic ways. If El Shaddai was not the name by which the patriarchs addressed the paternal covenant deity, that is at least what P consistently calls him, and we might properly use El Shaddai as the "type" of family deity.[64]

61. *In the Beginning*, p. 95f.
62. Roland de Vaux, *Ancient Israel: Its Life and Institutions*, pp. 293–294.
63. Albright, *FSAC*, p. 188.
64. *Cf.* Lewy, *RHR*, CIX (1934), p. 55.

The El-type and the paternal-type do not have the same divine function, economically speaking, and consequently they would not be thought of as overlapping or conflicting in the simple mind of the nomad. Belief in and worship of the two types of deity must have existed alongside each other, with appropriate attention and dignity allowed each, or the record, it seems, must be more unanimous. One thinks of the later Hebrews and their easy passage from the worship of Yahweh of the Exodus or of sacred warfare to the propitiation of the agricultural Baalim. Alt submits that parallel worship of national and tribal deities might well explain why the later shrine at Shiloh, an important center of national Yahwist worship, had no patriarchal connection, whereas all the other holy places of later times connected with the patriarchs are sites whose pre-Israelite settlement is well attested.[65] Within each category of deity it is conceivably impossible to classify each of the divine names of Genesis,[66] relegating each to its proper position as major or minor deity. What seems more significant for this writer is that we recognize the practical polytheism, the double-level idea of deity, which the Biblical and the extra-Biblical material suggest for the prevailing religious pattern of such people as the patriarchal Hebrews at their time.

The subsequent course of the development of Hebrew religion makes it clear that the creative aspect of patriarchal religion that was charged with greatest potential for future growth was, of course, the paternal covenant god. There is undeniable truth in the idea of God as ultimate reality, but the path of growth seems to have been through the relationship of man to a close-at-hand object of religion. The ultimate answer as to why this notion, neither original with nor restricted to the Hebrews, should be-

65. Alt, *GdV*, p. 59.
66. *Cf.* Lewy, *RHR*, CIX (1934), p. 64.

come so uniquely developed among them, is one of those things that *exeunt omnia in mysterium,* but it appears to have been this part of the patriarchal religious background that provided the context for the subsequent singular development of Yahwism.

One needs to give Woolley credit for his insight into this, even if much of his study of the patriarchal period has to be corrected by reference to work beyond his own. Woolley recognized in Abraham's family deity and Abraham's loyalty to that God the condition of the subsequent theological expansion of the knowledge of God, for this family God was "the god whose province was the hearts and minds of men," a God who could be "transplanted" from place to place. The Semitic religious genius took over in Abraham and brought to perfection a notion that never developed any higher in Mesopotamia.[67] That may be stating it rather humanistically, but it nevertheless recognizes the peculiar advantage of the paternal God and, theologically speaking, indicates the locus of providential activity.

Whether Abraham himself worshiped the God of his father remains problematical. We might expect it, in view of the Mesopotamian occurrences of the paternal deity in the time of Abraham, but the implicit suggestion of the patriarchal legends is probably a correct indication of what happened; namely, that the family religion as well as its fortune took a new turn with Abraham's journey to the new land. Thus the call of Abraham constitutes the inaugural experience of the cult that Abraham passed on to his children, and their probable experiences of similar sort fortified the idea that had sparked Abraham.[68]

The patriarchal period, then, finds the Hebrews at an uncritical and unsophisticated level of family-style poly-

67. Woolley, *Abraham,* pp. 238f., 251f., 257.
68. *Cf.* von Rad, *ATD,* p. 159.

theism. If the tendency toward monotheism was so strong among the great civilizations of the second millennium as is often maintained, and the Hebrews, by virtue of their way of life, lived without very much direct contact with the peoples around them, then they represent a lag behind the advances of their neighbors. So far as time is concerned, the people surrounding the Hebrews had achieved a social organization taking in more than the immediate family ties and a religious advance toward monotheism beyond that which we find in the patriarchal legends. The challenge that would bring about the sense of intertribal unity among the Hebrews and an awareness of the consecration of several tribes to one God lay in the future.

Worship in Patriarchal Religion

Biblical religion, once it achieves full stature, can be seen as composed of three large aspects of relationship between God and man: belief, worship, and ethics. Belief, in the restricted, largely non-Pauline sense, states more or less articulately, doctrinally, and systematically what one holds to be true about God. Worship we take here to mean one's formal, organized, cultic expression of devotion and loyalty to his God. Ethics embraces the principles of behavior by which one seeks to conform his living to the divine will. Doctrinal belief is more implicit and taken for granted in the Bible as a whole than stated outright, and that is true of the patriarchal chapters of Genesis. Concern with definite standards of behavior was not absent from even the earliest level of patriarchal religion, but, by comparison with the post-Mosaic development of Israelite religion, the characteristic tone of Hebrew morality was largely absent in the days of Abraham and his immediate descendants. It remains, therefore, to study the activity of worship by which the patriarchs expressed their faith.

Although worship has its mystical, contemplative side in later Yahwism, Judaism, and Christianity, the dominant note in patriarchal worship is that of action, things done. A full pattern of religious observance is not to be found in the patriarchal legends, of course, but many of the essentials of worship are plainly part of patriarchal religion: such basic actions as sacrifice, tithes and other offerings, prayer, and the establishment of places for doing these. This worship can be seen to have both its individual and its corporate expression, though it must be borne in mind that in the latter there is none of the established national cult that unites several families or tribes. While the personal acts of worship mentioned in the legends are such as can be observed on almost all levels of religious development, the corporate worship referred to is that of family devotion: this was the limit of reference in patriarchal religion, as with other aspects of their living.

Sacrifice in its essence is an acted prayer, in that it consists of something offered to God in acknowledgment of lordship and in testimony of the worshiper's indebtedness to God.[69] Sacrifice can be extended rhetorically, and with justice, to include all types of devotional acts, but in its strictest sense it is an act of offering something concrete and of real value. Self-denial is, of course, the means to this greater end and not the primary significance of sacrifice. In view of the importance of the institution of sacrifice in post-Mosaic Israelite religion, it is at first surprising to find that it plays such a small part in patriarchal worship: it is seldom mentioned. We have traces of or allusions to it in xii.7, xiii.18, xxvi.25, and xlvi.1.[70] The greatest development of sacrifice, however, came about apparently in the national cult and its competitors, not in family observance, as the later prophetic protests would indicate.

---

69. *Cf.* de Vaux, *Ancient Israel*, p. 451 and the excellent treatment of the subject as a whole at that point.
70. *Cf.* von Rad, *Theologie des Alten Testaments,* p. 177.

Also, there is in Genesis no mention of sacrifice in P and only a hint of it in J, since the P writer wished to derive all sacrifice from the instructions given at Sinai, and J had his own bias. The pre-exilic traditions, however, contain a few references to sacrifice that indicate some of its use among the patriarchs.

The sacrifices of Genesis are not carefully distinguished according to the later categories of animal, vegetable, or drink offering. There is the specific mention of the sacrifice of an animal in xxii.13 as the substitute for the near sacrifice of Isaac, and this is not surprising to find in the account of the doings of a herdsman, even if the story as a whole may be a polemical attack on human sacrifice. For whatever purpose the tale was told, however, it should be recognized as representing the sacrifice as an act of loyalty on the part of Abraham. Likewise, the drink offering of oil and (probably) wine of xxxv.14 represents an act of consecration of a place that is thereafter to be regarded as holy, and thus it comes under the general motif of dedication involved in sacrifice. The unspecified sacrifices of xxxi.54 and xlvi.1 may safely be assumed to have included the offering of both animals and vegetable products, since the patriarchs are represented by this time as gradually settling down to farming alongside their keeping of flocks. What is of more direct interest, however, is that both these sacrifices are offered to the paternal deity: the one accompanying an oath sworn by the God of the father in ratification of a solemn covenant, and the other invoking the blessing of the paternal deity on the ensuing journey.

These few examples are hardly sufficient ground for any kind of sweeping generalization about patriarchal sacrifice as a whole, but for themselves they have significant content. They show, first of all, that sacrifices occupied a definite place in patriarchal religion. They represent the sealing of the relationship between deity and worshiper implied in the phrase "acknowledgment of lordship." The effect of the offering of the sacrifices is felt to be a new (or perhaps renewed) closeness between God and man that brings man under the protection of or, as it may be, surveillance of God. In no case is it a matter of something done for the sake of the doing alone. The sacrifice, understood as acceptable to God, is accompanied by prayer and renders the petition, oath, or whatever acceptable by association. The question later raised by the prophets, of the faith of the worshiper as the guarantee of the acceptability of the sacrifice, has not yet come forth; the patriarchs offer their sacrifices in naïve belief that the gift will be pleasing to God, who will in turn grant the request or hallow the relationship presented with the oblation. This is to say, then, that the sacrifices in Genesis are what Christian liturgics would call *votive*; that is, they are not regularly arranged offerings made at certain stated times but rather special acts by which a special intention or situation is presented before God. We are not given enough references to sacrifice in Genesis to tell whether the patriarchs conceived of it as efficacious for the removal of guilt in the worshiper, but sacrifice is used as an avenue of approach to God when there is something important to lay before him: this is but a step removed from sacrifice for sin. The fellowship with each other of those involved in the offering of a sacrifice is not very clearly indicated in the Genesis occurrences, either, though there is a hint of it in the sacrifice of xxxi.54; the establishment of peace between Jacob and Laban is there solemnized by the offering of sacrifice.

The Genesis sacrifices, being family observances on special occasions, cannot be properly compared with the regular, established sacrifices of the later Israelite cult or with the official rites of neighboring national deities. Although the patriarchs appear to have recognized the

157

existence and dignity of the national deities of the peoples in whose midst they lived, the Genesis account does not represent them as participating in the cult of any of the Elim, at least in the matter of sacrifice. The ambiguity of the sacrifice to the paternal deity at Beersheba in xlvi.1 prevents our making any definite exception out of that incident: there may or may not have been some identification between a paternal deity and an El of Beersheba.

Comparison of patriarchal sacrifice with extra-Biblical mentions of sacrifice in similar contexts is entirely justified, however, and shows the popularity of votive sacrifice. At the outset it should be observed that the Genesis traditions are completely cleansed of any notion that a sacrifice represented nourishment for the deity to whom it was offered, if, indeed, the Hebrews ever so conceived of it. Mesopotamian myths are rather straightforward in their portrayal of the gods as eager for sacrifices, truly hungry for them.[71] Such crudity has been carefully removed from the Biblical idea of sacrifice, at least in the legends, even if the myth of the flood contains a probable reminiscence of expansive divine generosity after being well fed with a sacrifice (viii.21). The most that can be said here is that, in Genesis, God is represented as willing to accept a sacrifice but not as demanding it; the unique demand for a sacrifice in xxii is not the real point of the story and does not militate against the conclusion that sacrifices are offered by the patriarchs on their own initiative. In this sense, then, the canonical prophets were correct in their recurring harangue that God did not require sacrifice in the days of old, or at least not the kind they found in their own time.

Both Mesopotamian and Ugaritic material provide examples of sacrifice offered in the manner of the patriarchs.

71. Pritchard, *ANET*, pp. 69, 95.

158

Ut-napishtim's sacrifice after the flood is one of thanksgiving.[72] Ninsun offers incense along with her prayer on behalf of her son, Gilgamesh.[73] Keret offers animal and cereal sacrifices and drink offerings in company with his prayer for the son he desired.[74] Similarly, Daniel gives oblations to the gods when asking for a son,[75] and after the son's death he offers a mourning sacrifice on his behalf.[76] In each of these instances it is to be noted that the sacrifice is offered by the worshiper out of no compulsion but his own: he has a matter to present to his lord, and he approaches him not empty-handed. The process by which they felt the sacrifices would help bring about the end prayed for is not made explicit: whether the offering would serve as a divine meal spiced by incense is not stated, nor is any other, higher explanation given. Sacrifice is offered simply as the accompaniment of intercession or petition. What we have to deal with here is the universally felt and observed desire of man to render himself acceptable before God when presenting requests. Those of us who consider ourselves on a higher plane of religious development than Ninsun or Daniel or Jacob or Isaac should save our condescension toward them and recognize that the question is the same for us as for them, "Wherewith shall I come before the Lord?" Whether the offering is one of rams and incense or of a contrite heart, the motivation is the same. One does not lightly turn aside, as if in passing, to present his petitions to God, and the ancients realized this as profoundly as we do and took pains to approach God properly equipped. One does sense in the descriptions of sacrifice something of an ex-

72. *Ibid.*, p. 95.
73. *Ibid.*, p. 81.
74. *Ibid.*, pp. 143–144.
75. *Ibid.*, p. 150.
76. *Ibid.*, p. 155.

pectation of a *quid pro quo* reciprocation, but that may be purely due to their being ancient, so that we expect them to be less spiritual. It remains true, just the same, that bargaining with God is no old, outmoded, or outgrown behavior.

The patriarchal sacrifices and their Near Eastern parallels are not those of an established cult, as has been remarked before, and we consequently find no indication that they were offered by a regular priesthood or, for that matter, of necessity at a definite shrine. They represent individual or family devotions that are carried out in a context other than that of a temple. Canaanite and Mesopotamian temples had their priests, of course, as is well known, but these priests had their set duties in waiting upon the god in his holy place. It would appear that votive sacrifices were offered by the individual or the family with no thought of conflicting with the oblations and clergy of the temples.

The subject of sacrifice is not complete without notice of that type of sacrifice which is not consumed on the altar but is nevertheless true sacrifice, since it consists of the offering of something of value; namely, the tithe. The offering of the tithe is twice mentioned in the patriarchal legends. In xiv.20 Abram offers a tithe of his possessions to El Elyon at Salem, and in xxviii.22 Jacob vows to present his tithe in the future at Bethel, where God had confronted him. In both these instances the motivation is that of thanksgiving actual or promised: Abram had won a victory in battle, and Jacob vows to express thanks for future protection by offering his tithe. Direct parallels for this eucharistic attitude in giving the tithe are not available from the extra-Biblical sources, even if the thanksgiving idea is strongly emphasized in Ut-napishtim's sacrifice after his deliverance from the flood.[77]

77. *Ibid.*, p. 95.

Prayer

It has already been remarked that worship for the patriarchs was a matter of something done, and the prayer that accompanied sacrifice or was offered independently was of the same pattern. The acts of prayer that we find in the patriarchal legends are full-fledged, articulate actions of recollection in the presence of God and interchange with him, not the pious reverie favored by sentimental devotionalism. When Isaac is described as going out into the field in the evening to meditate (xxiv.63), it was probably not the same thing as we mean nowadays by "making a meditation," but it definitely was distinct from the direct utterances of prayer mentioned elsewhere in the legends of Genesis.

Modern manuals of the spiritual life customarily categorize prayer as composed of elements of praise, thanksgiving, penitence, intercession, and petition, and practically all of these movements of prayer are to be found in the legends, even if intercession and petition predominate. In this, of course, the legends reveal something profoundly true of human nature at all times. In Melchizedek's blessing of Abram (xiv.12–20), praise and thanksgiving are the whole content of the outburst, as with the prayer of Abraham's servant at the end of his journey (xxiv.26–27). Most often, though, the prayers in Genesis are of the asking type. In xv.2 Abram rehearses his situation before God in an indirect petition for a son. His servant in xxiv.12f. prays for guidance through an omen, just as Rebekah asks for an interpretation from God of the violent prenatal movements of her children (xxv.22). Isaac has only recently before that besought God that his wife might bear a child (xxv.21). Prayers of pure charity and generosity for the good of others are found in the intercession of Abraham on behalf of Sodom (xviii.23–33), the celebrated

161

and most extended dialogue of prayer in Genesis, and in his prayer for Abimelech and his household (xx.7, 17). The type of prayer contained in the paternal blessing of children has already been discussed in the chapter on family life.

Clearly the patriarchs believed in the reality and the efficacy of prayer; the power of the word spoken to effect what it said is taken for granted in this as in the pronouncement of oaths, blessings, and curses. It is true that the legends are cast in such a way as to make it explicit that God approaches man more often than *vice versa,* takes thought for his needs before man himself does, and fills those needs better than he can desire or pray for. The legends nevertheless are equally straightforward in asserting that, in placing his requests for his own needs and those of others before God in prayer, man has at his disposal the capacity for causing things to happen.

That this is no reading back from a later time of a more developed piety and understanding of prayer becomes evident with a survey of prayer as described in extra-Biblical records of the time. The famous hymn of Akhnaton has often been pointed out as illustrative of the monotheistic teaching of that pharaoh's religious reform, and it stands among the world's religious poetry as a classic example of pure praise of the Creator,[78] but its polished balance and measured composition mark it as prayer of the liturgical type and thereby not a useful comparison for the prayer of Genesis. Much closer parallels, some almost exact, can be found among the remains of Babylonia and Ugarit.

The story of Etana contains a touching description of the plight of the hero, who was supposed to found a dynasty but was childless. The story tells how he prayed daily for the offspring that only divine intervention could

78. *Ibid.,* pp. 370–371.

give him.[79] One thinks immediately of Abram in the early years of his story.

The importance of intercessory prayer offered by a holy man on behalf of others was recognized early in Mesopotamian religion. The story of Atrahasis, in those parts which appear to have separate existence apart from the Gilgamesh Epic, makes much of Atrahasis' extended intercession on behalf of suffering mankind.[80] The "effectual fervent prayer of a righteous man" is there represented as a distinctive duty of the godly man just as in Biblical religion: his greatness of soul is shown by his sensitivity to the needs of his fellow man and the readiness of his prayer on behalf of his brother. The same themes are present in the previously cited instances of Abraham's intercession on behalf of Sodom and Abimelech, and we thus have a very close parallel in the idea of the use of prayer. Von Rad protests the interpretation of the intercession for Sodom as a representation of Abraham as an exemplary man of God or "prophetic" intercessor, just as he cannot allow it to be some sort of argument from collectivism to individualism; he takes the episode rather as a simple study in the justice and mercy of God.[81] While he is probably right in denying to the story any theme of group versus individual, his interpretation fails to take account of the edifying moral purpose of legend and the obvious parallel between Abraham's intercessory activity and that of Mesopotamian legendary men of God. Here is an episode of the Biblical tradition whose full significance is most helpfully illuminated by comparison with similar material in extra-Biblical sources.

Of several occurrences of prayer in the Epic of Gilgamesh, the most interesting are the prayer that Gilga-

79. *Ibid.*, p. 117.
80. *Ibid.*, p. 106.
81. *ATD*, p. 182.

mesh himself offers to Shamash before his battle with Huwawa and the already-mentioned intercession of Gilgamesh's mother, Ninsun, on behalf of her son on the same occasion.[82] In a fully phrased outpouring, Gilgamesh requests Shamash to give him safety in the battle and success at the end of it, and the careful reader cannot miss the sincerity and earnestness of the prayer, without bombast or crudity. Even more appealing is the heartfelt tenderness of Ninsun's prayer for her son, for it is filled with the anxious concern of the mother who would like to see her son kept safe from harm and even removed from the constant dangers of fighting. One detail that adds unique interest to this whole episode is that it contains Gilgamesh's explicit request to his mother for her prayers for him. This is the earliest such request for intercession that this writer has found. It demonstrates a considerable degree of religious maturity to ask that the support of another's prayer be added to one's own, and this indicates the kind of prayer activity that was in the Mesopotamian background of patriarchal religion: the Hebrews could draw on a well-developed spiritual heritage there.

As in Genesis, so in the religious insight of the Hebrews' neighbors there was a lively awareness of the divine initiative and prevenience, by which the deity anticipates the desires and needs of mankind. Ugaritic legends contain a number of events that make us think of the divine appearances to Abraham and Jacob. El, for instance, is described as coming to the bereft Keret, who forthwith asks the god for a son.[83] Several gods visit Keret later on and bless both him and his wife.[84] There is also a divine visit to Daniel.[85]

82. Pritchard, *ANET*, pp. 80–81.
83. *Ibid.*, p. 143.
84. *Ibid.*, p. 146.
85. *Ibid.*, p. 151. *Cf.* Gordon's discussion of possible Ugaritic parallels in *JBR*, XXI (1953), p. 240f., and, on the divine visit type of story in general, von Rad, *ATD*, p. 174.

When one considers that the foregoing instances of prayer and other discourse between deity and man, both Biblical and non-Biblical, are out of a theological context of practical or outright polytheism, one thing emerges clearly: prayer precedes theology, so far as development is concerned. If monotheistic doctrine is a higher development than the polytheistic pantheon, and if vital, intimate interchange in prayer is more advanced than being afraid of the wind in the trees on a dark night, then progress in prayer comes before it does in ideas of God. The customary task of theology is to order, inform, and discipline the often-imaginative flights of devotion. This faster advance of prayer beyond doctrine may not be universal, but it does seem the proper conclusion to draw about the Hebrews and their closest Near Eastern neighbors. In their case, *lex orandi lex credendi* appears to be most appropriate: the way we pray shows what we really believe.

In view of the preceding, this writer must differ with the dictum of Albright, who has written that "the most exalted emotional experiences known to man, the experiences of religious conversion and mystical union with God, are unknown in the ancient Near East outside of Israel, so far as we can judge from our material."[86] This seems to overstate the case, perhaps in all commendable zeal to exalt the uniqueness of the experience of Israel. If the sense of closeness to deity whose ears are open to one's prayer and who takes thought for the needs of people constitutes union with God, then it is present in Ugaritic and Babylonian religion of the patriarchal period, too. Amidst the theological crudities in the remains of those religions can be discerned the warmth of the personal relationship of deity and man whose exercise is prayer, communicating back and forth. "Religious experience" is dangerous territory in which to claim uniqueness for Biblical religion at any level of its development, and especially so in the pa-

86. Albright, *ARI*, p. 24.

triarchal period, when the Hebrews were only beginning to approach the limits of the religion of the background.

For want of a more convenient point of classification, two events of the patriarchal legends must be considered here in relation, if not close relevance, to the matter of prayer: the destruction of Sodom and Gomorrah, because of its connection with the intercession of Abraham, and Jacob's experience of wrestling with God, because of the intimacy of the divine-human encounter in that story.

There is much about the story of the catastrophe at Sodom that smacks of the outright mythological, but investigation of the possible site of the wicked cities, now mostly covered by the southwest portion of the Dead Sea, has shown that the mythical element is to some extent aetiological and makes fair sense. Examination of the ruins indicates that sedentary life there came to an end, possibly violent, soon after 2000 and that the presence of gases (hydrogen sulphide and others) along with inflammables like asphalt and petroleum could have touched off an explosion whose violence could well be remembered in folk tradition as fire from heaven. The rock formation at Jebel Usdum has long been pointed out as having the figure of Lot's wife.[87] If the study of the supposed site of Sodom and Gomorrah dates the catastrophe too early for Abraham's most probable time, it at least demonstrates the possibility for explaining the event that has in the course of time come to be connected with the Abraham cycle and given a Hebrew moral interpretation.

The attempts of Biblical writers to remove as much anthropomorphic detail as possible from traditional stories are seldom more apparent than in the handling of the account of Jacob's wrestling with God (xxxii.24f.). Be-

87. J. P. Harland, "Sodom and Gomorrah," *BA*, V (1942), pp. 17–32, and VI (1943), pp. 41–54; and, more recently, Cornelius, *ZAW*, LXXII (1960), pp. 5–6, where a date around 1650 is given and the calamity, in earthquake country, compared to that which struck Ugarit and Alalakh.

166

cause of its importance as the aetiological account of the establishment of the sacred association of Peniel, the story could not be simply suppressed; so the handlers of tradition were reduced to trying to remove indications that the primitive story told of actually wrestling with God: success was not complete. Jacob's attempt to learn the name of his antagonist in this struggle (xxxii.29) does not succeed, at least as the story now stands, and it may be that we can see here some of the method of the Biblical writer. When the scheming Isis of Egyptian myth tricks Re into revealing his hidden name of power, Re is taken in by the ruse and reveals the name;[88] not so the God of Hebrew legend until he does so voluntarily with Moses. If the crude form of the Peniel story originally contained some revelation of a divine name, it has carefully been removed from the form of the story passed on by its literary custodians.

Sacred Places and Institutions

Patriarchal religion as described in the legends has already been characterized as chiefly that of an unsettled people whose paternal deity followed them about in their movements. This remains as our principal impression of patriarchal religious practice even after we have made due allowance for the bias of one or another Biblical author. There is truly little by way of actual use of sacred sites in Genesis. The legends tell of the setting up of altars or sacred pillars by the patriarchs at places of later importance such as Bethel and Hebron: xii.7, 8, xiii.18, xxviii.18, and xxxv.1f. The usual motive of such action is the commemoration of a theophany at the site where the memorial is erected.[89] Alt suggests that we have in

88. Pritchard, *ANET*, pp. 12–14.
89. *Cf.* de Vaux, *Ancient Israel*, p. 413.

such stories the sign of Hebrew acquisition of existing sacred places in Palestine upon their final settlement there, with the resultant identification of their paternal deity with the local god and of their ancestor as the founder of the cult at the shrine.[90] While the legends themselves show that the patriarchs were not ignorant of the Elim of the local sanctuaries, the principal focus of their religion was still the family deity, to whom prayer and sacrifice were offered, as a rule, wherever the occasion arose. Thus, while the legends associate the patriarchs with the establishment of several important centers of worship in Palestine, there is hardly an indication of their own use of them as continuing sanctuaries. Perhaps this is the reason for the absence of any mention of sacrifice in any direct way in J: in that document the patriarchs erect altars but never use them for the obvious purpose.[91] There is real plausibility to such a picture of patriarchal indifference toward established sanctuaries, since they failed to leave their mark on any of the known holy places of the period. In fact, as Albright points out, we have only slight knowledge of the religious buildings of the second millennium, although shrines from earlier times abound in almost all important centers.[92] What we do find, however, at the principal places in Palestine and Syria—pillars, roofed temples, altars, incense stands, figurines, carvings, and the like[93]—shows no sign of peculiarly Hebrew association. That all this would be in the background of patriarchal religion and known to the patriarchs through their occasional contact with it is more or less apparent from Genesis itself, but the association was a tenuous one until the Hebrews became a settled people in Palestine

90. *GdV*, p. 50, and the commentaries, which have long presented this view.
91. *Cf.* Skinner, *ICC*, pp. 1 (in Introduction), 246.
92. Albright, *ARI*, p. 48.
93. *Ibid.*, p. 42f.

after the patriarchal age. The worship carried on by the patriarchs appears to have followed no regular pattern in either time or space; just as they lacked a liturgical calendar, which sanctifies stated periods of time for worship, so they lacked the definite connection with specific places that concentrates worship at those locations. The institutions of religion are usually developed in response to the demands put on man by his actual situation, seldom in advance of them. So it is that we find the patriarchs leaving memorials of those crucial inaugural experiences in which God confronted them, memorials of some permanent character like stones, pillars, and altars. They set them up as markers of the location of what to them were important events, but they did not remain in the vicinity of them long enough to make use of them as continuing meeting places of worship with God. Abraham did not, so far as the story goes, offer sacrifices in commemoration of his covenant with God at the place of the original experience; as a matter of fact, he may well not have offered any sacrifice, in the strict sense of the word, at the initiation of the relationship.[94] Outside the one exceptional instance of XLVI.1f. the patriarchs did not go to a certain place to meet the God of their father; he came to them.

The realization of the untempled nature of the patriarchs' paternal deity makes all the more impressive the appearance in Jacob's dream at Bethel of what seems to be the classic type of Mesopotamian temple structure, the ziggurat.[95] The ladder leading from heaven to earth with the ascending and descending angels (XXVIII.12f.) is obviously thought to be connecting the heavenly residence of God with the earthly place of revelation, but there is no Canaanite counterpart for this, so far as we know. Mesopotamian temple architecture, however, provides us

94. Cf. von Rad, ATD, p. 157.
95. Finegan, Light from the Ancient Past, pp. 19–20.

with a source for the image in Jacob's dream that greatly illuminates its meaning and Jacob's reaction to it. For the Babylonians the ziggurat, with its ramps mounting upward, was the link between heaven and earth: at the top was the god's residence, and on the lower level was his earthly place of manifestation. If this is the scene that the story intends to portray, then Jacob's exclamation (xxviii.17) also takes on deeper meaning: he identifies the place where he had this experience both as the divine residence and as the appearance-place, "the house of God and . . . the gate of heaven." What frightens Jacob is that this place, Bethel, should be such a meeting point between heaven and earth, like a Mesopotamian ziggurat.[96] It is another question how Jacob came to know about a ziggurat, since that style of temple was unknown in Palestine, and the vision of the ladder appears to him, as the story now stands, on his way to Mesopotamia before he has ever had an opportunity to see a ziggurat. Either the Bethel story has been misplaced in its present position in the tradition, or we shall have to assume that Jacob knew about the ziggurats and their significance from such folk memories as those preserved in the story of the tower of Babel (xi.1–9), which is usually interpreted as having to do with the construction of a ziggurat.

Two great institutions that formed a significant part of the distinctiveness of later Hebrew religion, circumcision and the Sabbath, are of singular unimportance in the patriarchal legends. The only observance of the Sabbath in the entire book of Genesis is that by God himself at the end of his work of creation in the P account, and Old Testament study has long agreed that the late author is there trying to give divine and ancient sanction to what had become something primary by his time. Pre-Mosaic religion had nothing to correspond to what the Sabbath be-

96. *Cf.* von Rad, *ATD*, p. 247f.

came among the Israelites by the time of the Exile. The patriarchs did not even observe the Babylonian "Sabbath," since that feature of the Babylonian calendar never extended to the population at large and was by no means a day when business and labor were generally suspended. The extra-Israelite origin of the Sabbath is not yet successfully provable, but its Hebrew status as a joyful day of rest in recognition of the lordship of the God of the Covenant stamps it as peculiarly Yahwist all along and should withhold us from too-eager searching for approximations of it among those who were not in fact Yahwists.[97]

It is not exactly the same with circumcision. The P author makes the institution of circumcision as the sign of the covenant people one of the most extended and detailed events in his account of the tradition (xvii), and it is one of the rules of thumb of contemporary Biblical study that circumcision gained its quasi-sacramental character only later in Israelite life after patriarchal times. It needs to be observed, however, that circumcision had an important position in Hebrew life earlier. The requirement of circumcision in the Dinah episode (xxxiv.14f.) stands in the early J and E sources and is thus not to be lightly dismissed. The antiquity of circumcision as a rite of many peoples is well attested,[98] despite the tradition among the Hebrews that it was instituted for them at the time of the Exodus. We know, for instance, that the Egyptians practiced circumcision as a kind of initiation of the adolescent into adulthood in preparation for marriage, but we should note, as von Rad puts it, that even as early as the patriarchal period circumcision served to distinguish

97. T. G. Pinches long ago surveyed the difficulties of the problem in his "Sapattu, the Babylonian Sabbath," *PSBA*, XXVI (1904), pp. 51–56. Later studies of the unsuccessful attempts to connect the Babylonian observance with the Biblical Sabbath are in Barton, *Archaeology and the Bible*, p. 309; E. G. Kraeling, "The Present Status of the Sabbath Question," *AJSL*, XLIX (1933), pp. 218–228; and de Vaux, *Ancient Israel*, pp. 478–480.

98. *Cf.* Skinner, *ICC*, pp. 296f., 419f.

Hebrews from at least some of the peoples with whom they had contact.[99]

There is lacking in patriarchal religious life something else that gives later Hebrew religion much of its distinctive character; to wit, the phenomenon of prophecy. Perhaps the closest approach to it is the interpretation of dreams that helped Joseph on his way to success. Even so, the interpretation of dreams was not limited to regular visionaries, as can be seen from Mesopotamian remains: Ninsun and Enkidu are both spoken of as interpreting the hidden meaning of dreams.[100] While, of course, we do not look in the patriarchal period for the unique prophecy that burst forth in Israel in the eighth century, patriarchal life is remarkably devoid of semiprophetic activities like divination, with the exception of that of Joseph (xliv.5, 15). While the legends often speak of visions, they are usually a device of the author to temper a hint of anthropomorphism in the divine appearances. No one but Joseph in Genesis is represented as having greater insight into the meaning of things than the ordinary person, and no one among the patriarchs has the qualities of a *baru,* such as we know about from Mari.[101] The presence of seers, ecstatics, and the like in Mesopotamian, Egyptian, and Palestinian society of the patriarchal period is so well attested that we are forced to conclude that this widespread phenomenon of Near Eastern life did not enter the Hebrew sphere until after patriarchal times. The later author somewhat anachronistically refers to Abraham as a prophet (xx.7), but the only prophetic work that Abraham performs is to pray. If the origins of prophecy are to be sought in cultic surroundings, the absence of it in patriarchal life is not surprising, since the Hebrews of

99. *ATD*, p. 291.
100. Pritchard, *ANET*, pp. 76, 83.
101. *Ibid.*, p. 482.

Genesis had such a rudimentary development in that area. Whatever one may speculate about the ultimate origins of prophecy, no one achieves recognizably prophetic stature among the Hebrews before Moses. It may indeed be that activity of prophetic or semiprophetic types presupposes a more settled society than that of the patriarchs.

What, then, was unique about patriarchal religion? Its ideas of deity were much the same as those of neighboring peoples. It lacked the form and substance given religion by calendar and cult. Its ethical component was of the most elementary sort. It had no priests or official spokesmen for the divine word and only a trace of identifying marks. In fact, patriarchal religion was in many ways less developed than the religions of the more advanced peoples with whom the patriarchal Hebrews met. The patriarchs may have come in time after Mesopotamian and Egyptian religions had reached lofty insights, as Kaufmann eagerly insists,[102] but, living on the edges of culture as they did, they appear to have participated only passingly in it. The uniqueness of patriarchal religion, then, such as it was, must be seen as a uniqueness of opportunity, of potential. In the idea of the covenanting family God can be seen something of the germ of subsequent Hebrew religious development, as previously remarked, but the real distinctiveness of patriarchal religion can be found only by the eyes of faith, which discern the initiative of divine providence. Only that keeps the patriarchal legends from being merely one more collection of stories about another ancient people.

102. *The Religion of Israel,* p. 221.

✌ V

THE PATRIARCHS AND EGYPT

THE COURSE of the history of the ancient world was often one of movement back and forth through Palestine and Syria between the two early focal points of culture, Egypt and Mesopotamia. Armies, diplomats, traders, and nomads made their way along this avenue of history, and among them were the patriarchs as represented by the legends of Genesis. The story of the patriarchs opens with their departure from Mesopotamia, takes them through their wanderings about the western half of the Fertile Crescent, with semipermanent dwellings here and there in Palestine, and closes with their final settlement in the Delta of Egypt. If there were no sequel to the patriarchal legends in the story of the Exodus and the Conquest, it would indeed be one of the great ironies of history and literature that the story that began with high expectation of the inheritance of a Promised Land concludes, not with the possession of that land, but with the would-be heirs as a temporarily tolerated minority in another. As it is, though, all subsequent Hebrew tradition looks back to Egypt, that other land, as the birthplace of the national founder of Israel and as the scene of the crucial event that linked the Hebrews forever with their unique God. It is the Egyptian sojourn that formed the connecting link between the remote Mesopotamian origin and the ultimate emergence of the people of Israel. Therefore the story of the settlement in Egypt must be examined

174

for itself and against the archaeological background in order to determine what we may of how the patriarchs happened to go to Egypt and what happened to them there.

To and From Egypt in the Patriarchal Period

Travel in the ancient world was hardly a matter of vacationing tourism, seeking out interesting sights for the sake of diversion. If one traveled at all beyond his immediate environs, it was a case of his needing to do so because of war, politics, business, or some other pressing concern. By contrast with the modern world, it appears that the patriarchs sometimes traveled because they could not pay at all, now or later. This is not to say that travel was forbiddingly difficult or dangerous or that there was very little of it, for that was not the case. For instance, a Babylonian contract that has survived contains the stipulation that a wagon which is being hired is not to be driven to the Mediterranean coast;[1] there would hardly have been any need for such a prohibition if travel had not been quite common between Mesopotamia and the land far to the west.

As the expanding Egyptian power spread across the desert to the east of the Nile and northward into Palestine and Syria, as far as Qatna and Ugarit,[2] travel became increasingly heavy in and out of the Nile Valley. It had actually been a frequent occurrence since the third millennium, as the records show. There are mentions of Asiatics in Egypt early in the First Intermediate Period, between 2300 and 2050. In some detail the Ipu-wer text tells how during that time of weak Egyptian government foreigners moved into Egypt and were taking over land, and the same complaint about infiltrating nomads is

1. Barton, *Archaeology and the Bible*, p. 347.
2. Albright, *Archaeology of Palestine*, p. 85.

found in the invective of Nefer-rohu.[3] We know from the Egyptian execration texts of the presence of unsettled, restless peoples in Palestine during the late years of the third millennium and on into the nineteenth century.[4] The insecurity of their difficult lives was recognized even by the Egyptians, who seem to have reluctantly accepted the inevitability of these nomads' making their way into the Nile Valley, where living was easier.[5] Even after a strong dynasty took control of Egypt in the period of the Middle Kingdom, Asiatics continued to enter Egypt in various capacities, sometimes as mere slaves, sometimes as suppliants, entertainers, or traders: the celebrated Beni-Hasan scene shows Asiatic bedouin traders who have brought stibium, a favorite cosmetic of the Egyptians.[6] Egyptians traveled far and wide throughout the period, too, as we know from the adventures of Sinuhe, who made his way into Palestine and Syria.[7] On through the entire patriarchal period there was much crossing of the Egyptian frontier, as the surviving records of the border officials testify,[8] and in the fourteenth century a note is made of foreigners who have come to Egypt because of oppressive famine conditions in their homeland, just as Abraham and then Jacob did.[9] Mention has already been made of the appearances of Apiru as slaves in Egypt during the patriarchal period and of their increasing number of appearances in Egypt from the Amarna Age onward.

Such records as these from the second millennium, particularly its first half, enable us to understand the extent of the great movements of peoples that took place during that

3. Pritchard, *ANET*, pp. 227, 441, 445.

4. *Ibid.*, pp. 328–329; *cf.* Albright, *Archaeology of Palestine,* p. 82.

5. *Cf.* the twenty-second-century Instruction of Merikare in *ANET*, p. 416.

6. *ANET*, p. 229.

7. *Ibid.*, pp. 19–20.

8. *Ibid.*, pp. 258–259.

9. *Ibid.*, p. 251.

time. They were not confined to the mainland of Asia but passed with a fair amount of ease into Egypt itself, though it is not clear that they penetrated very far south, as a general rule. We do have the record of an official in Upper Egypt at the time of the Thirteenth Dynasty (*ca.* 1740) who had a number of Semites among his slaves,[10] but apparently the traders and herdsmen made contact only with the northern part of Egypt, like those Edomite bedouins whom Merneptah later allowed to settle in Goshen with their herds.[11] Of all the Asiatics who made their way into Egypt the Hyksos achieved the greatest political importance, since for a little over a century they were able to take over the monarchy and place their own kings on the throne. The picture that emerges from such details as these is one of frequent travel in and out of Egypt by both Egyptians and foreigners, despite the Egyptian resentment of the incursions of Asiatics and their toplofty attitude toward the displaced persons who made their way among them. Throughout our period the frontiers of Egypt were more open to trade and travel than we might ordinarily think. Customarily, when comparing the geographical situation of Egypt with that of Mesopotamia, we speak of the relatively "closed" Nile Valley, with an ocean to the north, mountains to the south, and a protective desert on both east and west. By comparison with Mesopotamia this is true, and it is acknowledged in the study of ancient history that this helped bring about the relatively unified civilization of Egypt. The homeland of Egypt was nevertheless open to travel both inward and outward, as is shown by the expansion of the empire, the arrival of foreign elements like the Hyksos and the Apiru, the references to foreign trade, and the almost successful later invasion by

10. W. F. Albright, "Northwest Semitic Names in a List of Egyptian Slaves from the Eighteenth Century B.C.," *JAOS,* LXXIV (1954), pp. 222–233.

11. Von Rad, *ATD,* p. 349.

the Sea Peoples. It is only reasonable that, when the Egyptians were strong and their nationalistic scorn for foreigners high, they would put up more resistance to the people who presented themselves at the eastern edge of the Nile Valley in search of land and a new life, but the exclusion of undesirable aliens was evidently as difficult to enforce in the ancient world as it is today. Most of them came peaceably, and many stayed on to become relatively settled members of the population in various states of life; a few managed to rise to important positions of wealth and influence, though this was by no means common.

The Genesis traditions are quite explicit in stating the reason for the journeys of the patriarchs to Egypt, and they fit very satisfactorily into the pattern of such trips into Egypt known from the extra-Biblical records, just as they display the same ease of actual entry into Egypt. Abram and Sarai are forced into Egypt during the time of a famine in Palestine (Genesis xii.10), just as the aged Jacob later moves his entire family to Egypt to escape a similar time of distress in Canaan (xlvi.6). Joseph, of course, is sold into bondage in Egypt (xxxvii.36). No part of the traditions allows us to date any of these trips to Egypt with precision, since the figures of xv.13, 16 are relative lengths of time only: "four hundred years" and "in the fourth generation." These figures are not to be ignored entirely, despite the unconcern of the ancients for statistical accuracy, but they are of general value for purposes of approximation without being pressed too closely. No Egyptian pharaoh or other official known to us from history is named in the legends, so that we lack both names and absolute dates. What the legends do provide is a general set of background details about life in Egypt at the time the patriarchs could have been there, at least in the story of Joseph.

The account of Abram's journey to Egypt is such a short one, told almost in passing and with primary emphasis on

178

the quick wit of Abram, that it contains no details that might help us identify the time in Egypt to which it refers. It is actually much easier, in the light of Egyptological study, to deal with Joseph's being sold in slavery in Egypt and the permanent settlement of Jacob and his family in the Delta than with the temporary sojourn of Abram there. To judge by the records we have of foreigners who came into Egypt in times of trouble abroad, it appears that they usually stayed there instead of returning to their former homes as quickly as Abram did. It is true that during the Hyksos period the signs of wealth in Palestine often point to a return from Egypt of men who had been for a time with the Hyksos,[12] but it is difficult to think of Abram as having lived as late as the Hyksos time. After having honestly faced the possibility that the story of Abram's sojourn in Egypt may be a duplicate of the later Jacob-Joseph account, we may still point to no particular instance of Asiatic invasion or settlement in Egypt as peculiarly appropriate to Abram's trip. Thus Peet's suggestion of the time around 2000, apart from the chronological difficulties of his attempt to correlate Abram and the time of Hammurabi of Babylon, is no more helpful than any other.[13] Perhaps the best we can say for the excursion of Abram to Egypt is that, long before the earliest suggested date for him, we know of Asiatics who made their way into Egypt to find a more stable and secure living.

There is more to work on in the story of Joseph. Egypt appears in that story as a prosperous kingdom enjoying peace at home and abroad: there is no mention of war or of civil strife of any sort. The government is apparently stable and, in the course of the story, gains a secure hold on all its territory. The legend does not designate which part of Egypt is the scene of its events, but the seeming close-

---

12. Albright, *Archaeology of Palestine*, p. 87.
13. T. Eric Peet, *Egypt and the Old Testament*, p. 47f.

179

ness of the Hebrews who settle in Goshen to the capital points toward Lower Egypt. The various classes of society are reasonably well defined: the pharaoh, his retinue of servants, scholars, officers, the clergy, the landowners, and the peasantry.

It would not be a justifiable interpretation of the Joseph story to say that it shows a time when Egypt was open to an unusual degree to immigration such as that of Jacob's family or that the attitude of the Egyptian authorities was more friendly toward foreigners than appears to have been customary. On the contrary, Joseph has to use the influence of his position close to the pharaoh to secure the privilege accorded his hungry family, and one wonders what might have happened to the old man and his family if Joseph had not been in Egypt and in a position to speak up for them (XLVII.1f.). Even Joseph himself reaches high position not as an Asiatic but as one who is named, dressed, and married in thoroughly Egyptian fashion. His own ability gains him the confidence and respect of the pharaoh, who then proceeds to make him as much an Egyptian as possible, as if to obscure his humble background. The travels of Joseph's brothers to and from Egypt are beset with no unusual obstacles, so far as actual entry is concerned, except for the trickery of Joseph himself, but their reception is to the end less than cordial. Thus, when it comes to finding a time within which we might place the events of the Joseph story, it is not so much a matter of locating a period when the Egyptians were exceptionally friendly toward Asiatics as it is of fixing on a time when people like Jacob and his family could have had a friend at court to intercede for them. Throughout the whole length of the patriarchal period, just as before it, it was reasonably easy for foreigners to make their way into Egypt; the time or times we need for the setting of the Joseph story would be a period when one of them could rise high enough to use his influence on behalf of the others.

180

Dating the Story of Joseph

Essentially two classes of problem confront us in studying the account of the adventures of Joseph and his family in Egypt: literary and historical. While it may be impossible to arrive at any conclusion that takes all aspects of these problems into account and sactisfactorily disposes of them all, it is still necessary to try to fit as many of them together as possible.

The first of the literary problems, perhaps the principal one, is that of adequately characterizing the type of story presented to us in the Joseph legend. To say that it is a legend at all is to attribute to it a purpose other than the merely historical; a legend aims to provide entertainment, inspiration, exemplary edification, or some combination of them, as we have already seen many times over. This means that the emphasis is to be found, not in the precise recording of facts and events, but in the more or less explicit presentation of a theological and moral lesson, of some theme such as that which von Rad suggests for the patriarchal legends as a whole, namely, the hidden but penetrating activity of God and his rule over events in the world.[14] Whether we designate the closing chapters of Genesis as the Jacob history, with von Rad,[15] or the Joseph history, the principal figure, humanly speaking, is Joseph, and his story is told with the purpose of showing the triumph of faith and simple virtue over great difficulties. This "rags-to-riches" motif has become trite in our day, but that should not stand in the way of our recognizing this wisdom-tale character of the Joseph story.[16] While something like this has to govern our handling of much of the patriarchal tradition, it is especially important to bear it in mind in reading the Joseph story, where various de-

14. *ATD*, p. 223.
15. *Ibid.*, p. 229.
16. *Cf. ibid.*, p. 380.

tails of Egyptian life are mentioned in such a way as to tempt us to take them very closely. In this story of Joseph, which of all the patriarchal stories bears the clearest signs of careful literary composition and polishing at the hands of the later custodians of tradition, we find alongside each other the authentic or plausible reminiscences of ancient detail of which legend is capable and also the decorative devices of local color that an artistic writer of a later age will supply to give vividness to his narrative. Again, this is not a unique problem of the Joseph story, but it is perhaps more a problem here than in the other legends, especially if we place the literary fixation of the tradition in a time when the Israelites were in close political and cultural relations with Egypt.[17]

If we satisfactorily deal with the first literary problem by acknowledging that the Joseph story is an exemplary fable told to extol an Israelite hero, then we introduce other, more detailed problems. We might suspect that, in a legend told with the point that morality brings success, the virtue of the hero is liable to be exaggerated, not for any purpose of deceit but simply for heightening the detail and making the point unmistakable. On this basis we look anew at the virtue of Joseph in his conduct toward Potiphar's wife and also have to face the possibility that Joseph's prowess as an administrator and even the extent of his authority over "all the land of Egypt" may be exaggerated. The easier way out of these literary problems is to adopt an attitude of hypercritical skepticism, which looks for nothing but the product of pious imagination in a schematic tale with local color, but this is to undervalue legend and its tenacity for fact.

There is also a literary problem of language that should

17. *Cf. ibid.;* also, Jozef M. A. Janssen, "Egyptological Remarks on the Story of Joseph in Genesis," *Jaarbericht van Het Vooraziatisch-Egyptisch Genootschap,* XIV (1955–1956), p. 63. (The latter is hereafter cited as Janssen, "Remarks.")

be mentioned. In a story that deals with people living in Egypt, one is naturally going to look for Egyptian terms and loan words in the account: technical terms and proper names as well as household words. Not only must we be satisfied that an Egyptian derivation can be demonstrated for such vocabulary items as these, but it is also of concern that we determine whether the Joseph story is particularly and distinctively characterized by a greater frequency of the use of Egyptian words than the other legends, or other parts of the Old Testament as a whole.

The historical problems are those of identifying people, places, and political and economic situations. In this we do not really seek to identify Joseph's pharaoh as a specific individual, though that is an attractive task to which many have devoted much effort, and several possible pharaohs have been suggested. It seems to this writer that we tend to try too hard to make this individual distinction because a few of the pharaohs are relatively well known to us. Actually few of them emerge as genuinely clear-cut individuals. Apart from the few really outstanding pharaohs of the second millennium—Tutmose III, Akhnaton, Seti I, Ramesses II, Merneptah—most of the pharaohs are little more than names in Manetho's list; we cannot expect one of the better known ones necessarily to be the pharaoh who was Joseph's friend merely because Joseph is important to us. It is more to our purpose to try to determine what kind of pharaoh was on the throne during Joseph's time, what his policies and acts were, and to restrain our disappointment if we cannot link a great pharaoh with Joseph. For that matter, if Joseph was the power that the legend says he was in Egypt, we might well expect the pharaoh to be a relatively small person, historically speaking; not a strong ruler in his own right but fortunate in having made a wise choice in his staff.

The question arises whether the reign of Joseph's pharaoh was a time of change and innovation. As it stands, the Genesis narrative seems to indicate that the centralization of landholding in the hands of the pharaoh was brought about within the single life span of this one pharaoh and his vizier. We expect a certain amount of simplifying and schematizing in legend, and we must consequently acknowledge the possibility that what is described in the Joseph story as the work of this one reign may actually have been a gradual process that took several generations to carry out. There is also the possibility that the absolutist arrangements already existed before Joseph's time and that what Genesis relates is merely the formalization of the existing fact.

If the time of Joseph was a time of radical change in ownership of land, as the story tells it, then it is reasonable to wonder whether the pharaoh in whose reign this was carried out was a native Egyptian or a foreigner. If he was the latter, say, one of the Hyksos kings, we might expect him to be more likely to upset the traditional Egyptian system than if he were in the line of a native Egyptian dynasty. Yet that expectation fails to coincide with the fact that one of the most revolutionary pharaohs ever to sit on the throne of Egypt was Akhnaton, a native son of Egypt, while the records we have of the Hyksos seem to demonstrate their desire to adapt themselves to Egyptian traditional ways. Whatever his ancestry, though, the pharaoh of Joseph's lifetime was different enough to have a foreigner as his vizier, a rather lowborn foreigner at that; that might, or might not, be of help in deciding the origin of the pharaoh himself. The problem still remains of finding record of foreigners in high Egyptian office.

Finally there is the question of the actual success of the administration of the pharaoh and Joseph. Was it in fact a time of prosperity or not? The general tone of the legend has it that it was, thanks to the ability of Joseph to foresee the future through successful interpretation of dreams and to take steps to ward off the evil consequences of the coming disaster. It could, however, be argued that the administration of Joseph was something less than successful because of the very fact that it was characterized by such extreme, emergency measures in its attempt to deal with a disaster it could not forestall.

In approaching the literary and historical problems connected with the location of the story of Joseph in a plausible time, one soon becomes aware that the literary aspect of the problem is more readily dealt with than the historical. As long as we hold legend as broadly, generally true to the time that it claims to represent—and there has been ample basis in our preceding chapters to justify this assumption—we are no more shocked by literary touches like overstatement than we are overwhelmed by the presence of proper names that ring true. This enables us to take in our stride, for instance, the matter of Joseph's encounter with Potiphar's wife. It looks very much as if the Hebrew tradition has taken unto itself a theme that also appears in a favorite story of Egyptian secular literature and has made its own use of it. What we find in Egyptian as the tale of the two brothers, Anubis and Bata,[18] an adventure story designed purely for entertainment, stands in the Hebrew tradition as an edifying tale that demonstrates the standards of sexual ethics that hearers of the story are supposed to follow. There is absolutely no facet of the story that indicates direct, conscious borrowing; it is so organically necessary in the development of the overall story of Joseph that the rest of the legend would make little sense without it. Strict virtue such as Joseph manifests in this situation meets adversity but finally triumphs. When we find such a close parallel as we do between this episode and the well-known Egyptian tale, the proper

18. Pritchard, *ANET,* p. 23.

185

conclusion is not that it is taken outright by the Hebrew author but that he saw in this event, present in the received tradition from irretrievable antiquity, something to be emphasized in order to present his lesson strongly. How this motif originally found its way into Hebrew tradition and attached itself to the character of Joseph is as unanswerable as how it made its way into Greek tradition in the story of Phaedra and Hippolytus and as striking as the way in which this universal theme appears in different contexts, now an adventure tale, now a moral fable, now a moving tragedy. There is even a bit of affinity to be observed in the account of Idrimi of Alalakh, a younger brother who disagreed with his elders, fled, practiced divination while living with the Apiru, and later returned to become master of the land.[19] What it all shows us is the literary method of the Hebrew author at work. If we wish to take the experience of Joseph with Potiphar's wife as factual, we might explain it as one of those actual experiences which people do have that are more like fiction than fact, but there is nothing about the story of Joseph or its parallel with Anubis and Bata that requires such a conclusion. Conversely, to find in the story of Joseph such a popular folk theme as this is not to say that all the rest of the story, which depends upon this turning point, is thereby to be discounted as having no contact with actual events and situation; it is simply to admit that whatever facts may be preserved about a conceivably historical Joseph are transmitted in a genre not every one of whose words may be taken literally. If this event at the beginning of Joseph's career in Egypt is taken as fictional, we are not thereby entitled to disregard the account of the subsequent course of his career on purely literary grounds. There the question enters the historical field and will be carried on below.

19. W. F. Albright, "Some Important Recent Discoveries: Alphabetic Origins and the Idrimi Statue," *BASOR*, No. 118 (1950), pp. 11–20.

It is another matter when we come to the question of language. The Joseph story contains several names and words that are satisfactorily Egyptian in their form and meaning, even if there are slight discrepancies in vocalization and division of syllables in the Hebrew. Thus we recognize in Potiphar, or its preferable form, Potiphera, the Egyptian *p'-di'-p'-r'*, "he whom Ra gave." Pharaoh represents the Egyptian *pr-'o*, which originally meant "the great house" but which from the Eighteenth Dynasty on was used as the title of the king himself. The Egyptian name given to Joseph in the process of his naturalization, Zaphenath-paneah, should probably be divided into syllables and vocalized as *tsapne-teph 'onh*, the god speaks and he lives." Joseph's Egyptian wife bore the name Asenath, which probably represents *as-neit*, "favorite of Neith" or "belonging to Neith." The acclamation with which Joseph was greeted in his dignity as vizier, *abrek*, remains a puzzle, but, if it is authentically Egyptian, the comparison with the Coptic *a-bor-k*, "prostrate thyself," may be illuminating. The name that Hebrew gives to the land of Egypt, *Mitsrayim*, probably does not reflect an Egyptian name but is closely akin to Akkadian and Ugaritic; the Greek *Aigyptos* is closer to the Egyptian than the Hebrew is.

The presence of such demonstrably Egyptian names is impressive, as is that of several loan words: *hartummim,* "magicians," *shesh,* "linen," *ye'or,* "river," and *ahu,* "reeds."[20] Here is a point for caution, however, for there are Egyptian proper names and loan words elsewhere in the Old Testament, too, and the use of them does not characterize any particular passage as distinct from other similar ones. There are no more Egyptian loan words in the Joseph cycle than in any other average part of the Old

20. Details can be found in the standard lexicons and commentaries. *Cf.* also, Janssen, "Remarks," p. 65; and Peet, p. 103.

Testament.[21] The presence of them in the Joseph story does not therefore entitle us to attribute an unusual knowledge of Egyptian life, language, and history to the sources of the legend; it would be most embarrassing if we tried to argue that it did, for the story has some inconsistencies in other areas that would be surprising if it were supposed to be based on intimate association with Egyptian lore. This realization spares us much trouble in considering the mention of "the land of Ramesses" in XLVII.11. There can be no doubt that it is anachronistic as it stands, since the land could not be so designated until the time of the Ramessids, beginning late in the fourteenth century.[22] The presence of this name, out of its proper time, no more fixes the date in the Ramessid period than it invalidates the possibility of an earlier era for the story as a whole. Likewise, the names Zaphenath-paneah, Asenath, and Potiphera are of a type not found in common usage until the Twenty-first Dynasty, after 1150,[23] but the same observation applies. What we have in the Egyptian names and words in the Joseph story is demonstration of the literary matter of appropriateness, just as in the case of the names of the patriarchs themselves.

In many ways the various aspects of the historical problem of the Joseph story interlock, to the extent that one does sometimes feel that he is arguing in a circle. For instance, the extent of the territory over which Joseph had authority can be specified if we assume that he held his position under Hyksos rule, but one of the chief arguments in support of dating Joseph in the Hyksos period is the assumption that he probably held sway only over Lower Egypt. Similarly, situations that we logically expect to obtain in one period are best known from totally dif-

21. Janssen, "Remarks," p. 68; Peet, p. 103.
22. Gordon, *Introduction to Old Testament Times,* p. 102.
23. Peet, p. 100f.

ferent times, as, for instance, the prominence of a foreign official during the reign of a native Egyptian pharaoh. This is probably inevitable when we try to seek points of contact between a legend written without concern for documentary accuracy and a reconstruction of history painstakingly worked out by the most exact scientific method.

The two most attractive hypotheses for the historical background of the Joseph story place it in periods two to three centuries apart: the one in the time of the Hyksos, roughly in the seventeeth century, and the other shortly after 1400, the time of Amenhotep IV in the Amarna Age. Both these theories can be reconciled with parts of the inconsistent chronological scheme of the Bible, and neither can be demonstrated to the total exclusion of the other. This writer suspects that a certain psychological atmosphere surrounds the respective arguments and determines the various writers' handling of the problem. Proponents of the Hyksos theory seem to have at least in the backs of their minds the known presence of Semitic elements in the Hyksos, which would supposedly make them favor other non-Egyptians for official positions. The preference for the reign of Akhnaton seems to be motivated by a readily understandable fascination with that thoroughly documented age, one of the most productive of material with which archaeology can work. No one operates without presuppositions, and these seem most likely for these two points of view.

If we wish to designate the Hyksos period as the time for the story, the following points serve the argument.[24] The Hyksos entered Egypt, not in one great armed invasion but by a process of gradual and often peaceful infil-

24. For this view, Alexis Mallon, "Les Hébreux en Egypte," *Orientalia*, No. 3 (1921); Speiser, *AASOR*, XIII (1933), p. 52; Albright, *Archaeology of Palestine*, p. 83.

tration.[25] This is not to deny their fierce military activity, which won them their domination over Syria, Palestine, and Lower Egypt, but simply to preclude the notion of their having had to fight step by step for every foot of the way into Egypt: the country was too weak by the time the Hyksos arrived to make that kind of entry generally necessary. By 1700 the Hyksos had secured control of Lower Egypt and had moved the capital northward to Avaris in the Delta, where their kings ruled.[26] The Hyksos were composed of as many ethnic elements as the Habiru, their contemporaries, and thus included Semites among their number. This many-blooded people made their way southwestward through Syria and Palestine along the route suggested by the gradual migration westward of the Habiru and in the same period, so that there is good reason to connect the Semitic element of the Hyksos with the Habiru, an earlier group than those Habiru known from the Amarna letters.[27] Whether the Hyksos would go out of their way to favor Asiatics for office or not, their very possession of the land with Semites among them would explain the occurrence of an official with an Asiatic name under Apophis, one of the Hyksos kings.[28] The mention of chariots in the Joseph story (*e.g.*, XLI.43) makes the Hyksos period our earliest *terminus a quo* for the story, since they introduced the vehicle to Egypt.[29]

The descent into Egypt of Jacob's family is entirely a peaceful one, such as would be expected of those accompanying the Hyksos movement, especially after the time had passed for whatever fighting had to be done by the Hyksos at first. The family as a whole never fully entered into Egyptian life but settled quietly in their new pasture

25. Mallon, *Orientalia*, No. 3 (1921), p. 54.
26. Pritchard, *ANET*, p. 231.
27. Speiser, *AASOR*, XIII (1933), p. 52.
28. Mallon, *Orientalia*, No. 3 (1921), p. 36.
29. Albert Edward Bailey, *Daily Life in Bible Times*, p. 68.

land and continued in their accustomed ways. Joseph had already been thoroughly Egyptianized, thus following the behavior of the Hyksos themselves, who, like the later Romans when conquering Greece, tried to identify themselves as much as possible with their new conquest, took new gods like Seth and Re, and assumed new names.[30] It might be remarked, somewhat aside, that nowhere in the Hebrew tradition is there expressed any shock over Joseph's adoption of Egyptian ways;[31] evidently admiration for his success covered everything.

It is impossible to prove precisely and absolutely when the land system attributed to Joseph's administration was set up in Egypt; it could be placed almost any time after the end of the Middle Kingdom.[32] At the beginning of the Eighteenth Dynasty, which wrested power away from foreign rule and restored it to Egyptian kings, the system was the prevailing one: the pharoah was the owner of all land in the kingdom with the exception of the temple properties.[33] Whether it was a benevolent system is not to be proven outright, and we need not expect to find any mention of possible civil unrest in the Biblical account: legend intended to praise the exemplary deeds of famous men does not function with the thoroughgoing honesty of the later historian, unafraid to tell the mistakes of his hero. Mallon considers the regime of Joseph a relatively unoppressive one that more or less gave a legal basis to a system already in existence and, having exacted its twenty percent from the people, left them to their ways.[34] Admittedly, twenty percent total taxation sounds positively millennial in the contemporary world, but it may have meant

30. Mallon, *Orientalia*, No. 3 (1921), pp. 54, 75. However, on the adoption of new gods, contrast Peet, p. 98.
31. Von Rad, *ATD*, p. 343.
32. Peet, p. 97.
33. *ATD*, p. 359.
34. Mallon, *Orientalia*, No. 3 (1921), p. 86.

more in ancient Egypt. It should be granted, however, that the Hyksos rule, like the Biblical period this argument compares with it, is not recorded as one of oppressive governmental demands on the people: the Hyksos were not the mighty builders of great monuments requiring forced labor whom Egypt had known previously and was to know again in the Ramessids.

There are certain advantages to this dating of the time of Joseph. The dividing line between Hyksos and other peoples of Semitic descent is impossible to draw; thus, whether the Hyksos when in power would have actively welcomed other Semites into Egypt or not, those other Semites like Jacob's family would have felt freer to enter a land where people like themselves were in control. The Hyksos dominion, extending from Lower Egypt through Palestine into Syria, must have made the entry into Egypt proper comparatively easy, and this fits with the apparent concentration of the Hebrews in Lower Egypt. The remains of the Hyksos period in Palestine indicate a relatively prosperous time there, and, if we may reason from that that Egypt was herself prosperous at the same time, it would serve well as a period to match the prosperity of the kingdom attributed to Joseph's administration. Perhaps the principal difficulty with taking the age of the Hyksos as our period lies in the generally acknowledged character of the Hyksos as fighting men, Mallon to the contrary. Their period of rule was not a peaceful one, as Albright has shown;[35] if Joseph had been vizier during this period, which knew many struggles in the northern part of the domain, he could hardly have ignored them, but the narrative in Genesis mentions no military activity. It would have made a logical part of the tradition about him to include an account of how he directed armies to keep down trouble when it arose, but we are told nothing

35. *Archaeology of Palestine*, p. 90.

like that about Joseph. For whatever it may be worth, it should be recorded that the Hyksos period is approximately four hundred years before the recommended date of the Exodus late in the thirteenth century, and that coincides with one Biblical dating of the entry into Egypt (xv.13).

The argument for locating Joseph in the time of Akhnaton has about as many plausible supports.[36] If we work backward from the time of Seti I or Ramesses II, either of whom could be the pharaoh of the oppression, and if we further read Exodus 1 as reflecting a short time of oppression soon after the time of Joseph, the age of Akhnaton emerges as a possibility for Joseph's time. Akhnaton had broken with the traditional religion of Egypt and its Theban priesthood, and thereby he must have lost the services of those priests and of their adherents. This would account for his making use of Joseph, since Akhnaton would have been forced to take his government ministers where he could find them. Akhnaton spent most of his time in the religious affairs that overwhelmed his attention, and a competent vizier like Joseph would have been able to take care of the affairs of the government and leave the pharaoh free to write his hymns and meditate on his doctrines. Once Akhnaton concentrated the religion of Egypt on the solar monotheism of Heliopolis (On), a marriage to the daughter of the priest of On, such as Joseph made, would have lent tremendous prestige to any man so fortunate. Further, the lack of attention to the constant pleas in the Amarna correspondence from the Palestinian governors for help against plotters and invaders makes sense if we place Joseph in power at this time: the pharaoh was not interested in such

36. For this view, H. H. Rowley, "Israel's Sojourn in Egypt," *BJRL,* XXII (1938), p. 279f., *Cf.* the preference for the Amarna Age for the patriarchs as a whole in Gordon, *Introduction to Old Testament Times,* p. 102f.

matters, and the vizier refused to send troops to fight off people to whom he felt himself akin.

It is clear beyond all doubt that Akhnaton did use non-Egyptians as his functionaries, for we have direct knowledge of at least two of them from the Amarna letters. The best known is Yanhamu, who turns up in over two dozen of the tablets.[37] He is the Egyptian overlord for Syria and Palestine and enjoys a position of high respect: all seem to admire his wisdom and capability and to hold him in real affection, something beyond the polite extravagances demanded in official manners. The Egyptians trust him, and the little governors in Syria and Palestine ask his intercession at court on behalf of their distressed situation. One letter speaks of Yanhamu as the only one who can save the land from the SA.GAZ. He is the dispenser of money, clothes, grain, and other commodities. We could hardly ask for an official who sounds more like Joseph than this one. Yanhamu's name is pure Semitic, and the way in which he is addressed by the Syrians makes it apparent that he is actually a kinsman of theirs of some sort. The name does occur in a list of names of Syrians on an ostracon of the Eighteenth Dynasty. Yanhamu makes his headquarters in Yarimuta, a site that cannot be located with precision but is most probably in the Delta, as Knudtzon takes it. For reasons that are not specified in the letters Yanhamu pays no heed to the request for assistance. Once we are told that he has even taken away troops that could have stopped the inroads of the SA.GAZ.[38] Whether we are justified in assuming that he took this action on the basis of actual favor toward the SA.GAZ is debatable, but there is no doubt that he did it, whatever the reason.

37. *Cf.* Knudtzon, p. 1169f.
38. *Ibid.*, p. 1336.

194

Another Semite is twice mentioned in Amarna letters as occupying a high position in the Egyptian court; this is Dudu, whose name is strikingly like the familiar Hebrew David.[39] We do not know so much about him as we do about Yanhamu, but he is of importance as another Semite in Akhnaton's service who resembles Joseph. This was not the end of Asiatic success in Egypt: a record from the time of chaos between the Nineteenth and Twentieth Dynasties (*ca.* 1200) tells how for a while a Syrian "made himself prince" and "set the entire land as tributary before him."[40] While too late for any direct tie with the period of Joseph, this record serves to illustrate how from time to time—usually when there was internal confusion in Egypt—Asiatics could take control.

Such a mass of relevant material for comparison cannot but be impressive, but there are real difficulties in making it the basis for dating the story of Joseph. Neither Yanhamu nor Dudu, for all their importance, is represented as enjoying the amount of prestige or exactly the type of office that Joseph had, just as neither of them appears to have served time as a slave in Egypt. In one important respect Akhnaton does not sound like the pharaoh of Genesis, either: Joseph's pharaoh does not have any unusual amount of interest in religious matters, and he does not appear to have been surrounded by anything resembling the resentful hostility that Akhnaton had to face throughout his reign. If Joseph's pharaoh was actually an innovator, it was in the area of government and economics, not religion. The dating in the times of Akhnaton has the advantage of chronology, since it is comfortably closer to the time of the Exodus, and the real advantage of the character of Akhnaton's reign with its

39. *Ibid.*, p. 1262.
40. Pritchard, *ANET,* p. 260.

195

"absentee pharaoh." His failure to attend to the customary duties of a king could have made for serious internal calamities as well as for trouble on the outer reaches of the empire like those in the Amarna letters. The famine of the Genesis tradition, for instance, could be the direct result of the preoccupied government's inability to control irrigation from the Nile or failure to repair the canals that made it possible.[41] The choice of the time of Akhnaton, however, has the distinct disadvantage of being unable to explain why Joseph is represented as vizier over all of Egypt in an age in which usually there were two viziers: from 1500 on till 1000 there was usually one vizier over Lower Egypt, another over Upper Egypt. There is nothing about the Genesis story to suggest that Joseph shared his power with anyone else.[42]

The question thus remains on balance: both the Hyksos period and the Amarna Age were times of movement of peoples, and both eras have certain characteristics that can be said to correspond with what is shown of Egypt in the Joseph story. If anything inclines us a little more toward the Hyksos period, perhaps it is the absence from the Genesis tradition of anything to correspond with Akhnaton's religious activity, the most distinctive trait of Akhnaton's reign as we know it.[43]

Egyptian Local Color in Genesis

In a carefully written story like the Joseph legend, dealing with what are to the writer and his audience an age in the past and a foreign land, one expects to find certain exotic details that make for the atmosphere of the long-ago and the faraway. These details of local color serve to heighten the entertainment value of the story and also to

41. Janssen, "Remarks," p. 69.
42. *Ibid.*, pp. 66–67.
43. No one but Breasted seems to have made much of Ahmose I, just after the expulsion of the Hyksos; *cf.* Rowley, *BJRL*, XXII (1938), p. 279f.

give it the illusion of reality. A careful author will work hard to attain accuracy in the use of these details, and the thoroughness of his research will be more or less indicative of the importance that he attaches to them.

The details of Egyptian life and custom that occur in the Joseph story do not bear the marks of laborious research on the part of the authors: minutiae are not to be found, and none of the references to Egyptian ways can be said to be recondite. The authors are not trying to demonstrate their erudition—by contrast with P, who often goes out of his way to record *recherché* items—nor are they attempting to prove to skeptical listeners that Joseph really lived at a certain time in Egypt and served with a particular king. There is consequently no need for them to document their story thoroughly. The result of this approach is that the items of Egyptian local color that stand in the Joseph tradition are there either for the sake of vividness, supplied almost offhandedly by the authors to increase the interest, or by reason of their being part of the received tradition and thus liable to have been remembered fairly accurately or, for that matter, informally simplified in passing from generation to generation.

The story has it that the traders who took Joseph to Egypt and sold him there were carrying gum, balm, and myrrh from Gilead (xxxvii.25). This puts them on a well-known trade route and attributes to them traffic in products highly valued by the Egyptians for medical and other uses, even if the mention of Ishmaelites at this point is probably anachronistic.[44] Such a detail as this will not help to date the story, but it is more important for the realism it gives to the account of Joseph's arrival in Egypt.

Joseph's servitude in Egypt is another detail that fits well with what we know about the various foreign ele-

44. *Cf.* von Rad, *ATD*, p. 310.

197

ments who made their way into Egypt. In addition to the pictorial representations of Asiatics as slaves we have the written record: there is mention of the transfer of Asiatic slaves in Egypt as early as 1800.[45] Slightly later there is the record of slaves who bear Northwest Semitic names, a papyrus from shortly before the beginning of the Hyksos rule.[46] It is a list of the names of the ninety-five slaves held by an official in Upper Egypt: some of them are Egyptian, but thirty-seven of them are Semites. There are more women than men, and several familiar names are found in the feminine form: *mnḥm* and *sk-ra-tu* correspond to Menahem and Issachar; *shp-ra* is a cognate of Shiphrah; *'sh-ra* corresponds to Asher. There is a Shamash name, *shmsh-tw*, and Albright finds in *'Aqba'* the root of the *Ya 'qub'-el* known from Tutmose III's list of captive towns.[47] The name of *'pr-rshpw* is probably to be connected with the Egyptian *'pr*, "provide," but not necessarily with the Apiru; perhaps it merely indicates the dependent status of the slave as one who received provisions from the master.[48] If this number of Semitic slaves can be taken as representative of a general pattern, then we have every good reason to assume that there was a flourishing trade in Asiatic slaves, of which the sale of Joseph would be a typical example. Again, it can be seen from the way this bit of local color is used that the purpose it serves in the story is not to date or otherwise document the account; by referring to a seemingly common occurrence, it provides a background of general plausibility for the story.

Dreams and their interpretation play a significant part in the story of Joseph, and we have indications that the

45. Pritchard, *ANET*, p. 229.

46. Albright, *JAOS*, LXXIV (1954), pp. 222–233; Janssen, "Remarks," p. 64.

47. *Cf.* Pritchard, *ANET*, p. 242.

48. *Cf.* John A. Wilson, review of *The Ḥab/piru*, by Moshe Greenberg, *JNES*, XIV (1957), pp. 139–141.

Egyptians shared the almost universal human interest in dreams. Portions of an Egyptian dream-book are available,[49] and Janssen points out the Egyptian coloration of some of the contents of the pharaoh's ominous dreams: seven was a holy number for the Egyptians; sacred cows occur in some Egyptian scenes, and the god of grain was sometimes represented by ears of corn or as wearing them.[50] Whether this adequately supports Janssen's interpretation of these details as a "malevolent allusion" on the part of the author to Egyptian ideas or not is debatable, but it does show how the Egyptian method of the interpretation of dreams is properly displayed in Genesis: each detail of the dream symbolically represents an event, circumstance, or some such. This must not be pressed too closely, however, for the method is not uniquely Egyptian.

The office and honors to which Joseph is promoted are spelled out fairly completely in the story, as are some of his activities in his position. It is customary to identify Joseph's status as that of vizier, because the record we have from one who was himself vizier of Upper Egypt under Tutmose III speaks of the place and dignity he enjoyed in a way reminiscent of the description of Joseph (XLI.40–43): he was second in honor in the kingdom, wore fine linen garments, and had the way cleared before him when he went about.[51] Likewise, when Joseph speaks of himself as father" to the pharaoh (XLV.8), his language parallels that in which a vizier of the third millennium, Ptah-hotep, was described as "father of the god;" i.e., of the pharaoh.[52] That the status of vizier is ascribed to Joseph is thus hardly to be questioned; the doubt that remains is whether it is conceivable that one of Joseph's background could have become vizier. This

49. Pritchard, *ANET*, p. 495.
50. Janssen, "Remarks," p. 66.
51. Pritchard, *ANET*, pp. 212–213.
52. Von Rad, *ATD*, p. 349.

has nothing directly to do with his being a foreigner, for we have seen that that in itself was no obstacle to attaining high position in Egypt. It is Janssen who raises the question: how could Joseph, untrained in the reading and writing of Egyptian, become even the master of Potiphar's household, much less vizier?[53] The use of scribes might make this less a problem than Janssen thinks,[54] but it is a question that cannot be ignored. We shall probably do well to allow Joseph no more dignity than that of vizier of Lower Egypt at the most. If someone like him had been vizier under the Hyksos, that would have been all he could control, since the Hyksos never gained the mastery over Upper Egypt. If under Akhnaton, probably no vizier would have been over both Lower and Upper Egypt, since by that time viziers usually came in pairs, one over each division of the kingdom.[55] In either event the reference to vizier is a reference to the office in its Egyptian form; the tradition cannot here be accused of transferring to an Egyptian setting something which the Hebrew kingdom knew only later. The Old Testament reference to a vizier in Israelite government comes relatively late, in Isaiah xxii.15f. and II Kings xviii.18, late in the eighth century and thus long after the Joseph legend had become well fixed in literary form and in whatever oral tradition persisted after the literary settlement.[56] There is no mention of a Hebrew vizier in the period when the J and E traditions were probably taking their shape.

Two matters of Egyptian local color are closely associated with each other in the Genesis tradition: the famine that lasted for seven years and the exemption of the clergy and their land from taxation. Genesis has it that, in the general context of Joseph's reorganization of the land in

53. Janssen, "Remarks," pp. 66–67.
54. *Cf.* Bailey, p. 84f.
55. *Cf.* Janssen, "Remarks," pp. 66–67.
56. *Cf.* von Rad, *ATD*, p. 330.

200

the time of emergency, he made provision to excuse the sacred precincts from the tax levied on the country as a whole. In this the story seems to echo Egyptian tradition that, in the form in which we have it, at least claims to be ancient. There is an Egyptian text that speaks of a famine of seven years, and the document mentions this in its substantiation of a priestly claim to certain land.[57] Another Egyptian text outlines certain privileges of the clergy of the temple of Osiris at Abydos, among them exemption from the levy of forced labor for the state.[58] If we can rely on these documents, then there may be reason for considering this part of the program of the legendary Joseph a legalization in his time of what had long been customary, or perhaps a revival of ancient usage.[59] The first of these two texts, however, is not to be taken too seriously, for it may date from as late as the Ptolemaic period and be merely a forgery, a pious fraud that claims great antiquity (it purports to be from the twenty-eighth century) but which cannot be trusted.[60] Janssen pleads for great caution here because of the real difficulty of properly interpreting the tax lists: the tax-exempt status of the clergy may be more ideal than real.[61]

Sometimes the Genesis tradition makes very obvious use of Egyptian lore; at other times it is subtly and unobtrusively mentioned, perhaps even accidentally. The average reader probably thinks nothing at all of the description of the last days of Joseph, in which he is shown living in great happiness, prestige, and prosperity and is finally gathered to his fathers at the age of 110 (L.26). If one's attention rests on that last verse of Genesis at all, it

---

57. Pritchard, *ANET*, p. 31.

58. *Ibid.*, p. 212; the translator (Wilson) there dates the text in the twenty-sixth century.

59. *Cf.* Mallon, *Orientalia*, No. 3 (1921), p. 86.

60. *Cf.* Pritchard, *ANET*, p. 31, and Janssen, "Remarks," p. 69.

61. Janssen, "Remarks," p. 71.

201

probably stays long enough to observe that no astronomical number of years is attributed to Joseph, by contrast with earlier figures in Genesis. When read alongside the ancient and popular wisdom book of Ptah-hotep, this verse takes on a new meaning; Ptah-hotep tells how he reached the ideal age of 110 at the end of a long and splendid career in the service of the king.[62] Perhaps this is only accidental, but the effect of it is to attribute to the vizier Joseph the length of life mentioned by the earlier vizier Ptah-hotep. It is difficult to think of this correspondence of the life span of the two viziers as completely accidental, though. The number 110 is not a popular sacred number either in itself or as a multiple, nor is it elsewhere made the length of life of an ideal hero like Joseph. It would seem that the Genesis tradition here quite subtly points out how fully Joseph measured up to the ideal pattern of Egyptian vizier.

Often commented upon is the way the Joseph saga mentions the etiquette and ritual purity of the Egyptians in dealing with foreigners (XLIII.32). Herodotus mentioned the care that Egyptians took in his time to avoid contamination of their persons or their goods by foreigners (II, 41), and we might also add that sitting to eat (XLIII.33) was a custom of the nobles of the New Kingdom.[63]

Other details have a way of escaping the notice even of the careful reader. Few have noticed the direction of the wind in the pharaoh's dream (XLI.6, 23). Janssen calls attention to it, however, as a detail that betrays a lack of acquaintance with Egyptian conditions on the part of the Genesis writers and perhaps a confusion of Palestinian with Egyptian climate. The parching sirocco that would blast vegetation in Egypt would come off the

62. Pritchard, *ANET*, p. 414.
63. Von Rad, *ATD*, p. 341.

desert to the south, not from the east as in Palestine.[64] Meteorological lore and interest were well developed among the ancients; so we cannot attribute this to mere carelessness. Perhaps the tradition has attempted to elaborate details of the pharaoh's dream and done so in terms that would be understandable to Palestinian people. Nevertheless, the rainless character of Egypt in ancient as well as modern times is amply recorded.[65] Must not moisture-bearing winds off the Red Sea to the east be regularly dehydrated by the desert they cross before reaching the Nile Valley?

The mention of embalming at the death of Jacob (L.3) and of Joseph (L.26) brings into the Biblical narrative the well-known Egyptian burial custom.[66] Though not practiced in early dynastic days, it came to be the standard procedure in the case of important persons by the time of the Middle Kingdom. Up through the Hyksos period only salt and soda were usually employed, though the process was growing more complex all the time, as can be understood from the practice of the Eighteenth Dynasty and afterward, when myrrh and spices were also used to fill the cavity left by the removal of the internal organs. This practice would assure a steady market for the spices imported by the traders who brought Joseph to Egypt. Embalming was an increasingly complicated process that would take a long time to complete; perhaps the forty days required to embalm Jacob, though a rounded off number, is not much of an exaggeration. Joseph, having occupied the position of vizier, received the high honor both of being embalmed and also of being placed in one of the multiple coffins in which prominent Egyptians were buried. In its mention of these burial customs

64. Janssen, "Remarks," p. 66.
65. *Cf.* Finegan, *Light from the Ancient Past*, p. 63.
66. Bailey, p. 80f.

the legend completes its account of Joseph's having reached the height of success in Egypt, the final flourish being his treatment after death with almost the highest honor Egypt could offer.

Before passing to the evaluation of the patriarchal tradition as a whole in the light of its archaeological context, we should take the time to assess the type and degree of correspondence between the Joseph narrative and what we know of Egyptian antiquity from other sources. The general estimate holds true here as in other aspects of the patriarchal legends: lives like those of the patriarchs can be duplicated "almost incident by incident."[67] We know how frequently Asiatics went to Egypt in times of trouble, and we know of a few Semites who held responsible positions in the Egyptian government when for some reason native Egyptian talent was not forthcoming for the job. Numerous customs and other local references to Egyptian life and practice in the Biblical material can be paralleled from extra-Biblical sources.

In this the Joseph legend is like the previous stories, but there is a special problem in dealing with the Egyptian section of the patriarchal tradition that does not exist elsewhere: that is the presence of the great number of references to matters outside the family circle, to an extent not ordinarily found in these legends. The other legends deal mostly with the intimate life within the family and the events within that limit; the Joseph story has a wealth of material about matters external to that family unit: the conduct of government, the doings of the court, the economic policies of the nation, and the like. Much of this comes under the division of local color, as the preceding discussion of the details has shown. The authors have, with perceptibly deliberate purposes, added to the outline of the narrative details that neither advance the course

67. Speiser, *AASOR*, XIII (1933), p. 43.

of the story nor contribute to its religious lesson; or, if the details were to some extent in the received tradition, the literary workers have embellished and emphasized them. The result of this is that the Joseph story contains a picture of external conditions in the land without counterpart in the stories of Abraham and Jacob.

If such details were intended to demonstrate the historicity of the story as a whole, we should probably be able to make a more coherent connection of them with a particular age than we are. The fact that two different eras, centuries apart, will serve almost equally well for the background of the Joseph story should indicate for us not only the literary purpose that accounts for the presence of these details in the legend but also the way in which we may properly use them in any reconstruction of the patriarchal period. They give to the story a vaguely Egyptian milieu that places it somewhere after the fall of the Middle Kingdom, generally speaking, and no greater precision of chronology should be forced upon the story. The Biblical authors attempted to count a definite number of generations from Abraham to Joseph, and from Joseph to Moses, and they did not succeed in producing a consistent scheme. The amount of their actual knowledge of Egyptian matters is debatable, even if they show remarkable acquaintance with the Egypt of a few centuries before their time. Perhaps we now know more about Egypt than they did, but not enough to allow us any greater accuracy than they achieved.

✎ VI

AT HOME WITH THE PATRIARCHS

THROUGHOUT this study we have worked with the estimate of the patriarchal chapters of Genesis common
to the standard commentaries that have appeared since
the rise of modern Biblical study: we have recognized
the patriarchal stories as legend, something distinct from
factual history on the one side and from poetic myth on
the other. To recognize the material as legend is to attribute to it a certain degree of historical verisimilitude at
the outset, at least that amount of historicity allowed
historical fiction in general. Purely literary study of the
patriarchal legends, as we have it in the standard critical commentaries, has made this clear. As a result of their
literary analysis of the legends, the critics felt free to draw
the conclusion best presented by Gunkel; namely, that the
movement of the patriarchs in the legends represent a
schematization of the wanderings of tribes personified in
the character of the patriarchs. This understanding of the
patriarchal legends has served throughout this study as
something of an irreducible minimum of significance for
the legends, and the writer is completely willing to let it
stand as that.[1] The over-all guiding purpose of this study,
however, has been to point out how far beyond that general interpretation we may justifiably go, to what precision
of detail we may press our explanation of the patriarchal

1. Kaufmann stoutly denies such a reading and asserts that the
patriarchs are "not tribal symbols but historical personages enveloped in
legend": *The Religion of Israel*, p. 219.

legends as containing historical reminiscences remembered with general dependability, so as to find more than the overcautious Noth will allow.[2] Having the precedent of the deduction of historical data from legendary tales by the great critics, the writer has aimed at the same goal, that of discovering what the legends can tell us of the actual life and times of the people of whom they speak. In this we have had the advantage of the vast body of archaeological findings, which enable us to reconstruct the life of the ancient world with often startling fulness, and we consequently find more data for history in the legends of Genesis than an earlier generation did.

We have now surveyed the patriarchal legends for what they tell of the origin, early experiences and contacts, and travel of the patriarchal Hebrews; for the glimpses they give us of life in the family and the conduct of its affairs; for the remembrances that they contain of the religious practices and belief of the time; and for the ultimate movement of the patriarchs from Mesopotamia through Palestine and Syria into Egypt. Comparison of these details with what we know from extra-Biblical sources compels us to draw the following conclusions.

All the events of the patriarchal legends that are not unmistakable anachronisms can be located within the period 1900–1400, give or take a few years on either end of that era. A shorter period demands that we arbitrarily restrict the area of possibility too much. The experiences of Abraham fit most plausibly into the earlier part of the period, his departure from Mesopotamia being most easily understandable in the unsettled time that came about with the Amorite invasions of eastern Mesopotamia soon after 2000. Semi-nomads like Abraham prefer to live settled lives as long as it is possible to do so, but their class is one of

2. Martin Noth, *The History of Israel*, p. 122f. *Cf.* John Bright's criticism of Noth in *Early Israel in Recent History Writing*, pp. 52f., 83f.

society's most easily uprooted and displaced. Thus the beginning of the wanderings of peoples around 2000, which put an end to the relative quiet of the preceding years, serves most helpfully as the background situation in which Abram became aware of his vocation to move to a new land and to begin life on a new foundation. Especially when we decide to place Abram and his family within the group known as the Habiru must we take this early a date for his original journey westward: it is precisely in this early part of the second millennium that the Habiru began their gradually westward movement, which extended on to the end of our period.

In view of this we must be willing to account the representation of Jacob as a grandson of Abraham a schematic shortening of the patriarchal period by the tradition, for the most satisfactory time for the Jacob and Joseph stories falls in the period of the Hyksos domination in Egypt—or perhaps, at the very latest, in the Amarna period. If there were ever traditional tales about the generations between Abraham and Jacob, they must have been dropped as not advancing in any significant way the story of the formation of God's People. The primary interest of legend is not in strict chronological accuracy but in the character and action of persons; consequently, we cannot make any use whatever of the patriarchal legends for the reconstruction of the precise chronology of the period. They show us the character of the age, with its populations on the move, and provide us with indications of the limits of the age; beyond that the legends have nothing to tell us about the extent of time between events and generations.

The legends do not provide us with dependable time fixes at any point, even in the names mentioned in Genesis XIV, the one juncture at which the Biblical author appears to wish to give a precisely detailed date. Both pre-exilic and postexilic sources, and especially the latter, take pains to color their narrative with authentic-sounding names of persons and places, but they are so often displaced or simply adrift in time and geography that we cannot use them to date any of the events spoken of in Genesis any more closely than to place them within our agreed broad limits.

The type of information contained in the legends is responsible for this lack of chronological precision which accompanies striking accuracy in other matters. The writer has previously had occasion to distinguish between "internal" and "external" types of information. By the former we understand details of an intimate, personal sort that tell of doings within the confines of the family; by the latter, events that happen outside that restricted scene: matters of government, law, and economics, of society at large. Both types of information are to be found in both the Genesis narrative and the extra-Biblical sources known to us, but the legends of Genesis contain primarily, all but exclusively, information of the internal variety.

From the reconstruction of history that our archaeological findings enable us to make we know of the first half of the second millennium as the age of the Amorite and Hurrian invasions of Mesopotamia, the age of the first great rise of the Hittites to power and their subsequent decline into obscurity, the time of the Habiru and their tramplike wanderings or depressed settlement in near-slavery, the time of the Hyksos ascendancy after the fall of the Middle Kingdom in Egypt and before the rise of the New Kingdom. This is external information about the period, and alongside it we have many intimate glimpses of the everyday life of the people: their domestic situations, their religious practices, their management of their property, even their family quarrels and other troubles. We know in many cases their actual names and the equivalent of their credit ratings. Archaeology presents us with both types of information.

Not so the Genesis traditions. Our Biblical sources for the knowledge of the period tell of a relatively small, (humanly speaking) unimportant family line, who utterly failed to leave any distinctive mark on the external history of their time, so far as it has been preserved to us. They knew the unsettled life of the period at first hand, having been swept westward by the course of population movement and the economic uncertainty of the time. They were a peaceful people, by and large, characterized by an independence that kept them at a distance from settled populations, who in turn looked on them as social inferiors; modest, poor but proud, simple people they were indeed. Since their descendants are the producers of the information about them, we have a thorough picture of the inner life of the family, in complete, often exhaustive, detail. Names, relationships, and episodes meaningless and uninteresting to anyone outside the family are fully recorded, while matters of government and public life hardly ever receive any mention. Only when one member of this family reaches high position in Egypt and enters public life to an extent far beyond any other member of his kindred does the narrative go outside the immediate family, and even then it is still a matter of background for the story of the family fortune. Our Biblical material is largely internal, and consequently the common area shared with extra-Biblical information is mostly in this sphere of life.

In the story of the Biblical Hebrews from Abraham to Joseph we have specific instances of things that we know from other sources to have been common between 1900 and 1400: their life is, so to speak, a miniature of what was largely true of their class of people throughout the Fertile Crescent at that time. The external life of the time is vaguely reflected in the Genesis traditions, but at many points the reflection is so diffused as to be without any distinct tangibility. Ancient peoples like the Hittites, the Horites, and the Philistines are mentioned as among those with whom the Hebrews met in Palestine, but the geography of the Hittites is stretched too far south in the first case; possibly it may be so with the Horites in the second; and the matter of time is simply impossible in the third. Either through the employment of the not too precise resources of folk memory or through drawing upon the type of history that is more anecdotal than factual, the Genesis traditions contain such details of time and place as are capable only of being placed in a very broad scheme of history. Within those broad limits of time, though, the placement of peoples and places is satisfactorily appropriate.

With the necessary caution, then, we can speak with greater respect for the "reliability" of the sources of the Biblical traditions of the patriarchal age. Both pre-exilic and postexilic sources took the trouble to provide a setting of plausible historicity for their events, mentioning places and peoples with whom the patriarchal ancestors could be connected. It was not the way of the tradition to supply this plausible historicity by the citation of definite dates, specific personalities, and the like, but rather to indicate the general location and the period that served as the background for the events being recited. In providing this material the J, E, and P editors were not thrown back upon their imaginations: they mentioned real nations and tribes in known places. Probably in the early, preliterary days, when the legends were still very close to the time of the events they relate, any such references they may have contained would have been much more accurate; the passage of time would make the mention of peoples and places broader and less precise. The character of the events related remained the same, though: they were presented as happenings in the historical course of life. The events that stand as the earliest in the sacred story of the Bible are presented, not as imaginary tales, but as real life accounts: a basis in history for the faith that the legends seek to teach. The legendary form that the stories take makes it impossible for us to find that precision of detail which to our contemporary minds means historical reliability, but their general picture of the time and of the contacts of the patriarchs can be trusted.

It is on the internal side of life that the patriarchal legends contain the sharpest details and are of most help in reconstructing the life and time of their period. When we find specific instances in Genesis of what are found to be generally or typically true of the patriarchal period, we may be sure not only that this was the area of the authors' principal interest but also that their dependability in relating what they knew of it is quite high. This dependability applies to all three sources of the patriarchal chapters: the early J and E, of course, and the late P, more than one might expect, as shown throughout.

The organization of the family and the exercise of authority within the family are clearly those patterns of life shared by ancient Near Eastern peoples as a whole. It is especially worthy of note that, at least in this early period, the Hebrews knew the custom of fratriarchal authority in family matters alongside the patriarchal rule. The arrangement of marriages was carried on in a serious manner in order to assure good relations between the two families concerned and a dependable supply of children to carry on the communally shared labor. The practices of the patriarchs in choosing mates, fixing the type and amount of wedding gifts, assuring the possibility of the birth of children through more than one legitimate means, and the distribution of wealth and position among offspring—all reflect those customs followed by the Hebrews' Mesopotamian neighbors.

Legend has a way of idealizing the past, and the legends of Genesis must be acknowledged as probably having raised the economic position of the patriarchs some distance above what people of their condition actually knew during the patriarchal period. The authors of the Biblical tradition, at least in the form in which we now know it, had only a dim remembrance of their origin in a large, undistinctive group occupying a lowly position just above hand-to-mouth existence: perhaps they were as unsure of the sociological meaning of "Hebrew" as we are. There is the possibility, of course, which has been mentioned earlier, that the records that we have of the Habiru of the towns show the fortune of only that segment of the class, whereas those Habiru who did not become servants or soldiers but lived at a greater distance from settled communities could have enjoyed more prosperity than their urban brethren without our ever knowing anything about it; they would seldom appear in written documents. It seems simpler, however, to recognize in the prosperity of the patriarchs the reading back by the later people of their well-to-do state of life to their ancestors' time—not through any conscious desire to deceive but purely as a result of the simplifying and idealizing tendency of legend.

Since the patriarchal Hebrews appear to have lived somewhat apart from the established life of their time, on the fringe of the civilization of their day, their religious development understandably lags behind that of the people who followed the established state religions of the time. The "trend" toward monotheism in the second millennium in the Near East may have been real, but the patriarchs' religion was largely untouched by the simplifying, unifying movement of the religion of the settled people. The obvious failure of a transparent attempt on the part of the

Biblical authors to conceal the traditions' remembrance of polytheistic practice coincides with the extra-Biblical record of religion at the time. While the paternal God was the deity who most filled the religious attention of the patriarchs, they nevertheless acknowledged the existence, presence and activity of the established, localized state gods and gave them the honor due them when the occasion arose. Where Genesis seems to indicate a single God for the patriarchs, we may be reasonably sure that we are dealing with the later age's attempt to project its own understanding and practice into the earlier time.

The absence from the patriarchal legends of the names of specific persons whom we may locate in history is balanced by the precision and accuracy with which the legends record the religious life and activity of the people of their time. Divine names of Genesis coincide with those of Mesopotamia and Ugarit, as has been shown, but even more striking is the way in which the understanding of prayer and sacrifice and of their efficacy is much the same in Genesis and in the material outside the Bible at the time of the patriarchs. If the patriarchal religion shown in Genesis traditions lacked the sophistication of the well-established cult of the official religions, it nevertheless shared the depth of their insight into the fundamental movements of the life of religion. We need to acknowledge, however, that the religion shown us in the legends of Genesis is by and large the family devotion of unofficial religion. Thus the paternal deity and the votive sacrifices and other devotions offered him by the individual and the family loom large in the foreground, while the official deities and cult, about which we know more from extra-Biblical sources, recede into the background, only occasionally reflected in the narrative. Genesis provides us with little we do not already know from elsewhere about religion outside the family.

When it comes to the fundamental question of how we may use the patriarchal legends for the reconstruction of the history of the patriarchal period, our basic rule is that legend may properly be used to sketch the history of the age for which historical documents, strictly speaking, are not to be had, but we have seen the areas in which the details of legend may be pressed closely and those where cautious generalization is all that we can allow. By showing us what is typical and characteristic of an age, archaeology provides us a context for understanding the specific instances of something general which we have in the Biblical narrative: not by "proving" or "disproving" a Biblical story but by illustrating it more amply. Thus we answer the subsidiary question of how we can intelligently and fair-mindedly make use of archaeological findings in the interpretation of the narratives of Genesis.

The use of legendary material for writing the history of our period, however, requires that we acknowledge that, legend being what it is and written for its purpose, it contains the folk memory of a situation of which our archaeological findings have shown us the same or a similar type of situation. The more closely connected with the inner life of the family our materials may be, Biblical and extra-Biblical, so much the more detailed are the resemblance and coincidence, or at least approximation, between them. Biblical narrative and archaeological discovery, legendary tradition and physical remains, are closest in their correspondence with each other in matters of family life, relationships, activities, and devotion. What we wish to know of the external life of the people of patriarchal times we must learn from archaeology almost entirely; what we wish to know of how the people lived at home, and particularly how the ancestral Hebrew family lived, worshiped, managed its property, and cared for its relatives and affairs, we can find both from archaeology and,

215

quite dependably, from the legends of Genesis. The purpose of the legends is actually much the same as that of the later historian: both aimed to provide a basis in history for the faith they sought to teach. In supplying this, the legends deal more closely and in greater detail with those inner matters of family experience which were the vital point of encounter out of which that faith originally grew.

❧ KEY TO ABBREVIATIONS

AASOR: *Annual of the American Schools of Oriental Research*

AfR: *Archiv für Religionswissenschaft*

AJSL: *American Journal of Semitic Languages and Literatures*

ANET: James Pritchard, ed., *Ancient Near Eastern Texts Relating to the Old Testament*

AO: *Der Alte Orient*

ARI: W. F. Albright, *Archaeology and the Religion of Israel*

ATD: Gerhard von Rad, *Das erste Buch Mose*

BA: *Biblical Archaeologist*

BASOR: *Bulletin of the American Schools of Oriental Research*

BJRL: *Bulletin of the John Rylands Library*

FSAC: W. F. Albright, *From the Stone Age to Christianity*

GdV: Albrecht Alt, "Der Gott der Väter"

Haverford Symposium: Elihu Grant, ed., *et al., Haverford Symposium on Archaeology and the Bible*

HO: T. J. Meek, *Hebrew Origins*

HUCA: *Hebrew Union College Annual*

ICC: John Skinner, *Critical and Exegetical Commentary on Genesis*

JAOS: *Journal of the American Oriental Society*

JBL: *Journal of Biblical Literature*

JBR: *Journal of Bible and Religion*

JNES: *Journal of Near Eastern Studies*

PEQ: *Palestine Exploration Quarterly*

PSBA: *Publications of the Society for Biblical Archaeology*

RB: *Revue Biblique*

"Remarks": Jozef M. A. Janssen, "Egyptological Remarks on the Story of Joseph in Genesis"

RHR: *Revue de l'Histoire des Religions*

VT: *Vetus Testamentum*

ZfA: *Zeitschrift für Assyriologie*

ZAW: *Zeitschrift für die Alttestamentliche Wissenschaft*

Zeitalter: F. M. T. Böhl, "Das Zeitalter Abrahams"

217

❦ BIBLIOGRAPHY

ALBRIGHT, WILLIAM FOXWELL. *Archaeology and the Religion of Israel.* Baltimore: Johns Hopkins Press, 1942.

――――. *Archaeology of Palestine.* London: Penguin Books, 1954.

――――. *From the Stone Age to Christianity.* Baltimore: Johns Hopkins Press, 1940.

――――. "The Names *Shaddai* and *Abram,*" *Journal of Biblical Literature,* LIV (1935), 173–204.

――――. "Northwest Semitic Names in a List of Egyptian Slaves from the Eighteenth Century B.C.," *Journal of the American Oriental Society,* LXXIV (1954), 222–233.

――――. "A Prince of Taanach in the Fifteenth Century," *Bulletin of the American Schools of Oriental Research,* No. 94 (1944), 12–27.

――――. "The Smaller Beth-Shan Stele of Sethos I (1309–1290 B.C.)," *ibid.,* No. 125 (1952), 24–32.

――――. "Some Important Recent Discoveries: Alphabetic Origins and the Idrimi Statue," *ibid.,* No. 118 (1950), 11–20.

ALT, ALBRECHT. "Der Gott der Väter," *Kleine Schriften zur Geschichte des Volkes Israel.* Munich: C. H. Beck, 1953.

BAILEY, ALBERT EDWARD. *Daily Life in Bible Times.* New York: Charles Scribner's Sons, 1943.

BARTON, GEORGE A. *Archaeology and the Bible,* seventh ed. Philadelphia: American Sunday-School Union, 1949.

BÖHL, FRANZ MARIUS THEODOR DE LIAGRE. "King Ḥammurabi of Babylon in the Setting of His Time," *Mededeelingen der Koninklijke Nederlansche Akademie van Wetenschappen afd. Letterkunde,* Nieuwe Reeks IX, 10 (1946), 341–370.

――――. "Das Zeitalter Abrahams," *Opera Minora.* Groningen: J. B. Wolters, 1953.

BOTTÉRO, JEAN. *Le Problème des Habiru à la 4e Rencontre Assyriologique Internationale.* ("Cahiers de la Société Asiatique," XII.) Paris: Imprimerie Nationale, 1954.

BRIGHT, JOHN. *Early Israel in Recent History Writing.* Chicago: Alec R. Allenson, 1956.

———. *A History of Israel.* Philadelphia: Westminster Press, 1959.

BURROWS, MILLAR. *The Basis of Israelite Marriage.* ("American Oriental Series," No. 15.) New Haven: American Oriental Society, 1938.

———. "The Complaint of Laban's Daughters," *Journal of the American Oriental Society,* LVII (1937), 259–276.

———. *What Mean These Stones?* New Haven: American Schools of Oriental Research, 1941.

CORNELIUS, FRIEDRICH. "Genesis XIV," *Zeitschrift für die Alttestamentliche Wissenschaft,* LXII (1960), 1–7.

DHORME, E. "La question des Habiri," *Revue de l'Histoire des Religions,* No. 118 (1938), 170–187.

———. Review of A.-G. Barrois, *Manuel d'Archéologie Biblique,* in *ibid.,* No. 122 (1940), 153–158.

DOSSIN, GEORGES. "Les Archives Economiques du Palais de Mari," *Syria,* XX (1939), 97-113.

———. *Correspondance de Iasmah-Addu.* (Archives Royales de Mari," V.) Paris: Imprimerie Nationale, 1952.

EISSFELDT, OTTO. "Der Gott Bethel," *Archiv für Religionswissenschaft,* XXVIII (1930), 1–30.

FINEGAN, JACK. *In the Beginning: A Journey through Genesis.* New York: Harper, 1962.

———. *Light from the Ancient Past.* Princeton, N.J.: Princeton University Press, 1946.

FORRER, E. O. "The Hittites in Palestine," *Palestine Exploration Quarterly,* LXVIII (1936), 190–203; LXIX (1937), 100–115.

FREE, JOSEPH P. "Abraham's Camels," *Journal of Near Eastern Studies,* III (1944), 187–193.

———. *Archaeology and Bible History.* Wheaton, Ill.: Van Kampen Press, 1950.

GELB, IGNACE J. *Inscriptions from Alishar and Vicinity.* ("University of Chicago Oriental Institute Publications," XXVII.) Chicago: University of Chicago Press, 1935.

GELB, IGNACE J. *Hurrians and Subarians*. ("Studies in Ancient Oriental Civilization," No. 32.) Chicago: University of Chicago Press, 1944.

GLUECK, NELSON. *Rivers in the Desert*. New York: Farrar, Strauss, and Cudahy, 1959.

GOETZE, ALBRECHT. "The City Khalbi and the Khapiru People," *Bulletin of the American Schools of Oriental Research*, No. 79 (1940), 32–34.

GORDON, CYRUS H. "Homer and Bible," *Hebrew Union College Annual*, XXVI (1955), 43–108.

———. *Introduction to Old Testament Times*. Ventnor, N.J.: Ventor Publishers, 1953.

———. "Parallèles Nouziens aux Lois et Coutumes de l'Ancien Testament," *Revue Biblique*, XLIV (1935), 34–41.

———. "The Patriarchal Age," *Journal of Bible and Religion*, XXI (1953), 238–243.

———. "The Patriarchal Narratives," *Journal of Near Eastern Studies*, XIII (1954), 56–59.

———. "The Status of Women Reflected in the Nuzi Tablets," *Zeitschrift für Assyriologie*, N.F. IX (1936), 146–169.

———. "The Story of Jacob and Laban in the Light of the Nuzi Tablets," *Bulletin of the American Schools of Oriental Research*, No. 66 (1937), 25–27.

GRANT, ELIHU (ed.) *et al. Haverford Symposium on Archaeology and the Bible*. ("Haverford College Biblical and Kindred Studies," No. 6.) New Haven: American Schools of Oriental Research, 1938.

GREENBERG, MOSHE. *The Hab/piru*. ("American Oriental Series," No. 39.) New Haven: American Oriental Society, 1955.

GUNKEL, HERMANN. *Genesis*, fifth ed. (Göttinger Handkommentar zum Alten Testament.") Göttingen: Vandenhoeck und Ruprecht, 1922.

GURNEY, O. R. *The Hittites*. London: Penguin Books, 1952.

HARLAND, J. PENROSE. "Sodom and Gomorrah," *Biblical Archaeologist*, V (1942), 17–32; VI (1943), 41–54.

HYATT, J. PHILIP. "The Deity Bethel and the Old Testament," *Journal of the American Oriental Society,* LIX (1939), 81–98.

————. "Yahweh as 'The God of My Father,'" *Vetus Testamentum,* V (1955), 130–136.

JACOBSON, DAVID. *The Social Background of the Old Testament.* Cincinnati: Hebrew Union College Press, 1942.

JANSSEN, JOZEF M. A. "Egyptological Remarks on the Story of Joseph in Genesis," *Jaarbericht van Het Vooraziatisch-Egyptisch Genootschap,* XIV (1955–1956), 63–72.

KAUFMAN, YEHEZKEL. *The Religion of Israel: From Its Beginnings to the Babylonian Exile.* Chicago: University of Chicago Press, 1960.

KAUTZSCH, E. (ed.). *Gesenius' Hebrew Grammar,* second Eng. ed. Translated by A. E. COWLEY. Oxford: Clarendon Press, 1952.

KENYON, KATHLEEN M. *Beginning in Archaeology.* London: Phoenix House, 1953.

KING, L. W. *Letters and Inscriptions of Hammurabi.* Vol. III. London: Luzac, 1900.

KNUDTZON, J. A., OTTO WEBER, and ERICH EBELING. *Die El-Amarna-Tafeln.* Leipzig: J. C. Hinrichs, 1915.

KRAELING, EMIL G. *Aram and Israel.* ("Columbia University Oriental Studies," XIII.) New York: Columbia University Press, 1918.

————. "Light from Ugarit on the Khabiru," *Bulletin of the American Schools of Oriental Research,* No. 77 (1940), 32–33.

————. "The Present Status of the Sabbath Question," *American Journal of Semitic Languages and Literatures,* XLIX (1933), 218–228.

————. *Rand McNally Bible Atlas.* Chicago: Rand McNally, 1956.

LEHMANN, MANFRED R. "Abraham's Purchase of Machpelah and Hittite Law," *Bulletin of the American Schools of Oriental Research,* No. 129 (1953), 15–18.

LEWY, JULIUS. "Ḥābirū and Hebrews," *Hebrew Union College Annual,* XIV (1939), 587–623.

LEWY, JULIUS. "Origin and Signification of the Bible Term 'Hebrew,'" *ibid.*, XXVIII (1957), 1–13.

————. "Les textes paléo-assyriens et l'Ancien Testament," *Revue de l'Histoire des Religions,* CIX (1934), 29–65.

MCCOWN, CHESTER CHARLTON. *The Ladder of Progress in Palestine.* New York: Harper, 1943.

MALLON, ALEXIS. "Les Hébreux en Egypte," *Orientalia,* No. 3 (1921).

MAY, HERBERT GORDON. "The God of My Father—A Study of Patriarchal Religion," *Journal of Bible and Religion,* IX (1941), 155–188.

MEEK, THEOPHILE JAMES. *Hebrew Origins,* rev. ed. New York: Harper, 1950.

NOTH, MARTIN. *The History of Israel.* Translated by STANLEY GODMAN. London: Adam and Charles Black, 1958.

OPPENHEIM, A. LEO (ed.) *et al. The Assyrian Dictionary of the Oriental Institute of the University of Chicago.* Vol. VI. Chicago: Oriental Institute, 1956.

PEET, T. ERIC. *Egypt and the Old Testament.* Liverpool: University Press of Liverpool, 1924.

PFEIFFER, ROBERT H. "Nuzi and the Hurrians," *Smithsonian Report for 1935.* (Washington: Smithsonian Institution, 1935), 535–558.

————, and SPEISER, E. A. "One Hundred New Selected Nuzi Texts," *Annual of the American Schools of Oriental Research,* XVI (1935–1936).

PINCHES, THEOPHILUS G. "Sapattu, the Babylonian Sabbath," *Publications of the Society for Biblical Archaeology,* XXVI (1904), 51–56.

PRITCHARD, JAMES (ed.). *Ancient Near Eastern Texts Relating to the Old Testament,* second ed. Princeton, N.J.: Princeton University Press, 1955.

RAD, GERHARD VON. *Das erste Buch Mose.* ("Das Alte Testament Deutsch," II–IV.) Göttingen: Vandenhoeck und Ruprecht, 1953.

————. *Theologie des Alten Testaments.* Munich: Kaiser, 1957.

ROWLEY, HAROLD H. *From Joseph to Joshua: Biblical Tradi-*

tions in the Light of Archaeology. ("The Schweich Lectures of the British Academy, 1948.") London: Oxford University Press, 1950.

ROWLEY, HAROLD H. "Habiru and Hebrews," *Palestine Exploration Quarterly,* LXXIV (1942), 41–53.

———. "Israel's Sojourn in Egypt," *Bulletin of the John Rylands Library,* XXII (1938), 243–290.

———. "Recent Discovery and the Patriarchal Age," *ibid.,* XXXII (1949), 44–79.

SCHILD, E. "On Exodus III.14—I Am That I Am," *Vetus Testamentum,* IV (1954), 296–302.

SCHOFIELD, J. N. *Archaeology and the After-Life.* London: Lutterworth, 1951.

SKINNER, JOHN. *Critical and Exegetical Commentary on Genesis.* ("International Critical Commentary.") New York: Scribner's, 1910.

SPEISER, E. A. "Ethnic Movements in the Near East in the Second Millennium B.C.," *Annual of the American Schools of Oriental Research,* XIII (1933), 13–54.

———. "New Kirkuk Documents Relating to Family Laws," *ibid.,* X (1930), 1–73.

STEELE, FRANCES RUE. *Nuzi Real Estate Transactions.* ("American Oriental Series," No. 25.) New Haven: American Oriental Society, 1943.

VAUX, ROLAND DE. *Ancient Israel: Its Life and Institutions.* London: McGraw-Hill, 1961.

———. "Les patriarches hébreux et les découvertes modernes," *Revue Biblique,* LIII (1946), 321–348; LV (1948), 321–347; LVI (1949), 5–36.

VIROLLEAUD, C. "Les Villes et les Corporations du Royaume d'Ugarit," *Syria,* XXI (1940), 123–151.

WILSON, JOHN A. "The 'Eperu' of the Egyptian Inscriptions," *American Journal of Semitic Languages and Literatures,* XLIX (1933), 275–280.

———. Review of Moshe Greenberg, *The Hab/piru,* in *Journal of Near Eastern Studies,* XVI (1957), 139–141.

WOOLLEY, LEONARD. *Abraham: Recent Discoveries and Hebrew Origins.* New York: Scribner's, 1936.

◆ INDEX

Abimelech, 162, 163
Abraham, 3, 15; ordeals and blessings, 5; archaeological claims, 20; ancestor of Biblical Hebrews, 29; story of divine action through human deeds, 31; desire to have family remain in Palestine, 37; lineage of, 38, 39; warlike Habiru compared with, 54; Habiru in Mesopotamia after Abraham had left, 56; dating of migration of, 58n; semi-nomadic life, 62; increasing prosperity of family, 64; purchase from the Hittite, 75; encounter with Philistines unlikely, 81–82; cognate in Mesopotamian documents, 82; polygamy of, 94; Jacob kinder to concubines' children, 103; servant as overseer of property, 117; name changed to show new status, 129; purchase of Machpelah, 121–123; El Shaddai the covenanting aspect of God, 132; El Olam and residence at Beersheba, 135; exacts oath in name of Yahweh, 136–137; a Yahwist, according to Gordon, 139; faith tending to henotheism?, 151; loyalty to family deity basis for expansion of knowledge of God, 153; sacrifice as act of loyalty, 156; prayer of intercession for Sodom and Abimelech, 161–162, 163, 166; destruction of Sodom and Gomorrah may antedate, 166; no sacrifices to celebrate covenant, 169; journey to Egypt because of famine, 176; prophetic work limited to prayer, 172; chro-

nology to Joseph imprecise, 205; and Amorite invasions of Mesopotamia, 207–208; see also Abram
Abraham's servant, 95, 111, 115, 161
Abram, 39, 87; in Egypt, 4; qualities, 4; vocation to go to new land, 4; and Hagar's son, 5; migration, 38; described as "the Hebrew," 51; property owner when leaving Haran, 59; wealthy on return to Palestine from Egypt, 60, 61, military man and Hebrew, 66; started journey of faith from Haran, 71; covenant with, 75; as theophorous name no key to linguistic root, 83; son by Sarai's maid, 94; authority as father, 107; Oriental etiquette, 115; land acquired by squatter's rights, 118; steps to assure an heir, 118–119, 120; adoption of servant reflects Hurrian culture, 120–121; made offering to God of Salem, 131; tithe to El Elyon at Salem, 160; blessed by Melchizedek, 161; prayer for offspring, 163; in Egypt because of famine, 178, 179; story of sojourn in Egypt may be duplicate of Jacob-Joseph story, 179; as part of the Habiru group, 208
Abydos, 201
Agade, 84
Akhnaton, 162, 183, 184, 194–196; solar monotheism in Egypt, 193; reign distinguished by religious activity, 195–196; two viziers in time of, 200
Akkadian, 41, 83, 90, 124–125, 132, 187; international language from

E Source (cont.)
as word for deity, 130; mentions
El Bethel twice, 133; ambiguous
as between El Bethel and paternal God, 138; no insistence that
patriarchs worshipped only Yahweh, 139–140; polytheistic traces
in, 142; no coherent record of
patriarchal religion, 150; circumcision, 171; no mention of Hebrew vizier at early period, 200;
historicity not the purpose but
dependable as to internal side of
life, 211–212; see also J and P
Sources
Ea, 144, 147
Ebeling, Erich, 44n
Eber, 38, 40
Edom, 71, 72
Edomites, 177
Egypt, 27, 28, 29, 38, 60, 72, 207;
Abram and Sarai in, 4; Joseph
in, 7; discoveries in, of Biblical
significance, 23; Hebrews' entry
into beginning of patriarchal age,
25; patriarchs in, because of
famine, 37; Apiru in, 50–51; Hebrews slaves in, 54; Habiru in
Mesopotamia before, 57; Hurrians entered, 69; references to
Hurrians in records, 71; Hittites
dealt as equals with, 74; of the
Ramessids, Hittites as strong as,
74–75; only foreign power to control all Palestine in patriarchal
period, 76; dominated Palestine
and Syria until 1800, 78; Hyksos
in lower, 78; Hyksos expelled
from in 1580, 79; Philistines in,
80–81; Jacob-type names in, 83;
defeat by Hyksos compared with
Genesis xiv, 86; unable to control Palestine steadily, 92; camels
in art as early as first dynasty,
116; religion a simplification of
inherited polytheism, 141, 143;
circumcision practiced, 171; seers
in patriarchal period, 172; religion more advanced that patriarchs', 173; link between He-

brews' origin and ultimate
emergence, 174; foreigners taking
over land, 175–176; travel to and
from, 175–180; Middle Kingdom,
176, 191, 209; relatively unified
civilization, 177; imprecise date
of patriarchs' trips to, 178–179;
Joseph's power over "all the land
of," 182; Mitsrayim in Hebrew,
187; Hyksos infiltration, 189–190;
Joseph's land system, 191; Semites in government, 194–195, 204;
a Syrian a prince ca.1200, 195;
Asiatic slaves in by 1800, 198;
New Kingdom custom for nobles
to sit to eat, 202; ignorance of
climate of in Joseph story, 202–
203; traders in spices brought
Joseph to, 203; New Kingdom,
209
Egyptian: epigraphic remains at
Tell el-Amarna, 12; records mention Habiru, Apiru, and Apirim,
26; language, 41; segregation of
Hebrews at meals, 52, 53; mythological god reveals hidden name
of power, 167; execration texts,
176; records of border officials,
176; literature's parallels to
Joseph story, 185–186; text refer-
ring to famine and priest claim
to land, 201; etiquette in dealing
with foreigners, 202
Eighteenth Dynasty, 187, 191, 194,
203
Eissfeldt, Otto, 133
El, 130, 133, 141, 145, 147–148, 150,
151, 158
Elam, 38, 86
Elamites, 27, 38; invasions, 27;
records, 86
El Bethel, 133, 138, 151
El Elyon, 131, 139, 160
Eliezer of Damascus, 119
Elim, 148, 158, 168
Ellasar, 86
Elohim, 130, 136
El Olam, "Everlasting God," 135,
151

Habiru (cont.)
through Amarna letters, 40; problem of identification with Hebrews, 41; linguistic argument for connection with Hebrews, 41–42; "foreign captives," 43; in Mari letters, 43; irregular auxiliaries in Egyptian armies, 43–44; slaves at Nuzi, 45, 46; troublemakers in Syria and Palestine, 45; settled at Aleppo, 46; special status among Hittites, 46; no nationality, 47; soldiers at Mari, 47; throughout the Fertile Crescent, 47; characteristics, 47–51; entitled to dole in Babylon, 47; variety of origins, 47; no single meaning, 49; as "the tramp," 49; in Aleppo, 51; occupational title of opprobrium, 51; total identification of Hebrews with impossible, 54; Greenberg's chart of time and place of activity, 55; position in Hittite records, 56; spread from southern Mesopotamia to northern Syria, 57; recognized from Sumer to Alalakh, 57; in Mesopotamia before being in Palestine and Egypt, 57; migration westward general but not exclusive, 58; Hebrew patriarchs a segment of, 58; Esau more typical of than Isaac or Jacob, 61; characterized by servitude, 64; Hebrews one group of, 67; slaves, soldiers, etc., 65, 67; the social and economic stratum out of which Hebrews came, 65–66; contrasted with Hebrews, 65–66; at Boghazköy in 15th and 14th centuries, 77; name means "not Egyptian," 78; philological problem, 89–90; Nuzi records reveal little about religion of, 146; contemporaries of Hyksos, 190; Abram a member of, 208; wanderings and settlement in first half of second millennium, 209; rural members may have been prosperous, 213; see also Apiru

Hagar, 93, 94, 103, 105, 119, 134–135
Ham, 74
Hamitic line, 39
Hammurabi, Hammurabi's Code, 27, 47, 55, 85, 86, 102–103, 110; view of marriage contrasted with that of Hebrews, 97; difficulties of dating Abram by, 179
"Hapiri gods," mentioned in Hittite documents, 146
Haran, 37n, 39, 56, 57, 59, 63, 99, 107, 121, 138; Abraham left early in 20th century B.C., 29; in Hurrian territory and departure point for Abram, 71
Harland, J. P., 166n
Harris Papyrus 55, 55
Hatshepsut, 50
Hatti-land, 74, 76
Hattusilis, 74
Hebrew, "to migrate" suggested root of, 38; same gentilic form as other words, 42; word designates social class, 42, 43; word first used in Bible for Abram, 51; word indicative of inferior status, 53

Hebrews: purpose of studying earliest history of, 14; in Canaan late in second millennium B.C., 17; dating patriarchal age, 25; akin to Apiru and Habiru, 25–27; looked to Mesopotamia as land of origin, 28; identified by social status, 29; no consistent picture of in Genesis, 36; originated in Mesopotamia, 37; leave Mesopotamia, 38; scattered through Fertile Crescent, 40; linguistic argument for connection with Habiru, 41–42; slaves at Nuzi, 45; writers thought of *Hebrew* as ancient name, 51; "land of the," 52; total identification with Habiru impossible, 54; similar to Habiru, 51–58; separated from Egyptians at mealtime, 52, 53; slaves of the Law, 54; at same times and places as Habiru and Apiru, 55;

Israel (cont.)
in eighth century, 172; Egyptian sojourn the link between origin and ultimate emergence, 174

J Source, 18, 24, 136; date of, 9; confusion in tracing patriarchal generations, 39; references to Hebrews, 52; doctrinaire about beginnings of Yahweh worship, 128; names do not suggest unified notion of deity, 129; mentions El Olam, 135; no insistence that patriarchs worshipped only Yahweh, 139–140; purpose to identify other gods as Yahweh, 139–140, 142; meaning of *Yahweh* not explained, 140; schematized picture of patriarchal religion, 140; dating of Yahwism, 146; no coherent record of patriarchal religion, 150; only a hint of sacrifice in Genesis, 156; mentions altars but no sacrifice, 168; circumcision, 171; no mention of Hebrew vizier at early period, 200; historicity, 211–212; *see also E* and *P* Sources

Jacob, 3, 15, 17, 159; ambition, 6; migration into Egypt in Hyksos period, 29; not to be buried in Egypt, 38; served Laban as relative, 54; trip to Haran from Palestine, 58; more settled than Esau, 61–62; animal husbandry, 62; names of this type in Mesopotamia and Egypt, 83; arranged with Laban and his sons for marriage to Rebekah, 93; polygamy, 94; dealings with Laban, 95–96, 98–102; relationship with Laban compared with Eshunna Code, 102; and children of concubines, 103; concern for youngest son, 109; fratriarchy in family of, 112; bowed seven times to brother, 116; controversy with Laban over property unusual, 118; Esau's sale of birthright to, 124–125; name changed to show new status, 129; deity revealed to at

Bethel, 133; at Bethel and at Peniel, 134; idea of paternal deity, 136–138; appearance of El Bethel to, 138; journey to worship the God of his father, 138; Laban's gods a sign of prestige, 139; sacrifice on making peace with Laban, 157; vows at Bethel to tithe in future, 160; wrestling with God, 166–167; Mesopotamian ziggurat in dream, 169–170; in Egypt because of famine, 176, 178; embalming of, 203; in either Hyksos or Amarna period, 208; schematic shortening of patriarchal period, 208; *see also* Israel

Jacobson, David: on Israelite marriage and family organization, 94, 96*n*, 99*n*, 105*n*, 106 and *n*, 118*n*

Janssen, Jozef M. A., cited: 117*n*, 182*n*, 188*n*, 196*n*; on Joseph's interpretation of Pharaoh's dream, 199; on Joseph's position in Egypt, 200, 201, 202

JE tradition: story of Jacob's farm life, 62; Hittites regarded as Canaanites, 75; Hittites' land promised to Abram, 75; Hittites in Palestine, 76

Jebel Usdum, 166

Jehovah-jireh, 129

Jerusalem, 76

Jirku, recapitulated by Greenberg, 57*n*

Joktan, 38

Jordan River, 87, 90

Joseph, 3, 15, 17; in Egypt, 7; referred to as Hebrew and servant, 51, 52–53; only short time in servitude, 54; settled farm life at time of, 62–63; compared with Habiru, 64–65; exceptional among Hebrews, 64–66; eminence in Egypt perhaps during Hyksos period, 80; extra-Biblical parallels of name, 84; two stories of his sale/abandonment, 112; interpretation of dreams closest to prophecy among patriarchs,

233

Ramesses II, 74, 183, 193
Ramesses III, 81
"Ramesses, the land of," 188
Ramessids, 50, 80–81, 192
Ras Shamra texts, 150
Re, 167, 191
Rebekah, 6, 108; arrangements for marriage, 93, 95, 111; fratriarchy, 112; observance of etiquette, 115; seeks divine omen, 161
Red Sea, 87, 203
"Relationship theology," 127
"Rock of Israel," 136
Rowley, Harold H.: philological aspect of relation between Habiru and Hebrews, 42n, 89n; associated meanings of *Habiru*, 49n, 51, 54n; on Semites among Hyksos, 78n; on locating Joseph in time of Akhnaton, 193n

Sabbath, 170–171
Sacred prostitution, 110
Sacrifice, 155–160, 168
SA.GAZ-Habiru, 41; sociological nature of names, 43; soldiers and shepherds, 44; appeals for help against, 194
Salem, 160; king-priest of, 4; God of, 131
Sarah, 108; birth of son, 5; name changed from Sarai, 5; treatment of Hagar, 103; *see also* Sarai
Sarai, 60, 118; danger of becoming an adulteress, 4; levirate marriage, 94; trip into Egypt, 178; *see also* Sarah
Sargon III, 132
Saul, 32
Schild, E., 140n
Schofield, J. N., 23n
Sea Peoples, 74, 79–81, 178; *see also* Philistines
Semites, 38; languages, 41, 83; nomenclature among Habiru, 47; Hurrians not, 69; strength after 1800, 78; many children desirable, 94; concept of name as summary of person, 129; slaves in Egypt, 176, 194–195, 198, 204; among

ethnic groups in Hyksos peoples, 190
Septuagint, 71
Servants, position of, 107
Seth, 191
Seti I, 50, 55, 183, 193
Shamshi-Adad I, 69
Shechem, 112
Shem, 38, 39
"Shield of Abraham," 136
Shiloh, 152
Shushan, 38
Simeon, 54
Simpson, C. A., 15n
Sinai, 128
Skinner, John, 33n, 34, 35, 63, 85, 111, 168, 171n
Sodom, 61, 110, 161, 163, 166
Sons, position of, 108
Sororate, 114–115
Speiser, E. A.: cited, 45n, 89n, 104n, 105, 109, 111n, 113, 114n, 120n, 125n, 190n, 204n
Steele, Frances Rue, 120n
Sumer, 57
Suppiluliumas, 74, 77
Syria, 11, 12, 27, 45, 51, 207; Ugaritic and Amarna references show Habiru in, 57; Hurrians in, 69; along with Palestine and eastern Asia Minor known as Hattiland, 74; Hittite power in, 74; Egyptian domination, 78; Hyksos in parts of, 78; Hyksos an example of movement through in second millennium, 79; places in Genesis XIV between Red Sea and, 87; worship of Bethel in, 133–134; paternal deities in, 148; deities known as El with some second name, 148; sacred places show no peculiarly Hebrew associations, 168; Egyptian power in, 174, 175; Egyptian travelers in, 176; Hyksos domination, 190; asked help against SA.GAZ, 194

Taanach, 60n
Tamar, 94–95, 104, 105

238